Christian Faith and
the Contemporary Arts

Christian Faith and the Contemporary Arts

EDITED BY FINLEY EVERSOLE

ABINGDON PRESS   New York—Nashville

CHRISTIAN FAITH AND THE CONTEMPORARY ARTS

Library of Congress Catalog Card Number: 62-16809

Cartoons on pp. 219, 220 by Jim Crane are reprinted by permission of motive.

"Willie," cartoon on p. 222, is from Agony in the Kindergarten by William Steig, copyright 1950 by William Steig, and is used by permission of Duell, Sloan & Pearce, Inc.

The cartoon on p. 224 is used by permission of Jules Feiffer.

"Art and the Renewal of Human Sensibility in Mass Society," "Thesis for a Playwright Still in Hiding," and "Demythologizing 'Peanuts,'" have previously appeared in motive.

"Camus: The Argument from the Absurd" first appeared in the December, 1957, issue of The Christian Scholar.

"Is the Creative Process Similar in the Arts?" was previously published in the Winter, 1960, issue of The Journal of Aesthetics and Art Criticism.

The paragraph by Bernard Scott, which appears on p. 6, was used by the permission of motive.

SET UP, PRINTED, AND BOUND BY THE
PARTHENON PRESS, AT NASHVILLE,
TENNESSEE, UNITED STATES OF AMERICA

To My Wife MARY ANN

The world is going through so crucial a change at present that one may well be perturbed if he finds unintelligible the poets and arts that are expressing that change.—AMOS N. WILDER

Might it not very well be that under God the arts, whether they understand it this way or not, are the spiritual alarm clocks for our day, to shake us up and bring us into focus, to check the phony tendencies of the heart, chill us with irony and wash us with beauty and preserve us in a selfhood that many things in our culture conspire to destroy. The arts are certainly full of bad theology, but they also give us the stumbling truth that the human heart is not filled easily. They have the virtue of being alive and the grace to wonder out loud. . . . I see the arts rushing into our vacuum claiming for itself a priestcraft it cannot perform but also cannot forever wait for from us.—BERNARD SCOTT

We all know that art is not truth. Art is a lie that makes us realize truth, at least the truth that is given us to understand.
—PABLO PICASSO

Man is fallen and his art can both manifest and analyze his sin. . . . Man cannot make a redemptive art but he can make an art that communicates what he experiences of redemption as a man and what he knows of it as an artist. God in his infinite wisdom may use an art work as an instrument of redemption but what serves or can serve that purpose is beyond the knowledge of man.
—JOHN W. DIXON, JR.

There are those who insist that beauty should be the aim of art, and that the proper function of the artist should be that of "creating beauty." . . . "Beauty" is not a biblical notion or term. The Scriptures speak to us of truth, justice, freedom, and love, but very little or not at all of beauty. They do not tell us that God is Beauty, but that God is Love. Neither does Christ say that He is the Beauty, but that He is the Way, the Truth, and the Life. This way is not beautiful, but rough and painful. This truth is not beautiful, but liberating. This life does not open into beautiful harmonies, but passes by the narrow gate of death.
—DENIS DE ROUGEMONT

FOREWORD

or, maybe not...

An artist is a man before he is an artist. So the fundamental relation of an artist to religion is that of a man to religion: the fact that the particular man is an artist is an accident. Artists have, on occasion, taken up with everything from neo-humanism, through communism, on up to the orgone box and table rapping—not for the sake of their humanity but for the sake of their art. Some have even taken up with religion for the sake of their art. This is triviality.

For more than a century the artist's sense of his alienation has been increasing. When he has seen his own work in the long perspective of time, against the monuments of the past, he has often felt cheated of some ease and spaciousness that made such grandeur possible. Knowing that art arises from some deep conviction, some heat of spirit, he has felt the need of "myth" to "integrate" and "canalize" his powers. He has often forgotten that you can't choose your "myth"; your myth has to choose you. He has also tended to forget that you have to believe in your "belief," or at least believe in your "unbelief."

When he has not forgotten these things he has prided himself on his tough-mindedness in not being willing to deceive himself, and then has fallen into that last soft-mindedness of taking his own historical situation as alibi. But sometimes, even as he has extracted the inestimable satisfaction of an alibi out of his historical situation, he has managed to create, from the giddy nausea of staring down into the depth of *nada*, his most poignant art. He has even managed to create it out of self-pity.

7

Face-saving alibi, self-pity, poignant art—the artist has that much out of his situation in the modern world. What more attractive can religion offer to him? Exactly nothing—that is, to him as an artist. Religion can offer to him exactly what it offers to anybody else. What he, as artist, can make of what it can offer to him is his business as an artist.

It is conceivable that he might make nothing of it. It is even conceivable that salvation of the man might be damnation of the artist. It might be.

He must do his own bookkeeping.

A deep art is bound to carry some shock to the devout, just as it carries some shock to the conventional. The devout man is committed to an order not of this world, and the conventional man is committed to an order of this world. Deep art implies a destruction of order for the sake of reordering. There is something incorrigible and anarchic lurking in art. The devout and the conventional are right. It is dangerous.

Let us speak of literature. Literature—when it fulfills itself—is apt to be, in some dimension, the enemy of received opinion. It is inductive. It tells, or implies, a story, and the story "tests" the received opinion. The opinion is put, by an act of imagination, into the acid bath of experience.

The story deals with the problematic—the better the story the more deeply problematic is what it deals with. It not only shows the reader a person confronting the problematic; it casts the reader back into the problematic from which he has been saved by grace or convention—with the painful necessity of reliving his own life. It awakens the lusts of the eye and the imaginations of the heart. They had not been absorbed, after all.

So now what?

Tragedy "tests" the received opinion by confronting it with "poetic injustice." In the end it affords only the reward of a secular "justification by faith"—the moment of reconciliation in courage and understanding.

But the reconciliation is a fraud—only, we feel grander for it because it is a fraud like truth, the truth of the capacity for grandeur. *Virtù* is the virtue celebrated by tragedy. It is not a Christian virtue. But both Christian faith and *virtù* have dimmed in this world.

Lesson in this?

The common term between the life of art and that of religion is humility. Both depend on revelation—and both recognize that revelation comes

8

only from a prayerful reverence for truth, especially from an unscared reverence for the shockingness of inner truth. Art, as Bergson put it, "brings us into our own presence."

St. Teresa said: "I require of you only to look."

ROBERT PENN WARREN

EDITOR'S PREFACE

"THE HUMAN RACE," SAYS GRAHAM GREENE, "IS IMPLICATED IN SOME terrible aboriginal calamity." It is this fact, reported and interpreted in the art of our time, which gives to the forms of contemporary art the appearance of "chaos." It is this fact also which forces upon the artists of the present age their prophetic role. Indeed, it is not the preacher or the historian or the sociologist who speaks to us most clearly of the "crisis of civilization" in which we are involved, but the artist. Our art, then, is an art of anguish and guilt, of isolation and emptiness, of doubt and damnation. Contemporary art has rediscovered the irrational—in the depths of the demonic! Yet our art has discovered, as the art of no other generation has, the meaning of freedom, of courage, of inwardness and honesty. Clearly, modern art is the child of the twentieth century! To receive it is to receive a mixture of blessing and pain.

The Christian may well ask why he should give attention to an art which embraces so much that is antithetical to his faith. Indeed, if Robert Penn Warren is right than art reawakens "the lusts of the eye and the imaginations of the heart"—which even the anchorite in the desert overcomes only with great pain and discipline—why should the Christian submit himself to the temptations of art, especially modern art? A great many answers will be given in this symposium, but I would like to take this occasion to offer four of my own.

For more than five centuries we have witnessed a gradual despiritualization and, finally, a dehumanization of man's life. Modern art, with its loss of God and the human image, is the drama of our age. Here we see what *really* is happening to man, to society, and to man's faith in God.

11

The artist's "sense of his age" gives his art revelatory power. In other words, art makes visible those images of society and self which we prefer to keep hidden. Contemporary art gives us the image of a lonely, anxious, and sometimes diabolical humanity. This image, however, is not of the artist's own making. It is the image which society itself offers to the discerning eye. Perhaps this is why we find it so difficult to look at today's art. For, as Goethe once said, "If a monkey looks in, no apostle will be found looking out." One value of contemporary art, then, is *its power to reveal us to ourselves.*

Ever since the wedding of the iconoclastic forces of the Reformation and the rationalistic tendencies of the Renaissance, says Samuel H. Miller, we have been almost entirely oriented to the conscious level of man. In doctrinal matters this has meant an almost complete rationalization of dogma. Worship has declined; sacraments and symbols have been rendered impotent. The church, says Miller, "remains without any tool fashioned to minister to men other than in the region of reason."

With the discoveries of modern depth psychology and existential philosophy—to say nothing of modern physics—the myth of rational, scientific man has suffered a major blow. The breakthrough of irrational forces from the unconscious mind, together with the growing anxiety of contemporary life, are facts which call for new forms of ministry. They also point to new, nonrational possibilities for life. Nor have artists been unduly reluctant to embrace mystery and the irrational. A case in point is John Ciardi's spirited defense of poetry which appeared a few years ago in the *Saturday Review:* "To call a poem obscure is in no way to damn it. The deepest in all of us is obscure. Freud is obscure. Every man's life is motivated, at depth, in obscure ways. What, for that matter, is any more obscure than the Bible? Its obscurity, together with its unmistakable sense of pertinence-in-depth, is of the essence of its greatness." [1]

A second value of contemporary art—which is a value for the church at this time of renewal of its own liturgical life—is *its ability to permit the nonrational to find an "order" properly its own.*

In a time when political and intellectual freedoms are being curtailed and religion discredited, the arts constitute the last stronghold for the protection of the imagination, without which *Life* is impossible.

Moreover, it is in the center of the imaginative life that one finds the most fruitful point of contact between faith and art—indeed, between faith and this age of unbelief! If one looks at the chief critics of Chris-

[1] *Saturday Review,* July 20, 1957, p. 11.

tianity in modern times—men such as Nietzsche, Marx, Hölderlin, Renan, Freud, Sartre, Camus—one is immediately aware that he is dealing with some of the most creative minds of the age. If, conversely, one looks at those Christians who have most successfully touched many of the most "alien" minds of our time—men such as Paul Tillich, Rudolf Bultmann, W. H. Auden, T. S. Eliot, and Graham Greene—one is again aware that he is in the presence of great, creative minds. Thus one is led to suspect that it is not the validity of the Christian gospel but rather the creative power of its spokesmen which accounts for the declining influence of Christian faith in our world. Nathan Scott points to the secret of T. S. Eliot's achievement when he says of his works, "The logic which we encounter is thus a logic of the Christian imagination rather than a logic of Christian concepts."

One of the exciting possibilities of our time is the possibility of establishing a new point of contact between faith and culture, between church and world, through "the logic of the Christian imagination." But if the Christian church is to speak so as to command the attention of our contemporaries, if it is to experience a renewal of faith in a post-Christian age, we cannot content ourselves with new "programs" but must seek *an increase of imagination* by means of which the biblical and historic faith may be translated into terms that are meaningful to men today. Intentionally or not, the artist, by virtue of his office as priest and conservator of the human imagination, is the church's ally in this task. A third value of contemporary art, then, *is its hold upon the imaginative life of man where renewal of faith and life alone take place.*

The contemporary arts, it should be noted in passing, are not without significance for the formal work of theology. Karl Barth, whose prophetic revolt against cultural distortions of Christianity triggered a major theological revival in the 1920's, has said that "there is no theological visual art. Since it is an event, the humanity of God does not permit itself to be fixed in images." Barth's Protestant dogmatism is now called in question by contemporary nonrepresentational painting and sculpture with their insistance that visual art, in Francis Bacon's words, "should be a re-creation of an event rather than an illustration of an object." Barth might have strengthened his attack upon visual art by pointing to the overtones of Docetism and Manichaeism in the works of a number of contemporary artists, but the Docetism in his own position precluded such a critique. Yet with all its limitations we have in contemporary art an aesthetic with far-reaching implications for a new understanding of sacramental and natural theology. For Protestant Christians this means that we cannot continue, as Gustave Weigel put it, "ignoring the fact that the encounter [with God] must take place in a material situation." A fourth value of contemporary art, then, is *its understanding of the material world as a realm within which event and meaning may find expression.*

These remarks may well be concluded with a statement of the challenge which this symposium presents to its readers, a challenge that is best expressed in the essay by Nathan Scott, when he says:

"[The] exciting and difficult challenge that is presented to us by the human scene in our time is that of searching the cultural experience of the modern period and the rich resources of the Christian faith for the first principles of a theology of the imagination that will be relevant to the spiritual crisis of the present time. And this . . . will require us to enter into a new and hitherto largely untried collaboration with the whole community of the modern arts."

The formulation of the title of the symposium as *Christian Faith AND the Contemporary Arts* permits each writer to see the relation of faith and art in terms authentic to his own experience. The great diversity of views expressed is evidence of the creative thinking that is taking place at the point of juncture which this symposium represents. The views expressed in the essays are those of the individual authors.

A word of thanks is due my writers for their patience and co-operation through many problems and delays. My chief regret is that Randall Stewart of Vanderbilt University had to withdraw from writing an essay for reasons of health and that problems of schedule prevented the inclusion of an essay by James Johnson Sweeney on "The Artist and His Media."

A special word of thanks is due Nathan Scott for many helpful suggestions and for reading the symposium in its entirety. Thanks is also due to Stanley Hopper, James Miller, Maurice Lavanoux, and Margaret Rigg for their invaluable suggestions; to George Pool for editing the chapters on music; to Dean Peerman and Keith Irwin for helping with the bibliography; to Eddie Lee McCall for proofreading the manuscript; and to Marion Garnsey for typing several of the essays. I wish also to acknowledge my indebtedness to *motive* magazine which, in the two years of my association with it, exerted a vital and continuing influence upon my interest in the arts. Finally, my appreciation for my wife and for the patience she exhibited as I spent many an evening poring over manuscripts finds expression now in the dedication of this volume to her.

FINLEY EVERSOLE

14

CONTENTS

15

16

LIST OF ILLUSTRATIONS

(BETWEEN PAGES 128 AND 129)

1. Paul Klee, *Mask of Fear*, 1932
2. Georges Rouault, *The Old Clown*, 1917
3. Pablo Picasso, *Guernica*, 1937
4. Graham Sutherland, *Crucifixion*, 1947
5. Jackson Pollock, *Cathedral*, 1947
6. Alfred Manessier, *For the Feast of Christ the King*, 1952
7. Clark Fitz-Gerald, *The Brothers*, 1959
8. Henry Moore, *Madonna and Child*, 1943-44
9. Theodore Roszak, *Anguish*, 1947
10. Seymour Lipton, *Sanctuary*, 1953
11. Le Corbusier, *Notre Dame du Haut at Ronchamp*, France
12. Marcel Breuer & Associates, *St. John's Abbey*, Collegeville, Minnesota
13. Eero Saarinen & Associates, *Concordia Senior College Chapel*, Fort Wayne, Indiana
14. William Wenzler, *St. Edmund's Episcopal Church*, Elm Grove, Wisconsin
15. Alden B. Dow, *St. John's Lutheran Church*, Midland, Michigan
16. José Limon Dancers, *Missa Brevis*

17

PART ONE

The Contemporary
Situation of the Artist

I

Art and the Renewal of Human Sensibility in Mass Society

NATHAN A. SCOTT, JR.

ONE OF THE MAJOR DEVELOPMENTS IN OUR CULTURAL LIFE OF THE LAST few years has been the steadily increasing insistence upon what might be called the crisis of the person in contemporary society. This is, in one degree or another, the message of David Riesman's *The Lonely Crowd* and of William Whyte's *The Organization Man*, of A. C. Spectorsky's *The Exurbanites* and of John Keats's *The Crack in the Picture Window*, of Vance Packard's *The Status Seekers* and of Wright Mills's *White Collar*, and of numerous other studies in the moral climate of contemporary American life. There is indeed a whole new literature appearing whose purpose is to insist upon the inauthenticity and facelessness of the life that awaits us in an increasingly standardized mass society where the individual is caught up "into the rank and file of some operational combine [or] . . . into some category of occupational concern with all its paraphernalia: code of behavior, standards of opinion, lingo, and so forth."[1] "Identification of one's function," says Erich Kahler,

is the admittance ticket granting the right to exist. And so people tend more and more to touch each other with that externally established functional part of the self, that part of the self that has the right to exist, while their indi-

---

[1] Erich Kahler, *The Tower and the Abyss* (New York: George Braziller, Inc., 1957), p. 23.

vidually human parts, for which no legitimate place is provided in our social structure, becomes increasingly isolated, unrelated and alienated from each other.[2]

Amidst this gray, dreary anonymity of "other-directedness" in which men's goals are given them not by tradition or by their own consciences but by the social groups in which they have their assigned functions—amidst this depersonalized life of the "public" mass, men live by what Karl Jaspers thirty years ago called "a conventional ethic of association"; that is, "courteous smiles, a tranquil manner, the avoidance of haste and jostle, the adoption of a humorous attitude in strained situations, helpfulness unless the cost be unreasonable, the feeling that 'personal remarks' are in bad taste, self-discipline to promote order and easy relationships whenever people are assembled in large numbers." [3] All this constitutes, in Dr. Jaspers' phrase, the "universal language" by which the faceless, anonymous inhabitants of our contemporary wasteland shuffle through the dreary rituals of their intermingling.

A Suggestion of Fatalism

Now despite the somberly prophetic character of the critique that begins to emerge from the new sociology, it does yet sometimes convey to us suggestions of fatalism that very sharply differentiate it from the *avant-garde* social criticism of the thirties. For in that earlier and simpler time the focus of aggrievance for radical thought was generally rather highly particularized. One knew precisely what it was that John Steinbeck was protesting against in *The Grapes of Wrath*; and one knew just who it was that a Norman Thomas wanted to call into question; and there could be no uncertainty at all about the identity of Walter White's opponents. Indeed, it was precisely because of the definiteness with which the source of the disorder was particularized that the critical traditions of the thirties often managed to be so genuinely radical. But the new social criticism of the Whytes and the Millses assumes that we are all involved in the malaise of an enveloping totalitarianism from which no escape is possible: it does not focus upon a particular flaw in our social structure, but rather calls into question the whole fabric and design of contemporary society. The charges that are made in books like *The Lonely Crowd* and *The Organization Man* are charges that implicate us all in the depersonalizing processes of mass society, and it is the very inclusiveness of this testimony that some-

---

[2] *Ibid.*, p. 42.
[3] Karl Jaspers, *Man in the Modern Age*, tr. Eden and Cedar Paul (Garden City, N. Y.: Doubleday Anchor Books, 1957), p. 49.

times blunts its urgency: we are all, it seems, touched by the facelessness and anonymity of an "other-directed" society; and the reign of the Organization is envisaged as a consequence of processes immanent within and made necessary by the exigencies of this present moment in modern history. The tragedy of self-loss is universal, and the new sociology sometimes seems to be saying that to suppose that any really effective resistance is possible is simply to surrender to the last illusion: no, it is sometimes implied, we are all doomed to be the helpless victims of a quietly omnipotent and unopposable totalitarianism.

Now the extremism of this new critical tradition is not, I think, excessive, for the fact of the matter is that if, indeed, our present situation is truly a "mass-situation," then it is by definition an extreme situation. When the crowd is no longer merely an occasional phenomenon but one of the characteristic forms of human life; when men no longer feel themselves to be subject to moral norms but only to the impersonal necessities of collective existence; when the things that they do are done not because they are natural or satisfying but simply because their Riesman "radar-mechanisms" tell them that to act differently would be to violate the impersonally established laws of the social collective—when this has become the shape and the stance of life, then the human situation is an extreme situation: which is to say that in some sense men have begun to know the meaning of hell. So it is not, I think, the extremist character of contemporary criticism that is to be objected to but rather the fatalism that it sometimes entails; and it is this, I believe, on which it is proper for us to exert a new pressure.

It is true, of course, that, when an enterprise of cultural criticism has as its object the specification of some particular flaw, of some particular disorder, in the fabric of our common life, it is relatively easy to avoid the tone and the accent of fatalistic resignation, for the very particularity of the disorder implies the existence of melioristic possibilities. But when we are dealing with a general disorder; when in some sense the tragedy is universal; when there are no longer any privileged persons and when everyone is equally distant from any sense of security— when this is the extremity of the situation that man faces, as indeed I believe it is in our time, then it is very difficult to do justice to the generality of the malaise without seeming to rob the human reality of its radical imperatives and to promote a kind of fatalistic euphoria. This is, I believe, an error that can be avoided only by our persistence in simplistically putting to ourselves the questions: What can be done? What concrete steps can be taken to halt the drift of life in our time towards increasing depersonalization? If the ubiquity of the Organization is a permanent feature of life in a technocratic culture, what can be done at least by way of making the Organization something less demonic and more humane? What can be done, what concrete steps can be taken? This surely is the basic question with which we must be finally concerned.

But, though I am convinced that it is a right attitude of the mind to resist the euphoria of fatalism, I am not at all certain that the *first* questions it will be most fruitful for us to contemplate in the religious community are questions of an immediately and urgently practical order. We must, of course, candidly face the issues concerning precisely how it is that the pressures of creative intelligence can be brought to bear upon the depersonalizing structures of life in a mass society; and we must not attempt any evasion of the concrete tactical issues of reconstruction. The Christian enterprise must seek a deeper understanding of the stratagems whereby it may participate in the defense and reconstruction of the human community, but surely the *first* question to which it ought to address itself is not an immediately practical question. It is rather a question involving what I should call a theology of the imagination, the issue concerning how the imaginative style of a people may be renewed and reinvigorated at the concrete level of sensibility and life-style. Indeed, the problem of life-style, of imaginative style, may well be one of the central issues facing the apologetic theologian in the years just ahead, and this is an issue to the settlement of which I am convinced he will not himself make any very helpful contribution unless he clearly perceives how closely he must co-operate with the most vigorous movements in the art of our time.

The Order of Sensibility and the Theological Task

I have been recalling on this occasion the testimony that is being made by much of the most trenchant social criticism of our period, that a new type of man has been emerging in the past generation or two on the American scene, a man the operative law of whose life is conformity and adjustment. Which is to say that he is a man who increasingly finds it impossible to make any real sense of such a motto as Dante's, "Go your own way and let the people talk." Nor can he make any sense of the life-perspective of biblical faith, with its notion of the "dedicated spirit" being "singled out" and standing "over against" the world in unwavering witness to what it has beheld to be the truth: the very notion of being "singled out," of standing "over against" the world, is resisted by him for whom adjustment and conformity define the ideal human position. Indeed, the "other-directed" man of our time seems to be without any real capacity for understanding the prophetic religion of biblical faith: he simply has not the imaginative resource for understanding what it is the Bible is talking about. He may be an ardent supporter of church or synagogue, and yet, paradoxically, the Hebraic-Christian faith in its moral profundity and radicalism is something that simply surpasses his imagination. Which is to say that the root-problem of our present religious situation may be one of renewing and reinvigorating that deep and interior order of human sensibility and human feeling.

But now what we must recognize in the theological community is that it is not within the competence of the theologian as theologian to deal directly with the order of sensibility. This is, rather, the order in which the artist takes the steadiest, the most permanent, and the deepest interest. For, as the Roman Catholic critic Father William Lynch has so finely said:

What the artist is essentially interested in is the expression, involving judgments but in the most visible and concrete terms, of the total life and movement of the soul as it engages with the reality outside of itself, especially with the reality of each current moment of history. I do not think it too much to say that . . . the artist wishes to "save" that soul in the sense that he wishes to keep its various acts of sensibility straight and real and ever moving with a freedom that really belongs to the children of God.

He searches for the rhythmic and spontaneous movements that will accomplish the freedom of the soul, for it is not a set of false or cheap eternities or seductions that will win to this great objective. He so arranges his sounds and images that they judge each other, though not according to the formal judgments of the immediate moralist. He discovers the human in a thousand corners and is the revealer of the non-human for what it is. It is by the inner light of his organisms that he lights up fantasy as fantasy and reality as reality, and reaches all his power by finding and following the lines of the latter. Therefore his work is a human act in the highest and the fullest sense of the term.[4]

In other words, what the authentic artist is concerned above all else to do is to make us see the fundamental order of the world; and the account that he renders of it is given, not in terms of propositions and measurements, but in terms of the rich and strangely irreducible particulars of existence. We speak of "synecdoche" as a device which the poet occasional-

[4] From *The Image Industries* by William F. Lynch, S. J. © 1959 Sheed & Ward, Inc., New York. Pp. 140-41.

ly uses when he wants to make an instance of something stand for the whole. But surely, synecdochism is not merely an occasionally stratagem of the artist but is, to some degree, always and essentially involved in his method of handling reality. Joyce's Leopold Bloom and the ghostly finale of the string pizzicati in Stravinsky's *Pétrouchka* and the cruelly impervious electric light that glares down upon the wreckage of man in Picasso's "Guernica" mural are all particulars that compel an act of attention upon themselves; but at the same time they tell us something about everything else in the world. And this is the perennial mystery of art; that it seeks to master the radically singular, concrete, individual aspects of reality and yet ends by somehow presenting them in such a way that they, in their concrete singularity, become resonant of the whole of reality.

St. Teresa tells us: "I require of you only to look"; and this is, in a way, the single requirement of the artist also. He asks us to look, indeed to stare, at *this* boy in love, at *this* plane soaring through the sky, at *this* soldier's fright before the advance to the front—and he asks us to contemplate *these* images so steadily and with such intentness that we begin to perceive the story or the fragment of a story in which they are interacting. Which is to say that he compels us to perform an act of judgment, and this not at the top of our minds but at the deep level of feeling, of passion, of sensibility, where the men and women of our generation are perhaps most in need of re-education. Of this I think Mark Van Doren is right in thinking that

> The simplest evidence is the behavior of audiences at movies which are trying to be tragedies. In proportion as the attempt is successful the audiences are embarrassed, for nothing has trained them in the emotions of pity and terror; they are afraid to be afraid, and they do not know whom to pity, or when. . . . The embarrassment expresses itself in titters or in audible signs of disgust; they came to be moved a little, but not this much. They brought quantities of sentiment which they cannot use, for the work of art before them is aiming at precision, and understanding is required.[5]

And not to know how to feel is to be at the mercy of dreams and fantasies and fears by which we may well be undone.

So we must say, then, that the creativity of the artist partakes of the creativity of religion—for here it is, in the creative forces of authentic art, that the religious community will find an indispensable ally in promoting that health of the imagination apart from which the integrity of man can in no wise be guaranteed. And since the order of sensibility does not lie immediately within the competence of the theologian, he cannot but regard the artist as one of his most natural partners, for it is the whole office of the artist to liberate the imagination and to train and educate us in the ways of feeling and sensibility. Indeed, perhaps one of the most constructive things that can be done in the theological community today in relation to the whole range of questions having to do with modern collectivism is to work through the first principles of what I have called a theology of the imagination. And this will, I should hope, be an effort that will result in the development of a generation of theological critics so skilled in negotiating the transaction between art and faith that they would be capable of convincing both the artist and the theologian that nothing could be more wrongheaded than the suspiciousness with which they habitually view each other. It is wrongheaded because, in quickening the imagination, the artist trains the human intelligence to make precise discriminations about the dimensions of experience that transcend the gross materialities of life, and thus he may become one of the theologian's best allies in the liberation of man from the predominant platitudes of a positivistic culture. It is also wrongheaded for the artist and the theologian to persist in their mutual suspicion of each other because, in his struggle against the blunting of our sensibilities that the popular arts of a mass culture are so skilled in bringing about, the artist might find in the high drama of the Christian story about reality a kind of support and encouragement. Furthermore, in turning their salvos upon each other, the theologian and the artist may simply all the more weaken their already none too secure status in the culture, when actually they should be jointly engaged in warfare against the increasingly insidious control of the American imagination by the kitsch that is circulated in a mass society through the powerful media of the popular arts, or of what Gilbert Seldes calls "the public arts."

This brings me to what ought to be a major focus of what I am calling a theology of the imagination. For not only ought it to entail an effort to understand what will be involved in the collaboration between theology and the high forms of art, but it ought also to involve an effort to submit to the closest critical scrutiny all the archetypes and symbols and rhythms that animate our popular literature and movies and music. Here it is that we discover the dreams the people feed upon and what the prophet Ezekiel called "the chambers of imagery" in which their souls are sometimes so insidiously enervated that the astonished observer, on contemplating the

27

mere "gigantic something" they have become, cries out with the narrator in *The Waste Land:*

> I had not thought death had undone so many.[6]

The Task of Reshaping a Life-Style

So, then, I am proposing that the theological community may well conclude that something very fundamental awaits doing before it begins to put its shoulders to any wheel of radical and active reconstruction of the "other-directed" culture of our period. And, indeed, I suspect that, increasingly during the next few years, the best theological intelligence will be coming to regard the deepest cultural problem of our period as the problem of reshaping a life-style. But a life-style is something which has its deepest sources in the order of sensibility, in a style of imagination. So, therefore, though the religious community must attempt to do many other things by way of rehumanizing the "mass-situation" of our period, I suspect that the chances of its doing something really constructive and redemptive will be greatly enhanced if it consents to begin by facing the question as to how the human imagination in a mass society may be renewed and reinvigorated. Which is to say that the exciting and difficult challenge that is presented to us by the human scene in our time is that of searching the cultural experience of the modern period and the rich resources of the Christian faith for the first principles of a theology of the imagination that will be relevant to the spiritual crisis of the present time. And this, I am suggesting, is a theological effort that will require us to enter into a new and hitherto largely untried collaboration with the whole community of the modern arts.

Finally, I should like to suggest that Christian reflection upon the themes of a theology of the imagination will deepen and instruct itself within the framework of reflection upon the liturgy. For, when it truly understands its own genius, it is through the actions and the implications of the liturgy that the church will seek to inform and purify the images and symbols and rhythms that constitute the imaginative style of its environing culture. Paul Tillich says:

It is not so important to produce new liturgies as it is to penetrate into the depths of what happens day by day, in labor and industry, in marriage and friendship, in social relations and recreation, in meditation and tranquility, in

---

[6] T. S. Eliot, *The Waste Land,* Part I, in *Collected Poems: 1909-1935.* Copyright, 1936, Harcourt, Brace & Company, and used by their permission and by permission of Faber and Faber, Ltd.

the unconscious and the conscious life. To elevate all this into the light of the eternal is the great task of cultus.[7]

And I believe that real progress will have been made toward the renewal of human sensibility in a mass society when the church not only rediscovers the good collaborators it may have amongst the great artists of our period but rediscovers also the powerful resources that it has in its liturgy for training the people in how, through the style of their life and feeling, "to celebrate the tenderness and the fierceness of the world into which the Creator has put them." [8] To be specific, we must begin our work in the theological community not only with such materials as Kafka's *The Castle* and Camus' *The Fall* and Eliot's *Four Quartets* and Picasso's "Guernica," but also with such texts as Romano Guardini's *The Spirit of the Liturgy* and Louis Bouyer's *Liturgical Piety* and A. G. Hebert's *Liturgy and Society* and the work of the Benedictines of the Maria Laach Abbey in Germany (and most especially the revolutionary essays of Dom Odo Casel in the Abbey's *Jahrbuch für Liturgiewissenschaft*).

[7] Paul Tillich, *The Protestant Era* (Chicago: The University of Chicago Press, 1948), p. 219.

[8] Jaroslav Pelikan, *The Riddle of Roman Catholicism* (Nashville: Abingdon Press, 1959), p. 166.

II

Literary Tradition and the Contemporary Writer

WALTER SULLIVAN

IT IS APPARENT, I THINK, THAT WHEN ONE SETS OUT UPON A TASK, HE SHOULD get all the help he can, and if it is at all convenient, he should consult his betters. Acting on this principle, I reread recently T. S. Eliot's celebrated essay on "Tradition and the Individual Talent." I was struck not so much by Eliot's erudition—I knew about that already—but by how far we had come in forty-five years, how much the world had changed. It is true that in 1917, when the essay was first published, there was a war going on; and it was a costly and vicious war, more terrible, probably, than any conflict which had been undertaken to that time. But behind the war there was a noble hope. Disillusionment would set in soon enough, but while Eliot labored on his essay, a good segment of the world's population did indeed believe that this war would be final: there would be no others. On the heels of this holocaust would come, as if by magic, a democratic world where justice would prevail.

The tone of Eliot's essay is very comfortable. He was not a man free of doubts—what human being ever could be? But he was sure at least—as we are not sure—that the world in which he lived would be standing in the morning. Man would still be sinful and man's civilization was becoming more hollow and more depraved. But there was leisure to

30

discuss the niceties of technique, to look at the past and savor its literary accomplishments, to work toward a definition of aesthetic principles by which the efforts of later writers could be guided and judged. There was quietness too in the poetry and the novels of that time. They were tough enough in their outlook, and pessimistic to be sure. But they were not frantic, which is what we are today.

Let me give an example. Last year I read *Set This House on Fire* by William Styron. Now, Styron is one of the most talented of our younger novelists, and in many respects this novel is as well written as any novel ever needs to be. But it is a high-pitched, almost a manic, work, and finally it disintegrates against the agony of the modern world. A drunken painter careers across Europe with his wife and children, falls under the influence of an obscenely evil and rich fellow American, becomes involved in rape and murder, and at last returns to his home in North Carolina. It is a violent, orgiastic book with an unsatisfactory end. "I suppose I should tell you," the main character says in conclusion, "that through some sort of suffering I had reached grace, and . . . found some belief. . . . But to be truthful, you see, I can only tell you this: that as for being and nothingness, the one thing I did know was that to choose between them was simply to choose being." [1] This is all he can say. The best he can hope for is just to keep on living.

Death: Our Existential Posture

This is not the only modern posture, but it is a typical one. And it is an image of our contemporary predicament. Cling to the present, we tell ourselves. The past is dead and death lurks in the future: death has become the super villain, the all-time public enemy number one. Old age, which connotes the approaching end, is by a trick of semantics swept out of existence: senior citizens do crafts at the neighborhood center and try to forget. We don't speak of death before children. We write new stories for them and change the old ones so they will not read of it in their books. Only the bad men die, shot down on the streets of Laredo, but for well-behaved and ordinary people, we urge the children to think there will be no end. Adults have their fictions, too. The corpse lies in the "slumber room" and rouge puts the bloom of health onto his cheeks. Even advocates of euthanasia have ironically mixed motives: by a desperate remedy they would spare us the agony of death.

Now the existentialists, who are by no means traditionalists in literature,

[1] William Styron, *Set This House on Fire* (New York: Random House, 1960), p. 500.

31

know that we are wrong in denying death. They know that life is defined by death almost absolutely. "Had we but world enough, and time," [2] Marvell wrote, and what he said in his poem applies not only to courtship but to all the other things we do besides. Time has meaning only because it must stop. If one could try over and over again, then who knows? Maybe in a millennium or two we all might be saints. But life ends, and both history and literature teach us that dying is the only thing that even a small segment of humanity does consistently well. Those who seem to have failed in life change the future course of history by dying. Socrates did this, and of course, Christ. Those who have blundered through the business of living die touchingly and well: Hamlet, who should have killed the king considerably sooner than he did. Heyst, in Conrad's *Victory*, who at last accepted his responsibility to act in the world. According to Nietzsche—who was a Hegelian at least, if not an existentialist—one of the sources of tragedy was man's individuation, his consciousness that because he was a part of unified and timeless nature, his time would end. The Greeks, too, knew that the conclusion was all-important. But simply to know that life stops is not enough.

The Writer's Paradoxes

In what seems to me a brilliant figure, Helmut Kuhn says that the existentialists take the road to Calvary. But when they arrive there, they find only the crosses of the two thieves. Existentialism, Kuhn goes on to say, is an "encounter with nothingness." [3] Think death, think death, think only death, it insists. And this is as bad as thinking only life. The two go together: they must not be fragmented. One of them wrenched free from the other becomes a distortion, the worst sort of lie, because once it was a participant in the truth.

Life and death are the fundamental paradox: all philosophy, all religion must start here. But for the writer there is another paradox that is almost equally important. In the same way that life and death define each other, past and future are part of the same definition. Without a future the past is meaningless, and only by the past can the future be foreseen. As for the present, it is much too small to try to live or to write by. If a writer is to communicate effectively to the present—that is to say, to his own contemporaries—he must always write with his eye on the future. He must write for those shadowy—and unlikely—people who will read him

[2] Andrew Marvell, "To His Coy Mistress."
[3] Helmut Kuhn, *Encounter with Nothingness* (Chicago: Henry Regnery Company, 1949), p. x.

fifty or a hundred or five hundred years from this moment; otherwise, he is doomed to fail in the here and now. How is he to write for the future? By aligning himself as best he can with his tradition: by making a close and intensive study of the past.

Most obviously, from an examination of past masterpieces a writer learns technique. If he is a novelist, he learns about point of view, what to do with chronology, innumerable large and small tricks of the trade. But more and more as time passes, I come to believe that the problem of learning the technical aspects of writing is much exaggerated. By and large, people who write poorly are either the lazy ones who won't take the trouble to do their job properly, or they are the ones who think poorly, perceive poorly, and in the end have poor things to say. It is no accident, I contend, that Shakespeare, who knew more about technique than anybody who ever wrote in English, also knew more about the nature of man and the world and the complex forces that govern it. Think of it this way: literature is different from other arts because it is made of words, and words are referential. Words stand for things, qualities, actions. They have meanings from which they cannot be separated. Therefore, a poem or a novel, unlike a painting or a sonata, must necessarily deal with—indeed, be built on—ideas and meanings too.

But, then, just as life is not life without death, and past and future cannot be separated, meaning depends for its existence on the image, the event, the dramatic vehicle, which is concrete, immediate, and in every way severely limited. Meaning must be timeless, but the dramatic surface of a work of literature is quite strictly rooted in a particular place and time. Facing this paradox, the writer has many problems: he must find the meaning that is worth talking about; he must find the image with which to talk about it; and he must be able to distinguish between these two parts of the whole and to keep them in balance. I can perhaps illustrate what I am trying to say by an example from Dickens.

Bleak House was a book written against the law's delay. To the disgrace of the English court system, the case of Jarndyce and Jarndyce—based, we are told by Dickens, on an actual litigation—goes on and on until the substance over which the action was brought has melted entirely away. During the months of the novel's first, serial publication (1852-53), no subject could have been more timely. The tardiness of chancery was a festering thorn in the body politic. The public sense of justice was outraged. Then, partly as a result of the attack in *Bleak House,* a reform of the chancery system was accomplished. The law no longer held back unreasonably. Suddenly *Bleak House* was flogging a dead horse. Herein lies the difficulty. No one wants to be bothered with the reformer after the reform is effected. We have only the most tenuous nostalgic interest in what were the burning causes and issues and preoccupations of another time.

But Dickens was a fine novelist and he knew about this. Behind the surface of court action are the attitudes of human beings toward material wealth. Mrs. Jellyby gives everything she has to the Africans, while her own children starve. Skimpole assumes an innocent simplicity and sponges on the generosity of his friends. Carstone declines to work while he waits for his legacy: he longs to spend and enjoy what he has not earned. And so it is with a score of other characters. Through these people and their attitudes toward an immediate situation, Dickens enlightens us about an aspect of the general human condition and about ourselves. Like the poor, the problem of stewardship is always with us. So, like the poor, *Bleak House* stays too.

The writer must be of his time and out of it simultaneously. To a greater or lesser extent he shares the attitudes of his generation; and even if he employs the historical image, goes back into the past to find his plot, the present shines through. Shakespeare's historical dramas reflect the confident nationalism of Elizabethan England as well as or better than many contemporary documents of that era. But this participation by the writer in his own environment should go only so far. I once heard Robert Penn Warren remark that a man who loved his country totally was out of business as a writer. One must feel toward his country, Warren said, as he feels toward his mother: he has considerable respect and affection for her, but he is exasperated by many of the things that she thinks and does.

The Problems of History and the Writer's Perspective

Anything to be understood must be put into perspective; and society may be put into perspective in one of three ways: it may be set realistically against the past; or it may be measured against an ideal age that is not yet accomplished; or it may be set against a combination of the two. According to Lord Acton, no historian thinks well of human nature; one's mind is turned to gloom by contemplation of the affairs of men. We would do well to reflect on this somber judgment. We seem inclined these days to ignore the fact that the choices history offers are always imperfect. War is evil; Hitler's Germany was insupportable; we searched for the third, good way, but we could not find it. A writer needs to know that from human beings he should not expect too much.

Yet from a few human beings always, and from all human beings occasionally, he should expect everything. And from life he has a right to expect some good things too. Novels by realists such as Howells and by naturalists such as Dreiser are powerful in their way and not as phony as *Pollyanna*, but essentially they are stacked. To say that human experience is all bad is as romantic as to say that it is all good. There are saints and the sun does sometimes shine on them. Satan may be the unintended hero of *Paradise Lost*, but, as Hegel pointed out, Antigone and Creon are both loyal advocates of the good, and the end of the play is a reassertion, a reintegration of the moral essence of the universe.

If a study of literature of the past teaches us anything, it makes clear that man is a paradox. His history is contradictory, and his motives are almost never pure. His fundamental nature remains the same, but his problems are never the same. Adversity presents a new face to each new generation. The writer must remember this and therefore be simultaneously conscious always of both past and present.

Marx, in his famous essay on Hegel's philosophy of right, said that religion was the opiate of the people. He was as wrong about this as he could possibly be. For religion does not deaden, it enlivens. And even when it makes its most glorious promises for the future, it requires of man the narrow, painful way. It demands a total commitment, a total sense of responsibility, a total awareness of the moral implications of every situation, and action in terms of this awareness every waking moment of every day. It is an intensely individual and personal and often lonely thing. But it has another aspect, and the Christian, at least, has a second area of responsibility: he has a duty to people whose names he does not know and whom he will never see. Without once losing sight of his individual problem of working out in his own life his own salvation, man must also labor to make the world at large as ethical and as good a place as possible. This does not mean that he must believe in the kingdom of God on earth, anymore than he must conceive of his own fleshly perfection. But he is obligated in both cases to do the very best he can.

Earlier, I indicated that the enduring success of *Bleak House* resulted from the ability of Dickens to put individual people with individual problems behind the facade of public action which gives the novel its plot. I should like now to point out that the facade is there and is as indispensable to a work of art as the underlying verities which support it. The public image changes, the nature of the public duty alters, but each generation must attend to its public duty, whatever it is. Allen Tate and others have pointed out that ideally the public and the private duty should be congruent. This should be true not only in history but also in literature. In either case, however, it is seldom, if at all, true. Hamlet's duty to avenge his father was equally his duty to rid the state of corruption, but nothing as fine as *Hamlet* has been written in a long time.

We, as writers, must do the best we can with what we have. And what we have is a situation so threatening, an alignment of world forces so terrifying, that a paralysis of the mind is likely to ensue. With the bomb hanging over our heads, it is perhaps small wonder that even extraordinary human experience shrinks and loses its intensity. Aware of what might happen to all of us tomorrow, we may cease to wonder that Styron's character could say no more than, "I want to be." But simply to say so is not enough. Overwhelming as our danger is, we must not quail before it. If life and history and literature are as paradoxical as I have made them seem in this essay, then it will not be unreasonable for me to say that because the present danger has never been so great, the past has never before been so important. The literature of the past can teach us about human suffering. It can teach us about ourselves, and this we must know if we are to understand ourselves and write about ourselves in the present situation.

If we are lucky, it might even teach us to be brave.

III

Art Tradition and the Contemporary Visual Arts

HERBERT READ

TRADITION IS ONE OF THOSE IDEOLOGICAL CONCEPTS WHICH ARE USED WITH very different meanings and very different intentions by different people. T. S. Eliot, quite at the beginning of his critical activity, tried to rehabilitate the concept by what is virtually an extension of the accepted meaning. For a static interpretation he substituted a dynamic one. I would not like to suggest that Mr. Eliot, even in 1902, had succumbed to the influence of Bergson, but the tradition in literature is seen as a changing order, a flux, an organism continuously modified by the introduction of new elements. "The existing order is complete before the new work arrives; for order to persist after the supervention of novelty, the *whole* existing order must be, if ever so slightly, altered; and so the relations, proportions, values of each work of art toward the whole are readjusted; and this is conformity between the old and the new." [1]

I was very impressed by this metaphor at the time of its first publication, but had some difficulty in reconciling it with my revolutionary zeal. A little earlier I had been equally impressed by T. E. Hulme's insistence on the *objective* character of ethical values and on the necessity for an order or hierarchy among such values that is *absolute*. But Hulme, too, had been

[1] T. S. Eliot, *The Sacred Wood* (London: Methuen & Co. Ltd, 1920), pp. 44-45.

37

a Bergsonian, and his view that art was essentially a breaking through conventional vision and conventional thought—a remolding of perception—this again seemed difficult to reconcile with a hierarchy of absolute values.

The Abandonment of Tradition

Philosophizing about the arts in the 1920's was a hazardous occupation because the arts were changing rapidly beneath our eyes. It might be possible to reconcile cubism with tradition—had not Cézanne, from whose practice it was to a large extent derived, declared that his purpose was to continue the tradition of Poussin. But the modern movement in the visual arts did not halt at cubism: from postimpressionism it developed by inevitable stages to expressionism and surrealism, and for the past thirty-five years it has moved rapidly and irrevocably away from any possible concept of tradition. It is no longer a question of modifying an existing order "ever so slightly": at the present extremes of the modern movement there is not the slightest trace of a pre-existing order; and even the material or technical formulas for the arts of painting and sculpture have been abandoned—the typical modern artist prefers to speak about his constructions or compositions rather than his paintings or carvings. Tradition, which always had some obvious relevance to the craft of an art like painting, was abandoned even in this sense: the modern artist has nothing to learn; he "envelops" his psyche in any material that comes to hand—rubbish, wastepaper, plaster, metal sheets or wires—anything will serve his purpose. We do not sufficiently realize that the traditional concept of the artist himself has been abandoned. In a sense more literal than was perhaps intended by Sri Aurobindo who invented the phrase, or by Coomaraswamy who gave it general currency, every man is a particular kind of artist.

It may be said that this is sheer nihilism—formlessness itself has become the aim of art (Nietzsche defined nihilism as "aimlessness in itself"). But at the same time there has been a corresponding development in a psychology and aesthetics which claims significance for the formless, the gestaltos. The absolute distinction between beauty and ugliness, on which traditional aesthetics rested, has disappeared. We now realize "that the two polar feelings of beauty and ugliness are not so far apart as they may appear to be; to repress unconscious symbolism is the dynamic function of them both." [2]

Art, it has often been argued in the past, receives its force and significance from its unconscious symbolism: art has been defined (by Susanne Langer) as the creation of forms symbolic of human feelings. But now we have

[2] Anton Ehrenzweig, The Psycho-analysis of Artistic Vision and Hearing (New York: Julian Press, Inc., 1953), p. 80.

the phenomenon of art anti-art, the nihilistic motive of the Dadaists, art as the destruction of forms that might symbolize human feeling. How can such art have any relation to tradition? Is tradition a meaningless concept in modern art?

Tradition in the Arts

Before we can answer this question we must return to the concept itself and try to define it a little more precisely. In the arts it has become essentially an intellectual concept, but it was not always so. We speak of craft traditions and of stylistic traditions, and in both cases we mean something that can be defined in practical terms. In the Middle Ages the craft of painting, for example, was controlled by a guild (usually dedicated to Luke, who was the patron saint of painters). The guilds may be regarded as the guardians of tradition: their regulations determined the kind of work a painter could accept, the nature and quality of the materials he could use, the organization of his workshop and his relations with his patrons.[3] Every detail of the process of painting was laid down by the guild regulations, with the result that a code of technical instructions and a standard of technical achievement were maintained unchanged for centuries. If one adds to this the conditions as to subject matter and treatment laid down by the patron (usually the church) which extended to every detail of comportment and costume, one can appreciate how confined was the framework within which the medieval artist was allowed to exercise his imagination. That he nevertheless managed to express so much personal idiosyncrasy and poetic fantasy is one of the paradoxes of our subject: a tradition does not necessarily imply frustration; it is compatible with some kind of freedom, though the kind has yet to be defined.

Craft traditions remained strong and efficient until the middle of the eighteenth century—Reynolds' *Discourses* are the final and most intelligent formulation of them. They were disrupted, not so much by the growing spirit of romanticism (for romanticism is as much in need of craft as any other ideology), but by economic and social changes. The social status of the artist had been rising ever since the fifteenth century, and he gradually divorced himself from craftsmen like goldsmiths and carpenters and assumed an independent position in society comparable to that of the scholar. Painting and sculpture became "liberal" arts or "fine" arts as distinct from applied arts or crafts, and with this change in status came a loosening of the control exercised by the guilds. Patronage, too, was

---

[3] For an excellent account of craft traditions in the art of painting see W. G. Constable, *The Painter's Workshop* (London: Oxford University Press, 1954).

changing; and instead of the universal church with its precise requirements, the painter had to satisfy a multitude of private patrons each with his individual whim. By the end of the eighteenth century the guilds had ceased to control either the quality of painting or the workshop practice of the painter, but the patron was still a dictator and would choose not only subjects after his own fancy but even the treatment he desired. Yet, as Professor Constable has pointed out,

the practice of painting for specific places and specific purposes continued until much later than is often supposed, and persisted throughout the nineteenth century. But at the same time, the painter played an increasingly large share in selection of subject, and became increasingly the final authority as to how it should be treated. Particularly was this the case with easel paintings, whose subjects were chosen without reference to any particular patron or purpose, the painter taking his chance of finding a buyer.[4]

As the guilds declined, however, there arose a new guardian of tradition, the Academy. The first academies were already established in Italy in the sixteenth century, and by the eighteenth century they had spread throughout Europe and had become as tyrannical and as jealous of tradition as ever the guilds had been. Not only did they succeed in confining state and court patronage to their members, but the prestige their members enjoyed meant that private patrons who could afford their services did so—it was a guarantee of quality. Technical standards similar to those of the guilds were enforced in the schools they established, and so the craft tradition was maintained without a break right down to the beginning of the modern period. In this sense Delacroix and Constable, Turner and Cézanne, are still traditional painters. Even painters like Gauguin, Van Gogh, and Rousseau, though their work is the foundation of all that is antiacademic in contemporary painting, nevertheless were very conscious of "the existing order" and deliberately strove to emulate it.

Tradition, Style and Individual Talent

It may be a little artificial to try and separate stylistic tradition from craft tradition, but the difference is perhaps obvious. Craft tradition is based on materials and their use, and on the right treatment of specific subjects—on workshop (and later academic) practice. Style is an intangible element and is communicated by personal example. Meyer Schapiro has defined it as "the constant form—and sometimes the constant elements, qualities and ex-

[4] *Op. cit.*, p. 13.

pressions—in the art of an individual or a group," [5] and he proceeds to show how intangible it is as a historical phenomenon. Perhaps one should admit that style and tradition are antithetical terms, for style is basically, in Mr. Eliot's sense of the term, individual talent. It spreads from one individual to another, it is contagious, and in that sense we can speak of a constant element in style. If it spreads far enough and deep enough, as did Michelangelo's style, then one can give a generic or historical term to the style, such as mannerism. I do not for a moment question the quality of the concept of style (on the contrary, as will be seen, I regard it as the basic concept in the arts). But a stylistic analysis such as that proposed by Heinrich Wölfflin employs categories—linear as opposed to painterly, closed as opposed to open form, the composite as opposed to the fused—all of which are *ex post facto* generalizations and, unless we are to suppose that a tradition can be unconscious (which would seem to be contradictory), are not, properly speaking, traditional. Indeed, when a style such as mannerism develops by contagion, it can be said to be antitraditional—it is a revolt against the prevailing classical tradition. Impressionism is a style in this sense, and it is a revolt against the prevailing academic tradition (a degenerate classical tradition). Other historical analyses of style, such as those of Paul Frankl,[6] would seem also to be generalizations from phenomena which are originally individualistic and disparate. Style remains, as Goethe defined it, an intuition of the inner essence of things—and as Riegl defined it, "an active creative process in which new forms arise from the artist's will to solve specifically artistic problems." [7] He may be helped to his solution by the knowledge of tools and materials derived from tradition, but the way in which he then solves his problems is peculiar to the artist, and this solution is his style. It is perhaps too late to attempt to confine the concept of "style" to what is personal or idiosyncratic in a work of art, but I do not find a generalization like "the Gothic style" very useful: I would prefer to speak of the Gothic *tradition* (technique, material, and function) and of the style of Giotto (or of the school of Giotto).

These distinctions are perhaps not very important for our present discussion, but it is easy to slip from an expression like the Gothic style to a much more imprecise expression like the Christian style in art. There is no such thing. There is doubtless a Christian tradition in art as in all aspects of the *vita activa*, and this tradition prescribes the form of the basilica,

[5] Meyer Schapiro, "Style," *Anthropology Today*, ed. A. L. Kroeber (Chicago: University of Chicago Press, 1953), pp. 287-312. Copyright 1953 by the University of Chicago.

[6] Paul Frankl, *Das System der Kunstwissenschaft* (Brünn und Leipzig: R. M. Rohrer, 1938).

[7] Cf. Schapiro, *op. cit.*, p. 302.

41

the design of church furniture, the way in which particular saints should be represented and the appropriate symbols for particular feelings. But the style in which the artist or workshop carries out these traditional commissions is the style of the artist himself. Even if we have a more generalized conception of style, the correspondence between style and religious content, as Meyer Schapiro admits, is not at all obvious.

If the difference between pagan and Christian art is explained broadly by the difference in religious content, there is nevertheless a long period of time— in fact, many centuries—during which Christian subjects are represented in the style of pagan art. As late as 800, the Libri Carolini speak of the difficulty of distinguishing images of Mary and Venus without the labels.[8]

Such historical facts are decisive.

Antitradition in the Contemporary Visual Arts

With these general considerations in mind, let us approach the contemporary scene. It is one in which tradition, in the sense in which we have defined it, does not exist in the arts. It was destroyed in a series of revolts to which we give the names futurism, Dadaism, surrealism, expressionism, etc., and which are all aspects of aesthetic nihilism. Only the ego and his own count in modern art, and though we may use phrases like the Paris School or the New York School, these are merely convenient indications of centers where artists congregate and perhaps influence one another stylistically. There have been attempts to establish a modern tradition—the Bauhaus in Germany is the most conspicuous example, and it failed. Only in architecture a negative tradition of functionalism (i.e., a tradition founded on craft or technique and not on spiritual values) has had some resemblance to the artistic traditions of the past. We sometimes speak of an "international style" in modern architecture; it is misleading. There is no style in modern architecture because there is nothing specifically artistic in the problems the architect tries to solve. The problems he tries to solve are technical. There is merely a prevailing conformity to technical standards —no problems of form, but only of building. As Mies van der Rohe has proclaimed: "Essentially our task is to free the practice of building from the control of esthetic speculators and restore it to what it should exclusively be: building." [9] Aesthetic speculators—such as the architects of Santa Sophia and Chartres!

[8] Op. cit., p. 305.
[9] Philip C. Johnson, Mies van der Rohe (New York: Museum of Modern Art, 1947), p. 184.

What happens when a modern architect ignores the advice of Mies van der Rohe and speculates aesthetically? The answer may be found in the church built by Le Corbusier at Ronchamp in France. This church conforms in certain respects to the Christian tradition in architecture: there is a nave with altar, side chapels, stained-glass windows, pulpit, porches— that is to say, it functions as a church. But for the rest, although it makes use of modern materials and modern methods of construction, it is a highly speculative exercise in aesthetic values. It has style—the style of the artist, Le Corbusier. I have no means of knowing how effectively it serves its purpose—only the priest and the congregation can tell us that— but when I visited it it was crowded with devout pilgrims who seemed to accept its religious atmosphere without question. No conflict, therefore, between this example of contemporary art and the Christian faith.

What of the other visual arts, more particularly the arts of painting and sculpture? Here the evidence is much more difficult to collect and assess. We have in England a church in the city of Northampton for which a statue of the Madonna and Child and a painting of the Crucifixion were commissioned some years ago. The statue is by Henry Moore, the painting by Graham Sutherland. The church itself is a pleasing example of the neo-Gothic "style" (there is some justification for using the word "style" in this context, because the church is an individual architect's interpretation of the Gothic tradition in architecture), and these two contemporary works look perfectly dignified and appropriately decorative in their setting. But they are not, of course, Gothic or neo-Gothic in "style": each is an expression of the artist's individuality. Both artists have accepted a traditional theme, but interpreted it in an untraditional manner.

It may be that when our descendants get far enough away from it, the riotous individualism of our contemporary art will have the appearance of another epoch of mannerism. Time has the effect of giving unity to what appears at the moment to be a multiplicity. But if at some future date the works of Picasso, Klee, Max Ernst, Kandinsky, Miró, Mondrian, Léger, Sutherland, Pollock, and hundreds more focus into some stylistic unity, a unity of style it will be and not one of tradition. Tradition demands what the modern artist rejects: discipline, conformity, humility. It may be an inherent tendency for the Christian to seek the security and the self-effacing service of an artistic tradition. But he cannot have it in our age, or in any easily conceivable future. It is not for me to speculate about the future of the Christian faith; I do not regard that future as necessarily incompatible with the irremediable individualism of modern art.

We have in England a beautiful and humble Christian artist (a poet as

43

well as a painter) whose name is David Jones. He has written with far more understanding of these problems than I, for he is not only a good artist but a devout Christian. I would like to conclude with the fragment of a poem which he wrote and abandoned about 1938—it seems to express the essential truth about the problem to which this volume is devoted:

> I said, ah! what shall I write?
> I inquired up and down
>   (he's tricked before
> with his manifold lurking-places).
> I looked for his symbol at the door.
> I have looked for a long while
>   at the textures and contours
> I have run a hand over the trivial intersections.
> I have journeyed among the dead forms causation
> projects from pillar to pylon. I have tried the
> eyes of the mind regarding the colours and lights.
> I felt for his wounds
>   in nozzles and containers.
> I have wondered for the automatic devices. . . . I
> have tested the inane patterns without prejudice.
> I have been on my guard to not condemn the unfamiliar
> . . . for it is easy to miss him at the turn of a
> civilization.[10]

[10] David Jones, "Art and Sacrament," in *Catholic Approaches*, ed. Lady Pakenham (London: Weidenfeld & Nicolson Ltd. & Barker Ltd., 1955).

IV

The Brave New World of the Modern Artist

FINLEY EVERSOLE

THE LATE MUNICH CLOWN, KARL VALLENTIN, ONCE ENACTED THE FOLLOWING scene: The curtain rises on a stage which is totally dark except for a small circle of light cast by a solitary street-lamp. Vallentin, with a long-drawn and worried face, walks round and round in the circle of light, searching desperately for something. "What have you lost?" asks a police-man who has entered the scene. "The key to my house," replies Vallentin. The policeman joins in the search until, after a while, finding nothing, he asks, "Are you sure you lost it here?" "No," answers Vallentin, pointing to a dark corner of the stage, "over there." "Then why on earth are you looking for it here?" "There is no light over there," says Vallentin.

This tragicomic drama serves us quite well both as a dramatization of the cosmic crisis which has obsessed the great artists of our age and as an instance of the "courage" of the modern artistic vision. Indeed, it is this vision of a dark world, a lost key, and a futile quest which in a variety of images has haunted the imagination of modern artists, as we see when we examine the themes which recur most frequently in modern literature and drama: exile, the wasteland, the descent into hell, the journey into night, the death of God, the lost father, the broken center, man's vertigo experience, the wanderings of Ulysses, the quest for justice, the inaccessible castle, and so on. The sensibility of the modern artist is defined by Erich

Heller with characteristic German exactness when, writing of Franz Kafka, he says, "Never before has absolute darkness been represented with so much clarity, and the very madness of desperation with so much composure and sobriety." [1] It is then the clarity, composure, and sobriety with which modern artists have represented the despiritualization and consequent dehumanization of our life which is the mark of their courage.

The Nature of Artistic Courage

It was Paul Tillich who first taught us to understand the courage of the modern artist as an expression of his "courage to be." Yet, while I have no wish to engage here in a discussion of ontology (the nature of being), it seems to me that to move *too quickly* from the existential experience of aesthetic courage to its "Ground" may be to render the nature of this courage unintelligible, especially to artists themselves. For the courage of the contemporary artist is essentially a *courage of existence*, a facing of the abyss by one who lives by the conviction of his own finitude, who sees himself, in Baudelaire's terms, as "exiled in the imperfect." The modern artist believes that "the conviction of damnation is all that is left of faith" in a world forever damned. The contemporary artist then is one who begins with the presupposition of damnation, with the encounter with nothingness, and seeks to wrest from the abyss some order of meaning and being. In the words of the ancient Chinese poet, Lu Chi,

> We poets struggle with Non-being to force it to yield Being;
> We knock upon silence for an answering music. [2]

The courage of the modern artist lies in his struggle to bring meaning out of meaninglessness, order out of chaos, sound out of silence and, as we see in Thomas Mann, to wrest the myths of eternal verity from that which is "uniquely interesting" in the here and now.

It is not, however, the philosophical character of modern aesthetic courage which concerns us primarily, but rather the substance of that courage as we find it in the recurring themes of contemporary art and literature.

The Broken Center

"Tradition," says Heller, "is the wise agreement not to ask certain questions, to narrow the domain of the questionable, to grant the mind a firm

[1] Erich Heller, *The Disinherited Mind* (New York: Farrar, Straus & Cudahy, 1957), p. 202.
[2] Quoted by Archibald MacLeish in *Poetry and Experience* (Boston: Houghton Mifflin Co., 1961), p. 8.

foundation of answers which can be taken for granted." [3] While tradition certainly is more than so negative a definition allows, nevertheless tradition, as a firm foundation of accepted values and beliefs in terms of which life and art may be ordered, has ceased to exist. The horizons of the world, as Nietzsche prophesied, have been wiped away, as it were, with a great sponge. The magnetic pole which once stood at the center of reality, drawing and ordering all things around itself, is broken. The result is a world of chaos, of unrelated fragments. So it was that the poet Hofmannsthal wrote: "Everything fell to pieces, the pieces to pieces again, and nothing could be comprehended any more with the help of customary notions. Single words, torn apart, floated around me; they coalesced into the eyes which stared at me, and made me stare back. Then again they became a vortex which . . . dragged me into bleak emptiness." [4]

The disintegration of the known forms of reality has made for a new openness and freedom which both allow and force the artist to define his own reality for himself. "The modern poet," wrote Friedrich Schlegel, "must create his works entirely from within his own self, and many have done it magnificently, but each in isolation, and *every work was a new beginning, and came as if out of nothing*" [5] [italics mine].

With unlimited freedom then has come a responsibility for the creation of new forms. The artistic imagination, says Baudelaire, "decomposes all of creation, and, with the materials gathered, set forth according to rules whose origin cannot be found except in the deepest part of the soul, it creates a new world, and produces the experience of the new." [6] To call these new forms distortions of reality, as the insensitive are wont to do, presupposes what we cannot: namely, that there still exists an accepted standard of reality in terms of which we may measure and judge our new art. Vallentin once ran about the market place of Munich measuring things with a yardstick, then measuring the yardstick with a second of different length. This, I suggest, is our contemporary situation, a situation which permits a Braque to say: "I do not have to distort. I start from formlessness and create form."

The freedom and self-sufficiency of the creative act, in a time when reality has lost its center of reference, is the measure of the artist's courage. The courage of artistic freedom in our own time has found its fullest

[3] Erich Heller, *Thomas Mann: The Ironic German* (Cleveland: The World Publishing Co. [Meridian Book], 1961), p. 16.
[4] Quoted by Heller, *ibid.*, p. 23.
[5] Quoted by Heller, *ibid.*, p. 211.
[6] From "La reine des facultés," *Salon de 1859.* Quoted in *The Journal of Aesthetics and Art Criticism*, June, 1960, p. 458.

expression in that peculiarly American school of painters known as the abstract expressionists, in such painters as Jackson Pollock, Arshile Gorky, and Willem de Kooning. It is in these men that we have, for the first time, the symbolic expression of chaos, the iconography of anxiety and despair. It is here that we have the development of an aesthetic appropriate to the extremity of our human situation, for it is here that we encounter the "feverish mood of crisis," "the fierce mood of nihilism." The truth of abstract expressionism is the truth of the void, the end. The brooding grays and running pools of black in Gorky's art create the sensation of nausea, of a sickness unto death, relieved only by the introduction of bright primary colors among his seething pools of gray and black. In Pollock the elements of unintentionality, incoherence, and meaninglessness find their fullest expression. Freedom is wed to accident, and control is employed only to convince of uncontrol. The absurd, of which Camus speaks, is here realized in the art of painting. Pollock's paintings are a reflection of the courage of the modern artist because they show the loss of the center of reality. The mazes which he constructs do not logically end at the edges of his canvas, but run on infinitely, reflecting infinite possibility and freedom in a world in which God is reported to be dead.

The fractured art of our day, with its lost center and unlimited freedom, is further characterized by a terrible sensitivity to that dizziness of soul which comes when every horizon has vanished. The dizzy sickness which attends man's vertigo experience is a recurring theme in modern literature, for example, in Rilke's The Notebooks of Malte Laurids Brigge. Nikolai Kuzmich suddenly becomes aware that the earth beneath his feet is swirling simultaneously in many directions in strange confusion. He freezes with terror, for Nikolai is unusually sensitive to motion, even to the point of avoiding trolley cars. He reels about in his room, as on a ship deck, holding to whatever objects come to hand. Suddenly he recalls something about "the slanted axis of the earth." This is too much. He decides to lie down and keep quiet, and from that day Nikolai Kuzmich has not dared to move! To do so would mean to risk falling into a sea of infinite nothingness.

His very insistence upon representing vertigo in his art is the artist's defense against the void which would engulf and destroy him. His courage before the abyss might well be compared to that of Father Donnisan in Bernanos' Sous le Soleil de Satan. Bernanos give us a picture of Father Donnisan suspended above the whole sidereal abyss, then says: "The intrepid man, as though bent and torn away by the tremendous appeal

48

of the Nothing, sees himself lost beyond recovery. And yet, even at this moment, his dominant thought was still dull defiance."

The Isolato

The isolation of the individual, which expresses itself in themes of alienation, exile, and estrangement, is, says Nathan Scott, "the pervasive illness of our age." It is an illness which, portrayed in all of the modern arts, beguiles the naïve into thinking that the sickness is that of art, not of man. On the contrary, the art of alienation is an interpretation of what Gabriel Marcel calls "our life."

We see alienation in Picasso's group portraits in the way individuals do not look at each other. We find it in Tennessee Williams' plays in characters who talk endlessly, but always at each other. We observe it in the "indifferent" love life of the typist in Eliot's The Waste Land, in the human unrelatedness of Meursault in Camus' The Stranger, in the dehumanization of Kafka's Gregor in The Metamorphosis and Mr. K. in The Trial and The Castle. One of the unforgettable passages on this theme is from Thomas Wolfe's Look Homeward, Angel:

Naked and alone we came into exile. In her dark womb we did not know our mother's face; from the prison of her flesh have we come into the unspeakable and incommunicable prison of this earth. Which of us has known his brother? Which of us has looked into his father's heart? Which of us has not remained forever prison-pent? Which of us is not forever a stranger and alone? [7]

Whatever its failings, existentialism has the advantage of being the only "philosophy" which enables one to apprehend the meaning of modern man's solitude. Ours is an age in which, like Dante descending by spheres into the center of hell, man makes the raw descent into the ego of his own self—for Kierkegaard has told him that "subjectivity is the truth." This existential descent, however, brings one to the center of an ego for which neither time nor community has any reality. Relationships are impossible, except as they are established by an absurd leap of faith which takes one to a point beyond time and community. Leap or not, the isolation of the individual within the historic and human communities remains an unalterable fact. All that remains of the ego, as Auden put it, "is a dream."

Solitude is not only the ontological situation of man hurled into existence. It is also the psychological and sociological state of the contemporary artist. Indeed, the isolation of the modern artist as an artist

[7] (New York: Charles Scribner's Sons, 1929).

intensifies all the more his isolation as a man, thus making him more sensitive than the average to the meaning of modern man's aloneness and alienation. In Thomas Mann's short story, "Tonio Kröger," the young artist, Tonio, whom one might think of as the alter ego of Mann himself, says:

Literature is not a calling, it is a curse, believe me! When does one begin to feel the curse? Early, horribly early. At a time when one ought by rights still to be living in peace and harmony with God and the world. It begins by your feeling yourself set apart, in a curious sort of opposition to the nice, regular people; there is a gulf of ironic sensibility, of knowledge, scepticism, disagreement, between you and the others; it grows deeper and deeper, you realize that you are alone; and from then on any *rapprochement* is simply hopeless! [8]

It is the ability of the modern artist to endure the isolation which accompanies his art, both as its subject matter and as his own existential state of being, which is the mark of his courage and his genius. The art of alienation will endure so long as estrangement is the state of man himself and so long as the artist has the courage to be faithful to his vocation.

The Loss of God

Some years ago students at the University of Chicago put up a poster which announced, "God will appear in the lounge tonight to answer questions about his divinity." When that sign was removed, another was posted in its place which read, "Jesus will appear in the lounge tonight to answer questions about the disappearance of his Father's posters."

Whatever the signs of God which were once discernible to the eyes of faith, these have disappeared for modern man. Men today agree essentially with Thomas Wolfe's statement that "the essence of belief is doubt, the essence of reality is questioning." Unbelief—I almost said "religious unbelief"—is the spiritual situation of modern man. And modern art is the drama of the grandeur and misery of man without God.

One of the most moving witnesses to the loss of God, one which still bespeaks the crisis of our time, is that of the poet Hölderlin:

But we, my friend, are too late. The gods, it is true, are living,
    Yet far above ourselves, away in a different world.
There they are endlessly active and seem but little regardful
    Whether we live or no, such is their tender concern,

[8] Thomas Mann, *Stories of Three Decades*, tr. H. T. Lowe-Porter (New York: Alfred A. Knopf, 1936), p. 104.

Knowing that fragile vessels like us cannot always contain them,
   Only at times can men endure the abundance of gods.
Life thereafter is but a dream of them. Yet our wanderings
   Help, like sleep, and anguish and night give strength.
                Meanwhile, it seems to me often
   Better to slumber than live without companions, like this,
So to linger, and know not what to begin or to utter,
   Or, in such spiritless times, why to be poet at all? [9]

The experience of the loss of God is not limited to those who stand outside the church. The preoccupation of contemporary theologians with the nature of the Christian revelation arises, in part, from a sense of the loss of God in the Christian church itself. The radical nature of our plight finds its voice in W. H. Auden, who says, "for us the problem of faith is not of lapsing into a childish magical conception of God but of despair, of believing that God has abandoned us." However we look at it, the central fact of our existence, whether we be Christian or not, is that of unbelief. That unbelief is the present state of "Christendom" is evident enough in our so-called religious art. One mark of a vital faith is its ability to permit itself to be represented in abstract symbols. The insistence, however, of the masses of Christians in our time upon "sentimental realism" in religious art is but a manifestation of that deeper loss of faith we find outside the churches. The pretty surfaces of our religious art hide a "ciphered nihilism" and are thus less honest than the art forms we have been discussing.

The courage of the modern artist, by contrast, manifests itself in his ability and willingness to accept damnation and represent it in his art, indeed, to represent it in abstract symbols, such as Roszak's "Anguish." In a remarkable passage in his essay on Baudelaire, T. S. Eliot says:

So far as we do evil or good, we are human; and it is better, in a paradoxical way, to do evil than to do nothing: at least, we exist. It is true to say that the glory of man is his capacity for salvation; it is also true to say that his glory is his capacity for damnation. The worst that can be said of most of our malefactors, from statesmen to thieves, is that they are not men enough to be damned.[10]

The artists of our time have shown themselves to be "men" in this respect. One thinks immediately of Kafka—whom religious critics have too quickly

---

[9] Quoted and trans. by Erich Heller in *The Disinherited Mind*, pp. xi-xii. Used by permission of Erich Heller.
[10] From *Selected Essays* (rev. ed.: New York: Harcourt, Brace & Co., 1950), p. 380. Used by permission of Harcourt, Brace & World and Faber and Faber Ltd.

interpreted as a new priest for the *Deus absconditus*. To read Kafka thus, to see in *The Trial* or *The Castle* the face of the Wholly Other, is to mis-interpret Kafka, who never once in his life, even in his most private notes, uttered the belief that the quest of his soul was directed toward God. Before Kafka's preoccupation with evil and estrangement, God retreated into utter transcendence, beyond the power of the imagination even to think. Kafka is the artist who is man enough to be damned, and *this* is his religious significance. Our response to Kafka is appropriately expressed in those words of Thomas Mann: "I am filled with awe in presence of the religious greatness of the damned."

Since we have no wish to be guilty of the "sentimentality" of pessimism, it is necessary for us to look also at those artists whose courage consists not in their acceptance of damnation but in their struggle to affirm something in defiance of hell itself. "Modern affirmation," says Amos Wilder, "is hard won." The quest for faith in a nihilistic age is Dantesque; it requires one to journey through hell, and the agony of this journey is nowhere more forcefully expressed than in writers like T. S. Eliot and Graham Greene. In Greene, grace almost always chooses to manifest itself in the depths of unbelief and sin, for example, in the "whiskey priests" of *The Potting Shed* and *The Power and the Glory*. In Eliot, the agony of a disquieted unbelief is wedded to the language of paradox (the paradox of doubt and faith) and antithesis (the antithesis of Word and world). Take "Ash-Wednesday":

> If the lost word is lost, if the spent word is spent
> If the unheard, unspoken
> Word is unspoken, unheard;
> Still is the unspoken word, the Word unheard,
> The Word without a word, the Word within
> The world and for the world;
> And the light shone in darkness and
> Against the Word the unstilled world still whirled
> About the centre of the silent Word.[11]

The descent of modern Christian writers into the depths of the demonic is itself a kind of affirmation of faith. As Eliot says in the essay on Baude-laire, Satanism itself is "an attempt to get into Christianity by the back

[11] From *Collected Poems: 1909-1935*. Copyright, 1936, by Harcourt, Brace & Co. Used by permission of Harcourt, Brace & World and Faber and Faber Ltd.

door. Genuine blasphemy, genuine in spirit and not purely verbal, is the product of partial belief, and is as impossible to the complete atheist as to the perfect Christian." [12]

The Wedding Day for Light and Darkness

The devout Christian who has lived in the modern world without entertaining doubt (I have not met him) will doubtless wonder why it has been necessary for us to invade the chambers of Satan and suffer the innermost agonies of modern art in order to win some small (perhaps too small) measure of Christian affirmation. The answer is twofold. First, as Sir Herbert Read has said, "The criterion of the modern artist is Truth rather than Beauty." Yet nothing less than *truth*, as I understand it, is permissible for Christians! In our nihilistic and unbelieving age, such truth requires coming to grips with the most nihilistic expressions of our culture and making ourselves sensitive to the spiritual crisis recorded therein. And this involves, among other things, coming to grips with contemporary art. This then is our present theological task. For as Paul Tillich has stated: "A present theology of culture is, above all, a theology of the end of culture, not in general terms but in a concrete analysis of the inner void of our cultural expressions. Little is left in our present civilization which does not indicate to a sensitive mind the presence of this vacuum." Second, the way of Christ himself involved abandoning the throne of grace and entering into the world of human sin and suffering, standing in silence before unjust judgment and crying out in despair at the moment of death, and finally enduring death and hell itself. In these "spiritless times," anything less than abandonment of the glories of theological certainty, anything less than entry into the depths of hell as it exists in the innermost heart of modern man, is *unchristian!* I find myself asking whether the Christian church today is able to believe those words of the psalmist: "If I make my bed in Sheol, thou art there!" (Ps. 139:8).

More specifically now, how does one respond to modern nihilism when, if one is himself a modern man and an honest one, he cannot flee the shock of the abyss or rely, as Kierkegaard put it, on cribbing the answers from the back of the book? Is not the answer the same for other men as for the poet, whose calling today, as Stanley Hopper put it, "is one of alienation and return—if he can make it"? The Christian is sent by his Lord into the world, not as the emissary of some anti-world, but as man redeemed

[12] Eliot, *Selected Essays*, p. 373.

in all his humanness and being-in-the-world. Whoever, then, fears alienation or despairs of return has not understood this essential fact of the Christian life.

Nietzsche once said, "The wedding day has come for light and darkness." The Christian, I suggest, may find here a *positive* principle for his own understanding and action. Karl Heim has suggested that secularism contains within itself the logic of its own end and that Christians ought, therefore, to *encourage* secularism and show what is happening in it. One might go even further and discover within the demonic symbolism of contemporary culture and art a manifestation of deity itself. Heller, with reference to Kafka, has said that the symbolic substance of his art, forced back in every attempt to attack from above, invades reality from below, bringing with it the stuff of hell. Kafka's symbolism, then, shows "two things at once, and both with equal assurance: that there *is* no God, and that there *must* be God." The dialectic of the demonic, like the dialectic of the Holy, may become the means for the reality of grace asserting itself, and that all the more vehemently through the power of its demonic antithesis.

A second way of approach is also suggested by Nietzsche when he says that "nihilism represents a pathological interim state." Nihilism is not finally a possibility for man, as Kierkegaard knew when he said that suicide itself requires an affirmation which undermines the nihilist stance. And every work of art which seeks to expose the *nihil* is, as we have suggested, a defense against the void and an antithesis to it. The only possibility open to the nihilist is "to go on living with the threat of the deadly abyss, to dwell on a thin crust of ice, and wait for something new to come. Nobody yet has ever lived in the water wastes beneath the ice. Life is rather an anxious existence 'between the times.' Nobody ever lives in non-time, in Nothingness." [13]

Finally, I would suggest that the Christian answer for our time lies not in the struggle to bring being out of nothingness, as Lu Chi suggests (for man finally cannot create *ex nihilo*), but in listening for some sound to come from the "silent Word." Rilke put it thus:

> Not that you could endure
> the voice of God—far from it. But hark to the suspiration,
> the uninterrupted news that grows out of silence.[14]

[13] Helmut Thielicke, *Nihilism*, tr. John W. Doberstein (New York: Harper & Brothers, 1961), p. 165.

[14] Rainer Maria Rilke, *Duino Elegies*, tr. J. B. Leishman and Stephen Spender (New York: W. W. Norton & Co., Inc., 1939), p. 25.

The abyss is *eternally silent!* The void has no word of revelation with which to make itself known to us as Ultimate! Being, however, has a Word, though in ages like our own this Word may choose to be silent before the "unstilled world." Despair then is only existential. Jesus, it is true, cried out of existential despair at the silence of the Ultimate. "My God, my God, why hast thou forsaken me?" Yet he *did* address God, and he found courage in death, and it is this which today's artists and Christians respectively must come to understand.

V

Is the Creative Process Similar in the Arts?

JULIUS PORTNOY

THE PSYCHOLOGICAL PROCESS THAT TAKES PLACE IN THE CONCEPTION OF A work of art is essentially the same, whether it be one art form or another. The creation of fine art, from its inception to the time of its expression, follows a definite behavior pattern. Artists vary in their mediums of expression because of differences in technical aptitudes. These techniques can to a certain degree be acquired and developed as part of a learning process. An artist's medium of expression is what Aristotle would call an accident rather than an attribute of his artistic nature. Artistic creativity cannot be taught or learned; it is basically an emotional phenomenon, even when appearances would seem to deny it. That artists are different from most men in nature and temperament was well known to the ancients and is commonly accepted now as well. But precisely why the artist creates—and how—is still, in part, unanswerable to this day.

Creativity as Divine Inspiration

The Greeks considered the artist to be a divinely inspired being who created his art in the same manner that the gods had fashioned the world, after the model of eternal archetypes. One of Homer's many fables is that artists are divinely inspired. Irrational poets rather than rational temple priests are the favorite mortals of the gods. Plato enhanced this

Homeric myth with his own belief that the gods take away the minds of the poets and imbue them with a divine frenzy so that when they are in a state of ecstasy they are capable of prophecy and supernatural wisdom. All artists create by the grace of the gods, but the gift of the bard is richer than that of any other artist. When Socrates went to the poets and asked them what they had said in their odes, he found that they were unable to give him a rational account of how they had come to create or what their creations meant. The gods had spoken through them, was their contention, and they were not in their right minds when creating. Socrates was poking fun at the poets, as he was at everyone else, but the implication is that the poets were more carried out of themselves when creating than other artists were. Had Socrates talked to artists in other fields about the meaning of their art he would have found that they were not very different from the poets, the favorites of the gods.

The Greeks were not the only ones to compare the artist to gods. The poet Browning likened the creative artist to the God of Christianity. Just as the God of Christendom created the world out of nothing, so the artist performs a lesser miracle in the process of creating something that had not existed before. The musician, like God himself, transcends natural law; he exceeds even the bonds of mortal creators, Browning believes. The finger of God has singled out the musician from all the rest, is Browning's theme in *Abt Vogler*; but it is questionable whether the finger of God is any more pointed at the musician than it is at the poet and painter.

Kant's classification of the arts gives credence to the notion that because there is a difference between the arts there is also a dissimilarity in the creative process. By placing the more emotive arts at the bottom and the less emotive arts at the top of his hierarchy he gives the impression that art forms which are closer to reason and understanding, like poetry in comparison to music, are produced by a mental process that approaches a philosophic discipline. Hegel practically says the same thing. But Schopenhauer and Nietzsche turn the Kantian hierarchy of values upside down. For them, the emotive arts are higher in importance than those that are able to express concepts. The more irrational the artist is, the greater are his insights, precisely because he is freed from intellectual restraint. To Kant, art born of contemplation is superior to what is produced in the arts by emotive eruptions. To Schopenhauer and Nietzsche, art is an expression of emotion, the animal, the irrational in man, resisting civilization itself.

Creativity as Unconscious Expression

Our analytic psychologists have gathered an abundant amount of clinical evidence that artistic ideas have their origin in conflicts and repressions of which the artist is not even consciously aware. Rank tells us that the artist strives for immortal recognition by creating something that will live after him. Horace, Shakespeare, Shelley give poetic expression to Rank's belief that the human craving for immortality is a driving force to create a monument of greater permanence than a fleeting life on earth. Adler is of the conviction that creating art is a means of compensating for organic deficiencies. In musical creation Beethoven unconsciously compensated for a physical infirmity, Schumann for a mental one, and Chopin for an imaginary one, according to this theory. Freud maintains that creating art is a sublimating process for realizing unfulfilled desires in the form of fantasy. The colorful canvases of Van Gogh and Matisse are an escape from the drab world that most of us know. Jung agrees with Freud as to why artists create, but he differs with Freud as to what their creations signify. He holds not only that the creation of art is more than personal wish fulfillment but that it is an expression of the collective unconscious, a symbol of eternity expressed in modern form. In the extended line of a Berlioz theme, in the plaintive lament of a religious chant, the voice of the past and present is heard, not just the voice of the composer. Bergler obverts the Freudian theory that art is wish fulfillment with his own belief that the artist creates to hide his actual feelings from us; art is a defense mechanism, not wishful fantasy. The novels of Hardy, Proust, and Gide are like protective cloaks behind which these authors hide their actual feelings and guilt. However varied these theories may be, one central theme yet binds them together. Artistic creation is the expression of the unconscious life of man which originates from conflicts and repressions. Artists may create for different reasons but they draw their strength from one source, the unconscious, and then follow a similar mental course in the process of nurturing and expressing their ideas.

It is doubtful whether any of these theories fully explain why man creates and how. The belief of the analytic school that the unconscious, the storehouse of past experience, hope, and frustration, is the never-failing source of all art is expanded by Jung to include all human creativity. A song of praise, a poem of hate, a social novel, a religious drama have their origin in the unconscious forces, but so do other human activities which are not artistic in nature. Not all creation has its origin in conflicts and repressions either, as the analytic school is apt to stress, but if we peruse the history of art we find that those who have made a lasting contribution have been men who have been burdened with conflicts and tensions, conscious and unconscious in character.

Young people are rarely original, their artistic contribution is mostly technical. They have not lived long enough to experience deep hurts, become embittered and envious. Their psychical disturbances will bring forth a delightful Mozartian Singspiel at best. Talented young people are virtuosos, master craftsmen at an early age. First they must live before they can create.

The ability to create is not the artist's alone. The scientific process of invention and the artistic process of creation are alike. The end products of scientific and artistic creation differ, but the creative process is the same for each. Poincaré's description of the role of the unconscious, the incubation of an idea and the illumination that follows in giving birth to a new mathematical formula could also fit Van Gogh's explanation of the creative process. The scientist relies on knowledge to produce something practical. The artist converts his repressed emotions into something fanciful. The artist may produce sheer nonsense, which is something that the scientist cannot afford to do. The psychological process that takes place in a mathematical discovery does not differ from the conception of a new way to depict nature in colors never known before. Working, waiting, lamenting, are common to scientist and artist alike before their ideas are crystallized. To create is to produce something new, whether it be a concept of a state or a new system of musical sounds. In this essay we are concerned with those who create fine art.

The Creative Temper of the Artist

Artists tend to be neurotic personalities. They cannot live with themselves or adjust to others. Even if others were to conform to them, they would not be able to accept the *status quo* for long. Should their neuroticism become overly severe, they would become unproductive altogether. They are cursed, and at the same time blessed, with a high degree of sensitivity. On the one hand, this sensitivity creates these very conflicts for them, and on the other hand, because they can resolve these conflicts in such a way that their art gives us a new vision of man, a novel interpretation of the world, they make a contribution to mankind. A man who produces one masterpiece and never another illustrates that the creation of art is not a continuous process. Where there is no strife and tension there is no art, in a pure sense. Scribes and hacks who produce continuously are like

59

parasites living on the ideas of others. They are men of good stability and so they bring forth nothing novel in the arts.

Artists are dedicated people who become so absorbed in what they are doing that they may well shut themselves off from the rest of the world. Still, an artist cannot live in isolation for too long a period of time, for then his art will become either symbolic of a vacuous life or it may develop into an overly refined type of expression. It is as though the artist were saying: "I wish to be as detached from the public in my art as I am separated from the ordinary run of men in my private life."

The stimulus which brings artistic ideas into being may come in response to an inner need, at which time the artist is practically aglow with the fires of creation. At other times in his career he may have a contract to fulfill and the mood to create eludes him. Having learned from past experience that sitting and waiting for the muse will leave him with nothing produced, he will try to evoke a mood which is conducive to creation; that will come with much effort, if at all.

The intrinsic merit of a work of art will have little to do with one method or the other, whether it be spontaneous or labored to meet the terms of a contract. In the spontaneous method, ideas which have long lain dormant will rise to the surface, each part in its proper place, to produce a unified whole. In the more labored method the artist tries to evoke a mood conducive to creation by contemplation and even stimulation, culling from his unconscious fruitful ideas for his needs. In one case, emotion erupts and the work of art emerges, perfect and complete. In the other, emotion is appealed to in order to break through restraint.

Artists draw upon life experiences or imaginary ones for their creations. There is no other source to draw from. They create for the same purpose, in the same way, in terms of psychological relief and unconscious activity. Their methods vary, their personal peculiarities differ, but the creative mechanism is as determined as the flow of blood running through their veins. They have no more control over this process than they have over the direction of a dream. Their art begins in the unconscious, is mulled over, elaborated upon, and then comes to the conscious level in response to a personal need, often involuntarily, or in response to some external stimulus. Because artists are controlled by forces they cannot understand, they are as mystified as we are as to how they come by their art and the meaning it conveys. Their descriptions of the creative process cannot be taken seriously. Like art, artists' diaries are written for posterity, a little less fanciful perhaps.

But when we find one dominant tone in all the explanations that artists have left us, however fanciful they may be, there is no brushing it aside. Their malady is the same; one need not be a wise physician to recognize their common symptoms, even when disguised. Consciously or unconsciously they gather material, comb the works of other artists for ideas. They are men of wonder who are impelled to search for what is beyond appearance itself. The material that they accumulate must be assimilated and become part of them. It is this phase of the process during which the artist is particularly restless, irritable, and vexed. Often, a gnawing sensation will not let him rest and then, all of a sudden, the whole world lights up and everything is clear and bright; with a minimum of effort it arrives, each part relevant, a thoroughly unified work. The same artist may sometimes work in a more arduous way. First he sketches and plans, repeats the process a thousand times, before a half-satisfying work begins to emerge.

The Unity of Creative Activity in the Arts

Artists have no qualms about using the forms of other arts when it suits their purpose. Maillol expresses a poem of life in a wistful statuette. Rodin expresses the concept of an architectural monument in the statue of a nude woman. Whitman writes a poem after the model of a musical symphony. Huxley plays one character off against another, in one of his novels, in the same fugal fashion that a baroque master planned a contrapuntal score. Liszt uses music to create a poetic image. Strauss depicts, as a storyteller would, a day of married bliss at one time in his life.

Ancient bards were both poets and musicians; there was no separation between them that far back in time. *Jongleurs* and *trouvères* perpetuated this tradition into the late Middle Ages of Western man. During the Renaissance there were some most exceptional artists who created in several fields without any variance in their creative process. Michelangelo was painter, architect, sculptor, and poet all in one. Leonardo's inventive disposition was just as fertile in scientific endeavors as it was in art itself. In more recent times, Wagner merged practically all the arts into his music drama, as though to belie any lingering belief that there is a difference in the creative process between one art form and another. Picasso works in ceramics, oils, and drawings, with a high degree of originality appearing in all three. Modigliani's preoccupation with primitive forms appears in both his paintings and his sculpture. The same idea comes through, be it in stone or on canvas. Eliot's artistic insights are just as evident in his plays as they are in his poems. The material that an artist deals with may be rigid or malleable, so that one kind of material may lend itself more easily to the expression of an idea than another. It is also true that artistic ideas that are expressible in one medium can be expressed in another—not so well perhaps, but expressible nevertheless. The psychological mechanism that is involved in creation is the same whatever material the artist may use. Artists resemble the original gods of Greece. Each god created like every other god, but one produced light, another darkness—one love, another war. The only difference is that the gods fashioned the world after eternal archetypes while artists draw their inspiration from a repository of repressed emotion and guilt. Creation is a gift that artists share together, as the gods before them did; and like the gods they contribute according to their specific interests to the making of a new world.

The evidence presented in this essay that artists create alike is surely not conclusive. If it serves as a reminder, however, that in our penchant for specialties and categories we are apt to lose sight of the common denominator in discussing the creative personality, then this essay has served a purpose. In essence, a creative experience may be spontaneous, like a crystallized witticism, condensed and apt for the occasion. It may be labored and drawn out as in the case of a man who works unceasingly until he achieves an effect that pleases him, although he did not know what he wanted or expected before he began his project. There is no evidence that one method has produced art of greater merit than the other.

The source of the artist's creativity has its origin in conflicts and tensions and a host of half-forgotten memories, painful and pleasant alike. It is from this past experience, so much of which has become latent and dormant over the years, that the artist primarily draws his ideas, whatever be his method. Nature's inexorable laws for begetting a work of art are the same for poet, painter, and musician. It is we who devise arbitrary classifications and separate one from the other.

VI

The Artist and the Problem of Communication

KEITH W. IRWIN

TO BROACH THE PROBLEM OF COMMUNICATION IN OUR DAY IS INEVITABLY TO deal with language and linguistic usage in some one of many possible forms. A course in communication skills would feature the development of clarity and persuasiveness in one's use of the spoken and written word. When the mass media of communication are referred to, one thinks of radio, television, periodicals, addresses, and sermons as the means whereby linguistic utterances are conveyed to audiences vast or small. A letter serves to communicate with an absent friend, a long distance phone call with one's family (no farther away than the nearest phone!). Language, oral or written, is used to describe states of affairs, to formulate scientific hypotheses, to express or evoke emotions, to invoke the sense of the Holy Presence, to articulate and sustain an ultimate concern, to command an action, to ask a question; and the enumeration could run on at length.

What about the arts, the artist, and communication? Poetry, the novel, drama—these are linguistic forms. Do they fall under any of the above functions? Are they used with the intent to make some item of knowledge common, to impart some wisdom or insight to others? Do they express in words some aspect of the forms our emotions might take in participation in and response to "the misery and grandeur of man" and his internal and external history? And what about the nonlinguistic arts of music,

63

sculpture, painting, the dance? What do they convey to their auditors or viewers? Like the literary forms, *they are made public*; that is, they are *meant* to be seen, heard, "appreciated." Paintings are exhibited, symphonies are performed, the poem requires that it be read aloud, the novel is reviewed by critics. Indeed, the artistic creation which is locked away, never to be subject to the inspection and consideration of others, is a contradiction in terms. Sebastian, in Williams' *Suddenly Last Summer*, in the creation of one "precious" poem a year, carefully hoarded from the vulgar and critical public, represents the perversion of creative talent. His is either a confession of cowardice or of failure, either an admission of impotence or, to carry out to its logical conclusion the metaphor suggested by his mother's comment that his work took nine months of gestation, the delivery of a stillbirth. But already in saying this much some of the most difficult questions in aesthetic theory have been either "begged" or glossed over. More careful statement is in order.

The Locus of Communication

Symbols are of many kinds and forms—words, events, actions, pictures, objects like flags and crosses, and the list could go on and on. Their common distinguishing characteristic is that they serve the function of mediating between a subject and that which is the object of his experience. They represent the point of juncture between the subject and his world where knowledge is born. Thus the most common abstract description of the situation or process in which communication takes place is in terms of a diagram of a triangle. The symbol, or vehicle for conveying symbolic meaning, at the apex of the triangle stands in relation to the "object" to which it refers at the right-hand corner of the base of the triangle, and to the person for whom it is a symbol at the left-hand corner of the triangle. There is no direct traffic across the base of the triangle from object to subject. Even the barest perceptions are given form when we "pick" them out of the flux of our experience by fastening attention on them, relate them to other percepts, give them names. What cannot be represented symbolically cannot be thought; what cannot be thought cannot be known.

Without going into the intricacies of the distinction between those meaning functions of symbols labeled "connotation" and "denotation," one can still distinguish from this too brief picture two additional dimensions of meaning which are of great importance for the problem at hand. This is the distinction implied by raising the question of what *a person means* when he uses a word or symbol in contrast to the question of what *the word or symbol itself* means. In the case of a work of art, a play, a poem, a sonata, the distinction manifests itself between what the artist (playwright, poet, musician) means or intends to express or communicate in his work and the meaning conveyed by the work in its own independent existence. At which of these two points does one locate the communicative function of art? To what extent is it necessary to examine the question of the artist's intent in creating the work of art?

An immediate suggestion for an answer comes from a consideration of those media which require reproduction, performance, in order to embody their proper form—musical composition, the drama, etc. The musician is not free to do anything he pleases with the piece he is performing. And the intention of the playwright, what he wants to express, is relevant to the problem of adequate theatrical performance. But the challenge to the composer or the dramatist is to embody in the work itself, through clarity of expression, adequate stage directions, indications of dynamics and tempo, what it is that he intends. No amount of statement from him will make it clear short of rewriting the text to make explicit the meaning intended. If a performing artist is in a quandary about what emphasis to give a passage in his text, words from the author might help him—which is why a playwright works with the rehearsals of a new play if possible. But even in as mundane a piece as this essay the burden on the author is to put the intended meaning in it as precisely as possible. If there are obscurities for which the text itself is responsible no amount of "But I meant to say—" will avail, short of a painstaking rewrite to give explicit statement to what was meant.

It is possible—and indeed actually the case—that an artist might not be aware of all that he has released in his work, either in terms of its deficiencies or of its positive values. Symbolic media, be they words, musical notations, or arrangements of color and form, are public property with a history and tradition of their own. They are a gift to the artist and have funded meanings, a richness of expressive capacity, a credit balance to be drawn on far beyond the conscious awareness of the user of the media. No artist, no critic, can restrict by fiat the meaning of the artist's work to his conscious intentions. There are implications of the sensory elements, the formal composition, the subject matter which the artist can neither restrict nor take back once they are released. Symbolic meaning is born out of community and the community is both directed to new meanings added by creative work and to read broader meanings and levels of meaning into the work than the artist was consciously aware of investing in it. This is why the yearling student of literature is improperly astounded when he expostulates, "But surely Milton couldn't have meant all that you've read into him!" Whether Milton was consciously aware of all those between-the-lines and between-the-words implications the learned professor teases out of him is a problem for the historian of literature to unravel, but when Milton drew on the English language to write *Paradise Lost*, he *did*, whether he wished to or not, release with his words all the fund of vested interest the whole linguistic tradition has put into them. Often the artist who merits our attention is one who knows the tradition, how much it has contributed to him, and how much he modifies and departs from it.

In short, once released, the work of art has an objective existence and an intentional character of its own. Even if the artist had *no* intention that a work be performed or exhibited but had developed it only to work out a technical problem for his own satisfaction or to satisfy an inner compulsion, once discovered, the work, if it has any merit, demands the appreciation and critical attention of all those who have a stake in those elements of the realms of symbolic meaning on which the work has drawn. In other words, it might well be that some works of art—akin to myth and ritual for Susanne Langer, and religious symbols for Tillich—are nonintentional *in their origin*, are expressions of acts of symbolic transformation necessary as ends in themselves for the artist, *but* once in existence they (metaphorically) cry out for the fulfillment of that second intentional or meaning relation to an interpreter which is inherent in any symbolic mode. Furthermore, it is possible that because of a failure to understand fully his own work, or out of a desire for publicity, or to shock a hostile or indifferent public, an artist might state his reasons for writing, painting, or composing as he does in a way that would seriously mislead the critic were he to take the statement at its face value.

From this discussion we might conclude that the *prime* locus of artistic communication is not in the artist's purposes but in the objective, intentional character of the work of art itself.

What Is Communicated?

One strong movement in contemporary philosophy has restricted the attention of the philosopher to language, and in particular to those conditions under which one particular kind of linguistic utterance could be said to be true, to convey knowledge—in short, to have cognitive status. Those utterances which don't have cognitive meaning—i.e., fail to conform to certain specified methods of intersubjective verification—are designated as meaningless, or, more kindly, as having emotive meaning. Their function is to express or evoke emotions; and into this basket are lumped religious, ethical, and aesthetic utterances. Aesthetic judgments communicate nothing about the external world, but rather something about the emotions or attitudes of the speaker. The only kind of information they convey is auto-biographical information!

This dichotomy between a kind of communication which is objective, theoretical, and scientific, in contrast to that which is subjective, expressive, and passional, has manifested itself in the traditions of aesthetic theory for many centuries past and has provided two different poles toward which such theories have gravitated. The mood of classicism in aesthetic theory has emphasized the formal elements in the work of art and the content of the work. Symmetry, balance of parts, repetitions of line and theme, an intellectually ordered and harmonious whole, in some cases even geometrically conceived, have been the criteria of judgment. Such apparently objective criteria have been used either to defend the aesthetic enterprise against the criticism of subjectivism or to avoid the dangers said to lie in subjectivism. Sensuous elements were subjected to the demands of formal structure; the passions, if admitted at all, were placed under rigorous rational control. On the side of content, formal theory emphasized the representational character of art; art was to provide an imitation of reality, but reality as ideal or perfect, screened of the ugly, the excesses of sentiment, the prodigality of nature by the control of the intellect. Music, drama, painting, architecture communicated through the sensuous manifold the underlying rational unities of a conceptual order.

At the opposite pole the romanticist movement might be seen as an attempt to assert the legitimacy of the material and sensuous character of reality in its own right. The contrast between Pope and Wordsworth, between Voltaire and Rousseau, between Mozart and Wagner, between Plato's critique of music in *The Republic* and Kierkegaard's Aesthete praising *Don Juan* illustrates in the latter member of each of these pairs the defense of sensuous appeal and the life of feeling. Art is the expression of emotion, the evocation of feeling and passion. The presentation of the sensuous manifold is released from the "sterile" control of reason so that nature in all its richness, its sensuous fecundity, its primal creative urges might find full play on the stage, the canvas, in stone, in sound, in the purple passage. The roman, the sentimental, rather than being given a negative critical judgment, became matter for praise.

The basic criticism of these two views is that the former subjects the artistic enterprise to domination by metaphysics and conceptual needs and the latter tends to a psychologizing of both the artist's work and the beholder's response. The former takes consciousness and becoming captive to the categories of rational being so that consciousness is shorn of its concrete particularity, and the latter mounts a revolt in the name of consciousness which ends in the chaotic anarchy of an almost undifferentiated and undisciplined sensuousness. One can use Christian terms here and say that the former commits the idolatry of ignoring the implications of the myth of the Tower of Babel and the latter commits itself to a more or less thorough antinomianism.

A more adequate view than either of these alone would insist that "Like the process of speech the artistic process is a dialogical and a dialectic one." [1] The two poles of conceptual or formal order and sensuous material need to be held in tension with each other, a tension dictated by the unique character of the artistic enterprise as contrasted with the scientific. The scientific enterprise is concerned to hold the hypothetical, conceptual component in tension with the empirical data, lest theory outrun verification so far that it becomes vain metaphysical speculation. But the creative factor in the scientific enterprise is contributed from the side of conceptual ingenuity. Science always operates within the framework of a theoretical component, and the task of the scientific mind is to generalize by means of hypotheses, to cast a conceptual net over expanding areas of experience and to abstract out those elements that can be given a common treatment. It is in virtue of fertile hypotheses, and a manifestation of them, that the periodic table of atomic weights, the reduction of qualitative to quantitative differences in spectrum analysis, the description of ideal bodies in terms of mass and inertia screen out and abbreviate reality so that a relevant set of common properties in each case can be isolated for study. The hypothesis has an explanatory and predictive role in relation to the facts that authorize it, but the definition of what constitutes authorizing facts undergoes constant modification to serve the needs of hypotheses at ever broadening levels of generality.

The artistic enterprise, we have said, is concerned to hold the same two poles of formal order and sensuous material in dialogical tension; but rather than aiming at abstraction and generalization it aims at the unique individual, at a concretion, a particularization of knowledge. This has been variously defined. Herbert Read has said, "The artistic activity might . . . be described as a crystallization, from the amorphous realm of feeling, of forms that are significant or symbolic." [2] One might distinguish here a twofold sense of the word "feeling": the reception of

[1] Ernst Cassirer, *An Essay on Man* (New Haven, Conn.: Yale University Press, 1944), p. 149.
[2] Herbert Read, *Icon and Idea* (London: Faber & Faber, Ltd., 1955), p. 18.

sensory material ("felt" experience), and the life of the emotions, our affective experience. The knowledge that art communicates is the awareness of particular formal significance which feeling in this twofold sense stirs in us. That the awareness is of significant form suggests that art yields its own kind of universality. The universality attained by scientific theory and the admiration of the logic of discursive argument which has made this universality possible has blinded many people to the fact that artistic expression has its own logic, that universality can be attained not only by attention to the general but also by attention to the unique, the concretely individual. Wheelwright, in his study of the language of symbolism, has listed eight basic assumptions characteristic of literal, "stenolanguage," representational discourse, in order to draw from them a comparable list of the logical principles of expressive language and to confirm this by reference to its mode of functioning in depth experience.

These eight assumptions of the logic of literal language fall into three groups. The first five deal with the logic of terms, the next two with the logic of propositions, and the last one with the character of logical system. In an abbreviated account these assumptions are: (a) the linguistic symbol is sufficiently distinct from the "object" of its reference that the two are never interchangeable; (b) the symbols of literal language are univocal in meaning; (c) vagueness is a fault to be avoided by striving for definiteness of meaning on each occasion of a symbol's use; (d) the literal symbol must retain an identity of meaning throughout any occurrence in a given argument—the assumption of semantic invariance; (e) the logical significance of a symbol is restricted by quantification as either universal or particular; (f) the truth-value assigned a proposition is equivalent for any true proposition or for any false proposition; (g) hence the law of contradiction holds—if any proposition (p) is true, its contradictory (non-p) is false; (h) ideally every true proposition is a member of a system of true propositions.[3] These assumptions define the universe of discourse, both the process and content of any possible communication in literal language.

By dialectical argument from these assumptions Wheelwright fleshes out what is barely hinted at in Susanne Langer's attempt to state the logic of presentational symbolism.[4] The eight assumptions of what Wheelwright calls "expressive language" he identifies as: [5] (a) The principle of

---

[3] Philip Wheelwright, The Burning Fountain (Bloomington, Ind.: Indiana University Press, 1954), pp. 55-59.

[4] Susanne Langer, Philosophy in a New Key (New York: Penquin Books, Inc., 1941), pp. 211-15.

[5] Op. cit., pp. 60-75. The following account is a very free summary of the passage, hopefully true to its content.

iconic signification which states that in addition to pointing beyond themselves expressive symbols are self-referential. "They mean by resembling," and hence their value is not merely utilitarian but intrinsic as well. This is, I take it, at least part of what Tillich has in mind when he says that "the symbol participates in the reality it represents." [6] Because of this intrinsic meaning, expressive symbols cannot be substituted for one another. (b) An expressive symbol may carry more than one reference. It is not that such symbols are equivocal, but that they have plural reference. (c) The principle of soft focus states that there are shaded edges of meaning, a "connotative fringe" for expressive symbols which makes a definite outline for their meanings impossible. This does not justify obscurity, but it is an acknowledgment of the subtlety, the richness, and the ambivalences of the realms of the sensuous and the emotive to which expressive language refers. (d) The expressive symbol reflects its context in the flux of experience in such a way that, though it retains a core of meaning in each instance, its full meaning will vary with and can only be found in its context. (e) The dimensions of universality and particularity which obtain in literal language have very limited application to expressive symbolism where universality is concrete and integral to the iconic character of the symbol itself. The cross as a religious symbol has such a concrete universality. (f) The assertorial tone of an expressive statement varies far more widely than a true-false dichotomy allows. There is a combination of delicacy and strength in the expressive statement such that "its truth is more fragile, and it asks no guarantee." (g) Expressive statement can employ paradoxical assertion on its surface, in the depth of its meaning, or in the relationship of statement and innuendo in which both sides of the paradox are necessary and acceptable. (h) The principle of significant mystery holds that there always remains a quality of meaning in expressive symbolism which eludes systematic explication; meaning always transcends any totality of explanations.

The rich development of symbolic logic as applied to literal and scientific language in this century has provided a basis for, and a delimitation of the content of, communicable knowledge within such language. A comparable effort in the area of the arts and the nature, criteria and limits of expressive symbolism is a necessity if in our time the arts are not to be stifled by the pressures of a discursively oriented public to make artistic communication translatable into literal language, nor to become the precious property of a totally noncommunicative coterie.

[6] Paul Tillich, The Dynamics of Faith (New York: Harper & Brothers, 1957), p. 42.

The way out of such an impasse is to extend the recognition that symbolic form in the arts does manifest itself at many levels. The level most readily objectified and most adequately dealt with in aesthetic theory is that of organized structure. The principles of symmetry and balance; unity in variety; theme and variation; relationship of part to whole; tension to resolution; the requirement of movement—all pertain in marked degree to every art form. A second level of the symbolic expression of form exists in regard to material in art. Though not of first importance, subject matter, where it occurs, gives determinate character to the work. But of first importance at the point of potentiality is the raw material used— stone, oils, instrumentation, words, the human body and voice in dance and drama. These set the challenge to the artist's capacities and set the boundaries, the physical limits, to what he can accomplish. Texture, surface, brilliance, empathy are indispensable components of the form and effect of the finished creation. At a third level the artist in the employment of his imagination provides a reconstruction of visual, auditory, kinesthetic, dramatic experience. As this reconstruction is determined by the artist's sense of the significant—both in terms of the "feel" of the sensuous field and of the forms of emotional response—the art work will have symbolic import as it directs the apprehender to a reappraisal of his own relationship to that reality now newly presented to him. At these three levels expressive symbolism embodies formal motifs of the type delineated by Wheelwright, and in terms of these it is possible to say that there exists a fourth level of form, the enunciation of such unifying functional principles or laws. What more complete pattern within which to locate the realities of communication in the arts could one want?

Postscript

The Christian, in his attempt to explicate the problem of communication, whether in literal language or the arts, will in the end inevitably have to view with jaundiced eye the ideal of a perfect univocal clarity of meaning, unless it be that universality of understanding foreshadowed by Pentecost and so imperfectly exemplified in the church today. In between the Tower of Babel and Pentecost our apprehension and our communication of reality is "through a glass darkly." For one who is himself a creature to observe the limits of a finite creative capacity is neither to sin boldly—to glory in artistic obfuscation—that grace may abound nor to be an icon smasher to assure the purging of all idolatrous pretension to have seen "face to face"; rather, it is to work out one's salvation through expressive forms with "fear and trembling."

71

VII

The Artist as Prophet-Priest of Culture

IN THE FAMOUS WORDS OF PAUL KLEE, "ART DOES NOT REPRODUCE THE visible; rather, it makes visible." That statement, which says something about all art, is supremely true of contemporary art. Painting, in its complex journey from impressionism and early cubism to abstract expressionism, has dug into nature and experience to disclose the patterns of color and line that the dull eye of normal experience misses. Literary and dramatic art, across the spectrum from stark realism to symbolic fantasy, have illuminated the experiences that men usually miss because of conventional insensitivity.

The Revelatory Work of Art

In the contemporary setting certain old disputes about the aim of art lose their meaning. Moralists have argued that high art should serve civic and ethical causes. Aesthetes have replied that any such purposes distort the purity of art, which has no purpose outside itself. Artists themselves have taken both sides in the debate. Too often the abstract arguments have only obscured the issues.

If art "makes visible," it has a revelatory function. It discloses hidden qualities in the outer and inner world. It awakens the perceptions of men to aspects of reality unrecognized by the jaded, habitual, or prejudiced eye and ear. The artist is false if he corrupts his calling in order to please a patron, win a political battle, or argue for his church. Yet his fidelity to art makes him, in one sense or another, a crusader.

Even the most reportorial art has its crusading character. Ernest Hemingway, commenting on his own early writings, has said: "I was trying to write then and I found the greatest difficulty, aside from knowing truly what you really felt, rather than what you were supposed to feel, and had been taught to feel, was to put down what really happened in action." [1] This very effort to eliminate everything extraneous or propagandistic provoked a crusade against the falsities that distort every man's report of his world and his own feelings. "To put down what really happened in action" turned out to be a work of revelation.

At the other end of the literary spectrum the works of symbolic fantasy —say Kafka's—perform the same function. Such writings do not in the everyday sense "put down what really happened." Yet the artistic imagination, unfettered by laws of cause and effect or logical consistency, is not an undisciplined imagination. Mediocrity is nowhere more helpless than in fantasy. Only superior talent can organize the seeming chaos of impressions and symbols so as to reveal the struggles of the human spirit in a world where the moorings are all lost. Again the writer is a crusader against the trivializing of life, the dehumanizing of man, and the false orders that pretend to give meaning to experience.

The Artist: Priest and Prophet

It is this revelatory function that makes the artist both priest and prophet of his culture. In word, in music, in visual images he celebrates the sacred qualities in the experience of his society and calls it to account for its failures.

As priest the artist mediates to a people a vision of the wonderful. His gift of genius admits him to the holy of holies, from which he returns to communicate to the rest of us an awareness of the numinous. Or he may move among humdrum events, alerting men to the unnoticed glories in their midst. He consecrates and enhances the treasured values of a people. He forms and transmits the symbols by which a society understands itself and its loyalties.

As prophet the artist unmasks the false sanctity that pervades every culture. He announces judgment upon the cheap and pretentious. He pricks

[1] Quoted by Malcom Cowley in The Literary Situation (New York: Viking Press, 1954), p. 34.

pride and complacency with a radical protest which is also an affirmation. His vision of what might be is often the occasion for innovation among things that are.

Thus the young Nietzsche wrote:

Only artists hate this slovenly life in borrowed manners and loosely fitting opinions and unveil the secret, everybody's bad conscience, the principle that every human being is a unique wonder; they dare to show us the human being as he is, down to the last muscle, himself and himself alone—even more, that in this rigorous consistency of his uniqueness he is beautiful and worth contemplating, as novel and incredible as every work of nature, and by no means dull.[2]

Nietzsche's statement shows the revelatory power of artists who "unveil the secret." Their priestly function is to mediate to men the sacred mystery that "every human being is a unique wonder." Their prophetic task is to condemn the "bad conscience" of mankind and to point to the holy truth distorted by customary symbols.

Many contemporary artists say roughly the same thing. Theoretically the artist is reluctant to explain his purposes and works. He prefers to let his art speak for itself. But in this "age of criticism," artists are often critics of their own work. When the artist tells what he is doing, he usually indicates in some phraseology or other his sense of a priestly-prophetic vocation.

Albert Camus is a clear example. Camus could make even pamphleteering an art because his method was not to beat the reader into submission but to "make visible" to him what he had missed. Conversely his novels had a persuasive effect because they induced insights of compassion and courage that prompted action. On the occasion of the Nobel Award in 1957, he stated the meaning of his art: "It is a means of stirring the greatest number of men by providing them with a privileged image of our joys and woes." He went on to define "the two trusts that constitute the nobility of his [the writer's] calling: the service of truth and the service of freedom." [3]

This statement unites the revelatory function ("service of truth") and the moral function ("service of freedom"). What if the two should conflict? Like the traditional prophet-priest, Camus lived by the faith that they

[2] Friedrich Nietzsche, from *Schopenhauer as Educator*, as translated by Walter Kaufmann (ed.), in *Existentialism from Dostoevsky to Sartre* (New York: Meridian Books, 1957), p. 101.
[3] Albert Camus, *Speech of Acceptance upon the Award of the Nobel Prize for Literature* (New York: Alfred A. Knopf, Inc., 1958), pp. viii-x.

could not. Shortly before the Nobel ceremony he declared this faith: "There is not a single true work of art that has not in the end added to the inner freedom of each person who has known and loved it." [4] Obviously not all artists define moral purposes with the clarity and passion of Camus. But the remarkable fact in our time is that so many do. And most of the rest share something of the same commitment to reveal to mankind in symbolic fashion a saving truth.

The Interplay of Roles

Priest and prophet traditionally struggle against each other. Yet the same man often follows both vocations. Recent biblical scholarship indicates that most, perhaps all, Old Testament prophets had a cultic role. Their denunciations of religious hypocrisy came from within the institutions of faith. In analogous fashion the artist mingles both roles. In any person or period one role may dominate. But at its most profound it merges into the other.

Most obviously, art is an expression of the culture of a people. The artist voices or depicts the ethos of a society. He is the mediator of its inmost spirit, the celebrant of its values, the high priest of culture. If we would know Athens, we not only study its battles and its politics; we gaze at its Parthenon. To investigate the Middle Ages is to look at its Gothic cathedrals, as well as to learn about its economy and social structure.

Art, though it has its universal qualities, speaks with the unique voice of its particular epoch. The Hellenic world is filled with gods. One can walk around the self-contained statues of Apollo and Venus and drink in their beauty from various perspectives. To enter further into the ethos of Greece, one studies the conflict between Apollonian and Dionysian motifs. The spirit of an epoch addresses the world through its art. The early church found the art of its times so expressive of pagan culture and religion that it felt a strong impulse to reject art.

But inevitably this church produced its own art. The medieval cathedral tells of a transcendent God. Gothic arches and towers reach upward, then point still farther beyond. The stained glass is not self-contained; it has no splendor unless a distant light shines through it. Thus the work of architecture, no less than the priest at the mass, mediates the grace of the transcendent God who enters into the life of society.

[4] Albert Camus, *Resistance, Rebellion, and Death* (New York: Alfred A. Knopf, Inc., 1960), p. 241.

In similar fashion we look to the literature of a people to learn of their spirit, and we compare the distinctive characteristics of different literatures from different ages. To take a single example, W. H. Auden, in a brilliant bit of criticism, has compared Herman Melville's Ahab with Sophocles' Oedipus.[5] Each author opens up the peculiar agonies and possibilities of healing in the tradition from which he writes. Each communicates some awareness of despair, some glimpse of glory.

Since pontifical language is often used of the classics, this designation of the artist as priest of culture may seem appropriate for the great tradition of art. But what about modern artists, who are close enough to us that we can see their human stubbornness, their earthiness, perhaps their insolence? We suspect that American artists in particular might reject the priestly role as pompous and false. Yet it may be that the American artist, living in a nonpriestly society, peculiarly assumes the calling of cultural priest. Such a suggestion comes from the special edition on "The American Imagination" of the *Times Literary Supplement*. The author—anonymous, like all authors in that periodical—writes:

The American heroes that we think of as characteristic . . . seem to have an especial quality that sets them apart from the creations of any English novelist. . . . They are myth-figures as the characters of no English novelists are, myth-figures in that they recapitulate within themselves deep and apparently abiding national experience, and that they are conceived by their authors with a lyrical intensity that seems to confer on them a more than naturalistic stature.[6]

We may waive the generous English comparison and the special tribute to American literature. The point remains that the great American novelists, past and present, are not *just* storytellers. They probe the pain and richness of the cultural experience, hallowing and symbolizing the human struggle.

In so doing they join company with artists of all times who by varying devices do the same thing. "Every writer tries to give a form to the passions of his time," says Camus. "Today, just as yesterday, art wants to save from death a living image of our passions and our sufferings." [7] In this powerful sense the artist is a priest of culture.

The priest, if he is very profound, inevitably becomes a prophet. He cannot celebrate the glories of a society without exposing its hollow claims

[5] W. H. Auden, "The Christian Tragic Hero," *The New York Times Book Review*, Dec. 16, 1945, p. 1.
[6] "The Limits of the Possible," *The Times Literary Supplement* (London), Nov. 6, 1959, p. xvi. Used by permission.
[7] Camus, *Resistance, Rebellion, and Death*, pp. 237, 238.

and false sanctities. As he "makes visible" hidden aspects of experience, he destroys illusory representations. He delivers judgment against pretense. He transforms cultural symbols and values.

Thus Aeschylus was both priest and prophet of Athenian culture. His great trilogy on the house of Atreus used old legends to celebrate the ethos of his society. The very performance of the plays was a cultic ritual in Athens. Yet Aeschylus was a prophetic reformer of faith. As Orestes defied traditional law on grounds of conscience, Aeschylus transformed inherited religion. The Furies, agents of torment, became Eumenides, spirits of mercy. By telling of the concordat between Zeus and Apollo, Aeschylus let the legendary polytheism express a virtual monotheism.

The contemporary artist usually has a harder time reconciling priestly and prophetic roles. No society has ever hired artists so profusely for purposes of advertising, illustration, and popular journalism. Thousands of artists make their living as priests of a commercial culture. Like Amazaiah in ancient Bethel, they are employees of the kings of the culture.[8] They do their jobs with more or less inner struggle and integrity.

Curiously, this very period when the artist is so often the voice and tool of cultural interests is the period when the artist is notably alienated from culture. If past artists were normally critics of culture, contemporary artists are devastatingly so. Paul Tillich has often been quoted for his saying that Picasso's "Guernica" is "the best present-day Protestant religious picture." The hot fury of the picture is not only a complaint against the cruel bombing of civilians. It also "shows the human situation without any cover."[9]

Literary artists verbalize their protest both in their art and in their comments on their own performances. America's greatest playwright, Eugene O'Neill, put the case in scorching prose:

I am going on the theory that the United States, instead of being the most successful country in the world, is its greatest failure. . . . Its main idea is that everlasting game of trying to possess your own soul by the possession of something outside of it, too. America is the foremost example of this because it happened so fast here and with such enormous resources. The Bible has already said it much better: "For what shall it profit a man if he shall gain the whole world, and lose his own soul?" [10]

[8] See Amos 7:10-13.
[9] Paul Tillich, "Existential Aspects of Modern Art," in *Christianity and the Existentialists,* ed. Carl Michalson (New York: Charles Scribner's Sons, 1956), p. 138.
[10] Arthur Gelb, reporting an earlier statement from O'Neill in a press interview, *New York Times,* Sept. 28, 1958, sec. 2, p. 1.

O'Neill's voice from a generation just past is reinforced by many contemporary writers. Robert Penn Warren, to take a single example from the many available, puts the issue with a sharpness again reminiscent of biblical prophecy: "If a man starts loving his country, he is practically out of business as a writer. He needs to have an argument with his country as shock lies behind all creativity." [11]

In a profound sense, of course, Warren does love his country. His novels and his poetry say so. His quarrel with his culture would not be so moving if it were not the protest of a man who cared deeply. Even the most nihilistic artistic protest—and contemporary art, which includes beatniks, angry young men, and despairing existentialists, can be as nihilistic as any in history—never rejects culture absolutely. As a work of culture, art affirms the worth of a cultural activity. Furthermore, its moral protest necessarily implies a context of meaning within which a complaint makes sense. Like the biblical prophet, the artist condemns with some element of compassion. He judges his world with a glimpse of a valid ground of judgment, and he despairs with a hope that repentance is possible.

Perhaps the best example of the interplay of prophetic and priestly vocations in the artist is the most discussed author of this century, James Joyce. Steeped in the life of Ireland, in memories of rejected Roman Catholicism, and in the Homeric tradition, he both transmitted tender impressions of his society and exposed its hollowness. "The reader of Joyce," says one critic, "is continually reminded of the analogy between the role of the artists and the priestly office." [12] Another critic lists him among the prophets of our time—among the "Christian voices, heretical, indeed, protesting against the narrowing and stifling of the Christian faith." [13] Still another sees him as an apocalyptic writer: "He rends the veil, and looks beyond this world and this life to the dark void once lit by faith and hope. . . . He looks upon the void and he dares to bring into conscious expression the fear which lies in the soul of the twentieth century, that the glory of man is meaningless." [14]

Yet the negation is not absolute. To quote Camus once again: "Even

[11] Robert Penn Warren, speaking at the annual literary symposium at Vanderbilt University. Reported in the Nashville Tennessean, April 24, 1959.

[12] Harry Levin, James Joyce (rev., augmented ed.; New York: New Directions, 1960), p. 29. Levin quotes Joyce's statement: "I imagined that I bore my chalice safely through a throng of foes."

[13] Amos N. Wilder, "Protestant Orientation in Contemporary Poetry," in Spiritual Problems in Contemporary Literature, ed. Stanley Romaine Hopper (New York: Harper & Brothers, Torchbooks, 1957), p. 253.

[14] Douglas Stewart, The Ark of God (London: The Carey Kingsgate Press, 1961), pp. 28, 38.

the work that negates still affirms something and does homage to the wretched and magnificent life that is ours." [15] Just as priestly ministration must move to prophetic protest, so prophecy and apocalypse must return to priestly mediation of the sacred.

The Artist and the Church

The prophet-priests of culture have a different vocation from the prophet-priests of the church. If the artist "makes visible," he usually does not issue a call to action. The aesthetic mood may be one of contemplation rather than of service.

The distinction is not absolute. The revelatory work of art, we have noticed, may also be a transforming work. In Erich Kahler's description, "A subtle interaction takes place between the flaring image and the experience that kindled it, whereby the image is capable of driving the experience farther, that is, of creating new experience." [16] The new perception and the new experience may generate new action. Many a person, in acquiring a new perception of other persons (e.g., someone of another race or the opposite sex), has changed his behavior radically.

Yet the distinction between art and religion is real. Christianity in particular is the faith of a community with a mission of healing, reconciling, and proclaiming the gospel. This mission constitutes its unique prophetic-priestly vocation.

Art, like religion, may be naturalistic, polytheistic, skeptical, Christian or heretical. Christian faith will, therefore, sometimes meet attack or support in art. But it will welcome the revelatory insight of all high art. Even the artist who scorns the church will, insofar as he explores and enriches the experience of mankind, serve God.

[15] *Resistance, Rebellion, and Death*, p. 239.
[16] Erich Kahler, "The Nature of the Symbol," in *Symbolism in Religion and Literature*, ed. Rollo May (New York: George Braziller, 1960), p. 73.

VIII

The Sensibility of the Church and the Sensibility of the Artist

JOHN W. DIXON, JR.

THERE WAS A TIME WHEN THE WORK OF THE ARTIST COULD BE DEFINED as his work within the Christian church, growing out of a Christian consciousness. At the present time the work of the artist and the work of the church proceed in virtually complete isolation from each other. These are historical and descriptive facts. It remains to be seen whether this relation is fixed in the nature of things or whether the intimacy of the relation that once existed can be recovered.

It is not enough to say that the situation at present is not so bad as it was in the immediate past; it is true to say that the church makes greater use of the work of creative artists than it has for a long time, particularly in architecture. It is nonetheless true that today the creative consciousness of the artist does not develop within the church but within the world of art. He comes into the church from an alien world and works for the church, creating monuments for the church's use. Creativity, however, is not in this activity but in the art world wholly outside the life of the church.

To deplore this situation is useless hand-wringing. To exhort the one to speak to the other is equally without purpose unless each can sense, not an obligation, but a possibility of enlivening his own work. It is demeaning to the artist and to the church to offer services to each other as alms.

A genuine relation can be restored only if it is a genuine relation, productive of understanding, acting as a channel of grace. Only such a relation is worthy of the high calling of the artist and the sacred mission of the church.

Obviously, the nature of such a relation and the nature of its present disorder is a complex human phenomenon. Thus it would be false to suggest that a simple definition suffices to describe it or a simple prescription suffices to cure it. But the concerns of the church and the concerns of the artist, disparate though they have become, intersect at one point; and to take hold of that one point is to lay hold of a central issue of the problem. That point is designated in the word "sensibility."

Sensibility: The Point of Contact

As an aesthetic term "sensibility" has a faintly musty air. We need not use it with its Bohemian accretions, however, and its nature which gathers in the concerns of the artist and the concerns of the church is not particularly complex; it refers simply to the manner of our response to the sensible world. It cannot be divorced altogether from a value judgment. Probably most people to whom the word means anything think of an ordered and intelligent response to the world of the senses; "sensibility" is more than the animal stirrings of stimulated nerve ends. It suggests heightened awareness and understanding. Its root meaning, however, continues to be "sense," and it can perhaps be defined as the human awareness of the world of sense.

Sensibility, then, defines the essential activity of the artist's preparation: his principal activity is carried on within the world of sense. The essential activity of all art is the intelligent ordering of sensible material. Most art incorporates into that fundamental act the awareness of the common world of experience and the translation of certain aspects of its sensible structure into the language of the work of art. The involvement of the word "sensibility" in the consciousness of the church is not quite so immediately evident, but it is no less important. The sensibility of the church is another definition of the church's response to the Incarnation.

Neither the theological nor the devotional life of the church is exhausted in its dogma. The Incarnation is a dogmatic fact because it is an historic event. More important, it is descriptive of the reality of creation for the Christian and therefore must determine his fundamental consciousness of the world, his sensibility.

The church is a divine gift, but its life in history is inseparable from the common life of man. Thus, much of its life has been defined out of its struggle with those who would warp its nature to destruction, and its dogma is partly fixed both in form and direction by the nature of the enemy. Thus the principal concern of the dogmas has been the defense of the center of the church's faith through the definition of the redemptive function of the Atonement. This concern has tended to obscure the fact that all of Christian doctrine is grounded in the Incarnation. If the Incarnation is not historic fact, then the Crucifixion becomes a dogmatic assertion without historical meaning. The Incarnation determines that the Crucifixion is not the suffering and death of a hero or the ritual act of a god but the transfiguration of the Incarnate Word.

Further, the nature and meaning of the Incarnation determine the relation of the person to the created order. Thus the Incarnation defines the sensibility of the church. The great heresies have centered largely on the nature of Christ. The ground of their formulation, however, has to do with the nature of the created order. Polarized schemes inevitably oversimplify the complexity of human motive and belief, but if Arianism and Docetism are not the only heretical formulations of the Christian faith, they do point the directions of heretical thought, and each summarizes an attitude toward the created order which violates the Incarnation. Arianism denies the mystery of nature: nature is fact and cannot serve as a vehicle of the divine. Docetism denies the goodness of nature: the corruption or finiteness of material means that the divine must keep itself insulated from it. The uniqueness of the Incarnation is that it secures for the consciousness and sensibility of the Christian the mystery and goodness—the holiness —of nature.

This is not to say that the Arian and the Docetic attitudes cannot produce fine art works. Any passionately held human conviction can engender works of art. But so engendered, the work is no longer Christian but expressive of another religion. Only as the work maintains the distinctively Christian sensibility can it be directly a part of the life of the church. Perhaps this principle is best demonstrated negatively: when the tension of mystery and goodness is lost without being replaced by another religious attitude, the result is the dissolution of the art work. The temptation of the Western church has always been toward Arianism, and the heresy toward which its art tends is a sentimentalized naturalism. The temptation of the Eastern church is toward Docetism, and its heresy is a dehumanized formalism.

Thus the term "sensibility" applied to the church is not simply analogical. It is partially analogical since it ascribes a personal function to what is more than personal. Nevertheless, the analogy is sound. Thus it is possible to say that there is a corporate sensibility in the church and that this sensibility grows out of the church's real belief (as distinct from articulated doctrine) about the nature of the Incarnation.

Consequently, the relation between the artist and the church is real only if it involves the sensibility of each. Otherwise it is irrelevant whether the relation is one of enmity or amiable friendship.

Restoring Communication Between Artist and Church

Nostalgia is no answer to the problem of the work of the artist in the church. Those who look back to a medieval relation between the artist and the church usually sentimentalize it out of all relation to the fact. Even so, the relation was a close one, and it is not likely to be recovered in our time; nor could the recovery of the particular relation be harmonious with the spirit or the intelligence of our day. The dissociation of the artist and the church cannot be healed by defining the work of the artist as institutional obedience or the adoption of a new series of ecclesiastical themes for his work. A man finds his humanity within the work he does. The church must meet the artist as an artist, for within his work he finds the fulfillment of his own distinctive humanity.

It is not different with the church. The church seeks its own identity and finds it only within its character and function as the church. It cannot bend the artist arbitrarily to its will. It cannot subserve the interests of the artist any more than the interest of the rest of the society, if it is to find its own character and its own mission.

Hence, the task in restoring communication is to find how the artist can be an artist and the church can be the church and still have meaningful communication with each other. This task, if successful, can add immeasurably to the catholicity of both the artist and the church. A church which defines itself only as an institutional expression and then attempts to engulf all men to the obedience of its institutional representatives is not truly catholic. An artist who defends his integrity by denying his context and his responsibility is not catholic. The restoration of the relation between them is a task worth undertaking.

In the accomplishment of this task both the artist and the church must realize the nature of the artist's work and the source of his creativity. Obviously the church must, else the church inevitably will abuse that work, but the artist might be tempted to put off the rightful claims of the church if he is not articulate about the nature and the possibilities of his own work.

The particular province of the artist is not the illustration of literary themes but the making of forms. His peculiar responsibility is to take a given body of physical material and bring it into a form embodying the order which makes it both intelligible and meaningful. That this order can include one of the literary themes (a subject matter) should go without saying, but in the present state of opinion about the arts it does not. The public demands a subject (as its requirement upon the artist), and the artist in turn is tempted to dismiss subject matter too quickly simply because the uniformed press it on him. It can be used as a part of the material incorporated into form, but in the work of the artist the meaning of his achievement is in the form, or it is nowhere. The nature of the artist's work is to establish coherent order in a physical material. This work is not describable in terms of some other responsibility, nor is it replaceable by any other work.

This reply does not, of course, fully answer the question the church can rightfully ask. It might be granted even that the nature of the artist's work is to make an object embodying a coherent order, but this concession does not fully meet the next question: Is the order thereby created of any real significance in the life of man generally, much less the church? Even expanding the definition to include the term "significant order" or even "relevant order" still would not meet the problem as it is lived beyond the bonds of logical coherence, for few in the public are likely to be convinced by the definition alone. It was possible for a long time for the public to find a point of contact with the art work because, in addition to and by means of its primary responsibility to form, it did communicate directly to the ordinary experience of the average person. Thus his sensibility was unconsciously trained. It remains a fact, uncomfortable for the artist, that bad paintings of Christ have served liturgical needs as well as have good paintings. It may be historically accurate to say that in many past periods many people could respond intelligently and sympathetically to the real work of the artist and that these persons make up a disproportionately large part of the formers of taste and the makers of decisions; it is equally true that the average person responded to art only to the extent it represents things in his own experience. When those who shared this average taste gained a position of control in society, it was possible for that taste to be satisfied by artists who could provide only the representation without the form and thus continue the general debauching of sensibility. Simultaneously, the creative artists were increasingly defining their work in terms of formal structures without significant subject matter and finally without any objective reference to the outside world at all. The general public, then, cut off from such means of formal training as had been available to it, believing that the democratic principle applied not only to

84

political decisions but to taste, and finding that its taste could be satisfied, was increasingly cut off from any serious communication with the artist. The artist, in turn, contemptuous of the uninformed taste-makers, resentful of the attempt to force him to violate his integrity, and concerned with problems in themselves cut off from the common concerns, was content to remain within this situation and even intensify it. This situation, general in Western culture, applies with particular force to the church. Much of society dispensed with the artist altogether, but the church continued to make use of visual images of one kind or another, and the process of formal disintegration of the public sensibility which took command in the nineteenth century continues under the enthusiastic sponsorship of the church.

Thus, the church and the artist are faced with a thorough dissociation from each other, and the artist is dissociated from the common life of man. Before this alienation can be healed we must do more than assert a new definition. We must find the grounds on which the relationship can properly work itself out.

In part, this grounds for association can best be pointed to negatively: the absence of it has consequences which make us sensitive to that which is absent. The work of the artist, however, deserves greater dignity than so negative a statement permits. It is necessary to make certain assertions which obviously deserve more detailed exploration: the order, which is the essence of the structure the artist makes, is significant and relevant both extrinsically and intrinsically.

It was once possible to say that the artist's work informed us significantly of essential characteristics of the world outside, common to us all but seen by the artist with considerably greater intensity and insight. This is still far more often true than the average observer—or even the average critic—realizes, for the artist continues to nourish himself on the experiences of the physical world. To a greater degree than was generally true in the past, he tends to isolate these experiences from those objects which first embodied them in the visible world, and thus he rejects subject matter. But this does not mean that he is less nourished on the natural and human order. In fact, the differences are really very slight, even when the artist does not begin with some sense of the world he sees and feels: the material he works with in making his structure is itself a part of the natural order and much of the work he does is the exploration of the possibilities of that material and the using of his discoveries in the creation of a newly ordered structure. Thus it is still possible to assert, with only slight modification of our language, that although his work is rarely recognized in this

85

way, the artist is informing us significantly of essential characteristics. This has always been and will remain one principal quality of the artist's work: he explores, he learns, he embodies the result of his research and his experiences in the form of constructed objects, and they become thereby part of the common experience and the common core of knowledge.

The church is still under no compulsion to support such formal research if it is irrelevant to its own life. It may intensify its relevance to know that the artist's knowledge is never knowledge seen in isolation but that it is embodied in an ordered structure. The order itself is a quality more directly relevant to the work of the church since any increase in the coherence of life is part of what the church would seek to perform. The relevance becomes acute once we see that the sense of order which governs the work of the artist proceeds from the very deepest places of human consciousness. Style is the fundamental concept in the study of the arts. Style is the individuation of the form of art, that which makes the form distinctive of a person, a place, or a time. The order which the artist makes of a work of art is the essence of his style, and it grows out of what he is basically as a person, a consciousness, a sensibility. Thus the investment of the church in the arts is an investment at the very center of its being and its work, not in ornamentation or illustration. The parish of the church is the deepest place of personality, and all that affects that place lies properly in the shape of the church's work. The relation is reciprocal: the church itself is not a person, but it has its own life and its own possibility of creativity. Its common life grows out of its devotion and its service, not out of formal creativity. But the involvement of persons in their own sensibility is so acute that a disorder of sensibility will reflect itself in a disorder of the common life—unless it is counterbalanced by strict discipline elsewhere.

Artist and Church: Their Common Disorder and Design

It is too simple to link causally the heresies of the church with the various disorders of sensibility that have afflicted mankind. The possibilities of distortion which are so much a part of the life of men are so extensive, so intricate, so well developed that it would be impossible to trace the one of these to the other. Neither would it be possible, at any given moment of history, to trace the direction of cause. Did the disorder of sensibility reflect itself in theological or devotional consciousness? Or did the disorder of that consciousness reflect itself in a disorder of sensibility? Some historical problems are beyond the range of man's conceptual tools. Yet it is still possible to say of the heresies which continually afflict the life of the church that they are a reflection of, and certainly correspond to, the disorders of sensibility that cause the dissociation of the artist from the general human work.

The work of the artist grows out of his communion with the natural order. By the nature of his act the artist assumes the goodness of nature, for it is the materials of the world with which he works. In the order of his art he grasps the glory and the mystery in the created order. Whether the absence of these elements of informed sensibility cause the heresies of the church, they certainly characterize them.

Arianism loses the sense of the mystery of nature and flattens the Christian experience into a rationalism incapable of producing more than inert naturalism in Christian art. Docetism loses the goodness of nature and is incapable of producing an art at all and can only use visual forms of the most idealized type, "idealized" here meaning less a stylistic quality than simply the denaturing of the material, removing it as far as possible from the substantial reality of the earth from which it came. This inevitably produces a sentimentalized stylization incapable of affecting the deep springs of consciousness. In either case the church is denying the Incarnation, the mystery and holiness of God's entering and thereby sanctifying the material of the earth.

Again it is neither possible nor necessary to say that the one causes the other historically. They do accompany each other in a significant fashion, and it is of the highest importance that the history of the church during the past 150 years has been a period of an almost complete dissociation of its sensibility from its faith, resulting in the production of some of the worst art in human history. During this same period the church has struggled, almost vainly, against a renaissance of the most ancient heresies, and it is both symptomatic and symbolic that the disorder of the inner life of the church is such that it is difficult to disentangle Docetism and Arianism and all their assorted relatives.

This break between the church and the artist has damaged not only the church but also the artist. The development of his sensibility is part of the artist's development of his tools; it is part of the very nature of art; so his problems are different. The break between artist and church, unless the place of the church is taken by some other worthy setting, dissociates the artist from context and purpose. It is of the nature of a work of art that it can, for a time, provide its own purpose, for the doing of it is good. But it is not self-sustaining. It is nourished out of the inner resources of the life of the artist, and if he does not have some context and purpose to give his loyalty to, he is weakened in his struggle with his principal temptations, materialism and the demonic. In the first he finds the source of creativity in the mystery at the heart of matter, and he makes the material of the earth into his god. In the second he finds the source of creativity and the justification of creativity wholly within himself and succumbs to the temptation to the demonic and the idolatry of self.

Thus the artist and the church have a responsibility to each other and the dissociation becomes a concern of both. The church cannot tell the artist how to make his work. The church can, however, nourish him on its common life, give sustenance to the rhythms of his redemptive ritual. Its service can give him purpose. It can restore him to the sense of the holiness of the earth and sustain his conviction of the goodness of nature. Its words can guide the articulation of his purpose.

The artist has much to give to the church. Where its building affirms the irrelevance of the present and the governance of the past, he can recall the life of the church to the community of which it is a part. Where its prayers are flaccid, its services without form, he can give rhythm and shape. He can restore to the church the sense of the Incarnation, the sense of the holiness of the earth, the rootedness of the Christian life in the substance of things as they are. The life of the church must develop its own grace and discipline and rhythm if it is again to shape the consciousness and the sensibility of men. The work of the artist is not the only requisite to the attainment of this goal, but it is a vital part of it.

Each, then, can give to the other rhythm and structure, context and purpose. Each can help restore to the work of the other the sense of a redemptive order, of a holy earth, and of the glory of God.

PART TWO

The Contemporary
Scene in the Arts

IX

What Is Christian in a Christian Literature?

HANS EGON HOLTHUSEN

WHAT RILKE TRIED TO EXPRESS IN THE PARABLE OF THE PRODIGAL SON IN *The Notebooks of Malte Laurids Brigge*—that modern man has abandoned the old home and refused to return to the arms of his father—seems to fit not only Rilke himself but also many other writers of our time. Today's man is an "unsheltered man." His consciousness, in Erich Heller's formulation, is that of a "disinherited mind." Yet the preoccupation of such writers as Baudelaire, Dostoevski, Mann, Valéry, and Camus with a parody of Christian myths and symbols ought to convince us that the unsheltered and disinherited sons of the Christian tradition are still its sons. Which brings us to the question: What exactly is Christian in a Christian literature? To what extent can Christian thought and belief become manifest in terms of literature? This is the basic question for Christian literature in our own or any age.

The Relationship of Christianity and Culture

What Christian poetry really is, is a question that can hardly be answered without our first achieving some degree of clarity about the relation of Christianity and culture in general. In distinguishing between Christianity and culture, we imply that the establishment of Christianity—in the Christian view at least—was not an achievement of human cultural capacities. Culture implies a worldly opposition to the gospel. It is to be understood as identical with "the world." The Christian faith, on the other hand, is literally derived from the active involvement of God in human history. Even with all the gross and fine worldly silt precipitated over two millennia by man's efforts to round out with a "Christian culture" the destiny of God's Word on earth, the reference of faith, love, and hope has always been to a realm "not of this world." Christianity is not the same as culture. Nevertheless, Christendom without culture is unthinkable. When the Fourth Evangelist wrote, "In the beginning was the Word," he assumed that his readers knew the traditional meanings of the word *logos*—in other words, that they were cultured.

Ever since New Testament times, the opposition of Christianity and culture has been one of the leitmotifs in the European history of ideas. There have been periods of synthesis, of intimate connection and mutual influence, and there have been periods of *diastasis*, of hostile separation. But never have Christianity and culture reached a state of complete fusion —nor can we expect such a development in the future. Such a fusion is a logical and historical impossibility, for the primal origins of man's culture-creating capacity are never identical with the primal origin of his attitude of faith and adoration. The brilliant Catholic essayist, Theodor Haecker, in an effort to interpret the divergent origins of culture and faith, said: "No creations of nature or of culture are ever the immediate creations of Christianity and its spirit which is the Holy Spirit. Rather, they are creations of the power of nature, which was in turn created by God, and of the human spirit, likewise created by God." [1]

Haecker's view is a model of arch-Catholic interpretation which solves the problem by harmonizing opposites by means of the all-powerful key of analogy. Just as nature and grace, natural light and divine light, correspond to and complement each other, so also do genius and holiness, man's culture-creating capacity and his capacity for conversion and discipleship. There is, says Haecker,

a mysterious analogy, a relationship in fact, between genius and holiness, since no perfect genius (as distinguished from mere talent) can be imagined without a perspective immediately opening out into the wholly different sphere of holiness, regardless of how far its human carrier may be removed from the latter. And, what is more significant, all perfect holiness will always have an aspect which cannot be adequately described other than by the word "genius," regardless of how far its human carrier may be from attaining any sort of

[1] Theodore Haecker, *Christentum und Kultur* (München: J. Kösel und F. Pustet, 1927).

92

cultural achievement. Surely this has to do with the fact that genius and holiness are both original primalities. Mysteriously, they are at the same time a natural gift and a divine grace. Hence the genius has an immediate relationship to the demonic character of nature's creative powers, and the poet, in particular, to the metaphysical sources of language.[2]

Protestant thinking, determined from the start to emphasize the opposition between nature and grace and to forego the idea of analogy, has always carried more heavily the burden of human worldliness than has Catholicism. As in political theories, so in cultural theories Protestantism has been torn constantly between a solid love for the world and an equally solid hatred for it. Seldom has it been able to keep to a proper middle road. On the one hand, all liberal Protestantism has tended finally to become "cultural Protestantism" in Schleiermacher's sense—that is, it has mingled piety with culture all too freely. All orthodoxy, on the other hand, has been tempted to tear Christianity and culture wholly out of a common context and to consign the works of genius to the flames of heresy.

The tensions which a Protestant conscience must withstand when gifted with religious genius may be seen in the passionate writings of Kierkegaard, with their absolute polarization of the "aesthetic" and the "ethical" principles. At thirty, Kierkegaard composed his famous paean on Mozart's *Don Giovanni* in which the Don was portrayed as the perfect embodiment of "sensuous genius," which Kiekegaard also claimed for himself. At thirty-five, he screamed into the calloused ears of the easygoing, philistine Christendom of his day, "What our time needs is not a genius but a martyr!" Not in spite of, but because of, his being so deeply moved by the unmediated quality of genius, he was able to define its absolute opposite, holiness, so compellingly. And only because he was so deeply experienced in matters aesthetic-erotic was he able to decide with such desperate passion for the totally other.

Analogy or contradiction, no matter. Genius and holiness have never been one and the same thing. Genius wants to make beautiful things or to do great deeds. The saint wants neither beauty nor grandeur. His only concern is self-sacrifice, love for God and for his neighbor. Between these two extremes spreads the landscape of a Christian culture.

It has often been said that the greatness of the European way of life lies in the strength and abundance, even in the unconciliatory nature, of its contrasts. Its psychic and spiritual vitality is kept up through the power of its most marked contradictions: papism and imperialism, individualism

[2] *Ibid.*

93

and statism, Protestantism and Catholicism, philosophy and theology, science and faith, skepticism and mysticism, humanism and iconoclasm, or, to use proper names, Erasmus and Luther, Kant and Hamann, Savonarola and Botticelli. The "and" between these terms and names signifies an antagonism which cannot be reconciled at the level of history. Only to the backward-looking eyes of its inheritors will this "and" stand for a real addition, an overwhelming summation of powers. And only Christianity's relentless claim to exclusiveness has made it possible for all these contradictories to retain their absolute significance. It is within and because of our Christian culture that these conflicts have been driven to extremes.

The Christian Poet and the World

One must have in mind this background of multiplicity and disagreement if one would comprehend the situation of the Christian poet within his culture. Poetic truth is not religious truth. And a poetic prayer is not the same as the prayer of a devout life. Ignoring for the moment everything that makes a poet Christian, we must explain that the poet as poet acts from a different primal source of insight into the world than does the religious man, be he priest, layman, or saint. The latter penetrates the mystery of God by way of the life of prayer, love, and suffering. But for the poet, bliss and despair are his life and work! His happiness is that of the master craftsman. His weeping and gnashing of teeth are signs, not of readiness for repentance, but of being shaken by those creative powers which the theologian defines as "demonic." This is not to say that the poet is an aesthete or a formalist or a man of mere sensibility, or that he is able to attain at will a cynical distance from the prayer which he writes, the song of praise, or the cry from the depths. The poet has material, content, ideas. He is an ethically and, at times, a politically responsible human being. He is, when he writes, present in his whole person with numerous nonaesthetic interests. Hence, if he is Christian his poem is an expression of his faith, though it is first of all an expression of his love for language and of his struggle with the angel of language. To use Paul Claudel's terms, there is in the Christian poet a conflict between "muse" and "grace."

To understand the poet, one must enter his world. Whoever reads Shakespeare, for example, does not leave the ground of Christian culture. But certain questions no longer bother him because, in the face of the poet's work, they lose their meaning. Shakespeare's world is fashioned from fantasy and love and unfathomable knowledge of the human psyche, penetrating the secret of our being-on-earth! Some say that tragedy is impossible since Christ's existence on earth and the triumph of Easter over

94

Good Friday; that the antitragic principle of redemption once and for all is victorious. But he—our Shakespeare reader—ignores this as pure abstraction, for he recognizes in his poet the greatest tragic poet since the author of *Oedipus Rex*. Shakespeare, to be sure, exhibits Christian features (think of *Measure for Measure*). But is he on that account a Christian poet? And if not, can we call him an unchristian poet? Is he a pagan of titanic stature wandering through the morally dissolute Christendom of his time? He is neither the one nor the other. He is, quite simply, the greatest dramatic poet of a particular Christian culture.

There are aspects of genius which are beyond the saint's judgment—which are, in fact, a refutation of saintliness. The saint's role is that of breathing spirituality into the nostrils of an all too worldly Christendom, of imparting the vitality of faith to the body of Christian culture. Finally, however, Christian culture requires more than saintliness; it requires genius. Nor is the genius simply endured for the sake of culture. Indeed, Christian culture needs, demands, and above all loves the genius. It follows then that our search for the Christian poet is illusory unless joined by the quest for the *greatest* poet.

The Situation of the Christian Poet Today

The question now is whether in our day the Christian poet still exists and how his proper place may be determined within the spiritual situation of our time. We are all agreed that the cross is no longer erected visibly before the eyes of all. The Englishman Osborne, author of *Look Back in Anger*, puts on the stage a brawling young man who is driven to frenzy by the sound of church bells and gives free reign to his neurotic compulsion to blasphemy. This purely emotional testimony seems to me to be more instructive than the monotonous speeches of a thousand culture critics on the subject of Nietzsche's thundering "God is dead!" Many of us speak quite decisively of a post-Christian civilization. Others insist that even today we stand on the ancient soil of Christian culture (though perhaps a soil eroded by the widespread secularization of our forms of thought and life) and that it would be a hopeless and senseless venture to seek to replace the faith of our fathers with a non-Christian system of values.

The alternative of faith or the disavowal of God is not new. What seems new, however, is the serious doubt whether there exists any longer a common language which the opponents might use to attack and call one another into question. What is lacking is the sense of a common culture or a common understanding of the historical situation such as still existed in the time of Voltaire between freethinkers and believers and which made possible—indeed, produced—a marvelous synthesis in Mozart and in Goethe.

The Christian poets of our day live in the midst of a Christendom which, among the masses, is neither Christian nor pagan in feeling. They must struggle, at least in the non-Communist countries, against a paralyzing tolerance which exposes their eccentricity in direct proportion to the degree of indifference shown them. Yet the distance separating one Christian poet from another is as great as that separating the Christian from the unbelieving world. The German poet Konrad Weiss is separated by worlds from Graham Greene. Compared to T. S. Eliot, R. A. Schroder and Reinhold Shneider belong to another century. The Hofmannsthal of *Das grosse Welttheater* and the Bernanos of *Monsieur Ouine* go together like fire and water. Only someone insisting upon purely philosophical categories of criticism, such as the Marxist aestheticians, could discover a kinship between these wholly different authors.

Werner Haftmann, in discussing contemporary painting, has advanced the thesis that the authoritative content of modern art, in contrast to the politically harassed pseudo art of the Communist countries, can be found in the unlimited freedom given to each individual artist to define his own reality. I should like to borrow this proposition and say that the poet of our epoch also possesses this highly precarious freedom, a freedom which one does not so much enjoy but to which, like Sartre, one is doomed. Here we see the new situation for the Christian poet as well. The "openness" of his horizon has changed its meaning. Once upon a time his freedom consisted in being worldly under the magnanimous protection afforded by a Christian culture. Today his freedom lies in being religious amidst people who do not know what he is talking about. He is the offspring of a society no longer warmed by the devotional ardor of the saint, a society which, at the ringing of church bells, can scarcely control its neurotic impulses. How *innocent* today seems the worldliness of those worthy men in ruff and bands to whom we owe the still-flourishing poetry of the baroque hymn. They were, to be sure, the matchless eulogizers of God and completely beyond suspicion in their vital piety and in the touching sincerity of their religious speculations. And yet they were, like as not, the victims of the baroque Venus as well. Nevertheless, how *guilty* by contrast the Christian poet of our day looks—guilty, along with everyone else, of godlessness, of nihilism, and of every conceivable heresy and apostasy of our time. His very bones are guilty by virtue of his contemporaneousness. We have all had certain metaphysical and psychological vertigo-experiences which were not yet dreamt of in Voltaire's day. And between the old-fashioned naïve piety of the *bien-pensants* and present-day authorship come of age stands Nietzsche with his test of intellectual integrity. Whoever cannot pass it does not count, at least for the *critical* reader, who seeks in a poetic effort the expression of a radical and precise historical consciousness, the sensuous language acquired in the *here and now*. Whoever tries to hit a note which, three hundred years ago, expressed the language of the historical moment misses the language of today's historical moment. The preacher, for example, may take recourse in the argument that the congregation understands him when he uses the vocabulary of the past. Theology must take this argument seriously. But then the preacher must face in all fairness the counterquestion: What is wrong with a congregation which has not found the poetically valid expression for its extreme need or, still worse, has not even missed it—a congregation, in other words, which suffers political history and lets linguistic history slip into neglect? All the grief of contemporary theologians over the linguistic inadequacy of the sermon refers to this question.

But is it still possible to reconcile this ominous "modern consciousness" with the claim of a two-thousand-year-old faith, the claim of the credibility of divine revelation? Or is the man who takes his baptism seriously today reduced to pitching his tent in a sort of preserve for the harmless, apart from the main stream of modern intellectual life?

Let us look at the Frenchman Bernanos who, with polemical fury, exposes the scandal of contemporary society with its pseudo culture and its *imbéciles* too dull to experience the mystery of faith at the tremor of the abyss. Let us see how, at the same time, he is fundamentally related to this culture through similarities of motif structure, style of thought, heat of feeling, and the inescapability of a common historical situation. Bernanos would consider as *imbéciles* such thinkers as Heidegger, Freud, and Mann. An analytical study would show, however, that Bernanos himself, by means of a powerful transformation, a kind of theological mirror writing, has assimilated and clericized these writers. In psychological radicalism, he outdoes the devil's dialogue in Thomas Mann's *Dr. Faustus* in his effort to "know the depths of Satan" (Rev. 2:24). Indeed, he abandons everything that the church stands for as he exhibits a familiarity with the demonic which causes the theologian to make the sign of the cross and ask himself whether the poet's genius can ever be caught and tamed in the baptismal font. Here is a scandal from any point of view, but it is this scandal which seals the unity of Christianity and culture.

Or let us take the Englishman T. S. Eliot. There is no nihilist of greater sensitivity and intellectual acumen. Yet he does not let the clumsy *nihil* pass without exposing its clumsiness. Through meditation he seeks to transform nihilistic indifference into a mystical indifference which is open to future being. Consider this passage from the *Four Quartets* ("East Coker"):

> I said to my soul, be still, and let the dark come upon you
> Which shall be the darkness of God.   As, in a theatre,
> The lights are extinguished, for the scene to be changed
> With a hollow rumble of wings, with a movement of darkness on
>   darkness,
> And we know that the hills and the trees, the distant panorama
> And the bold imposing façade are all being rolled away—
> Or as, when an underground train, in the tube, stops too long between
>   stations
> And the conversation rises and slowly fades into silence
> And you see behind every face the mental emptiness deepen
> Leaving only the growing terror of nothing to think about;
> Or when, under ether, the mind is conscious but conscious of
>   nothing—
> I said to my soul, be still, and wait without hope
> For hope would be hope for the wrong thing; wait without love
> For love would be love of the wrong thing; there is yet faith
> But the faith and the love and the hope are all in the waiting.
> Wait without thought, for you are not ready for thought:
> So the darkness shall be the light, and the stillness the dancing.[3]

In Eliot's work faith does not exclude doubt, nor does doubt exclude faith. They stand in a relationship like that of the government and the loyal opposition in a parliamentary republic. One cannot say, moreover, that such an attitude is less lawful or appropriate than the obstinate singlemindedness of a Paul Claudel. What is Christian in a Christian literature is not decided by a single believer or a generation. A century of Christian theological interpretation cannot settle the question.

The mystery of evil and the experience of total alienation and meaninglessness—never before have both of these been conjured up with such unrestricted sincerity as in contemporary Christian literature. Can anyone deny that the Christian poet shares in the suffering from the godlessness, theologically speaking, of our epoch, or that he profits, aesthetically speaking, from the same godlessness? The Christian poet, like the secular writers

---

[3] From "East Coker" in *Four Quartets*, Copyright, 1943, by T. S. Eliot. By permission of Harcourt, Brace & World, New York, and Faber and Faber Ltd.

of the present age, is given a freedom and a responsibility to "define his own reality." He too feels a melancholy emancipation of spirit, the dizzy free-floating freedom of the godless. Whatever is human moves him, but it does not shock him. He must grapple with it. Yet how is it possible for him to sympathize with the godless at the same time that he contradicts them in God's name? Can it be that truth no longer wishes to be recognized in the knowable, in convictions, in logical relationships? Is it rather to be found in the shifting "events" of the soul, in scandalous self-contradictions? "Ambivalence of concepts," Gottfried Benn has called it: "Fusion of everything with its opposite." Benn was himself one of the grimmest opponents of Christian culture, the lyricist of the "final pleasure," the cynical denouncer of all the so-called sacred values of the Western tradition. This same man, as he grew older, took the liberty of frequently reading his Bible. There he found Jeremiah's lament: "He hath hedged me about, that I cannot get out: he hath made my chain heavy. Also when I cry and shout, he shutteth out my prayer" (Lam. 3:7-8). To this passage Benn returned again and again. He said to himself, "This is what I am." Show us the contemporary apologist who would not gratefully seize these words with a triumphant "Hah!" (For he takes the arguments where he finds them.) For today's poet, the image of the self hedged about, the "walled-in" self, is a concrete and therefore irrefutable matter. And truth for him is the hidden mystery which reveals itself from time to time in the events of speech. Truth is ever an open question, and this openness is what the poet's powers of insight and feelings ultimately desire, whether he be Christian or not!

X

Christianity, Myth, and the Symbolism of Poetry

CLEANTH BROOKS

THE CURRENT CONFUSION OF THE ROLES OF POETRY AND RELIGION AND poetry and science can be dated at least as far back as the mid-nineteenth century. Matthew Arnold's pronouncements typify the confusion, though it would be unfair to suggest that Arnold alone was confused or to fail to take note of Arnold's attempt at clarification. He was confident that though religion could not survive alongside modern science, poetry could, and that poetry could be made to take over the essential function performed in earlier ages by religion. Hence, the now-celebrated prediction that "Most of what now passes with us for religion and philosophy will be replaced by poetry."

Arnold's "solution" did not, of course, win general acceptance. The more aggressive positivists were to put poetry firmly under the thumb of science itself and to define its function as the recommendation of naturalistic values. Nowadays, we are inclined to associate such blunt simplifications with the discredited "Marxist" criticism of the thirties, but they continue to flourish. The Luce publications, for example, simply stand the Marxist position on its head and urge the production of novels that will frankly make out a case for the American way of life. The recent violent attack by Karl Shapiro upon the modern poetry he dislikes as "theology ill concealed" finds the approved alternative, as his In Defence of Ignorance

100

makes abundantly clear, not in theology so thoroughly absorbed into the body of the work that it is "well concealed" or theology discarded altogether, but in an advocacy of Shapiro's own "theology"—that is, his own set of values. Arnold, it must be conceded, more than invited some such preoccupation with moral content: why otherwise all the fuss about his "high seriousness" which the greatest works of literature possessed but lesser works, including Chaucer's, lacked?

At any rate, Arnold's statement of the problem remains for us the classic statement, and subsequent discussions of the problem—down to the present—are right in continuing to invoke Arnold's name. One would like, however, a more concrete statement of the problem, the kind of statement that a poem provides, and we can find one apt to our purpose in Arnold's "Dover Beach." When the listener hears the "melancholy, long-withdrawing roar" of the ebbing sea, he associates it with the ebbing of faith, and turns to the loved one to give and to exact a pledge: they must be "true" to each other precisely because the sanctions of religion have been withdrawn. Because the world is really blank and grim and not the world that Christianity had depicted it to be, the lovers must find their refuge in each other.

So much for the "situation" in the poem: sufficient, be it said, on which to found an admirable poem. But here we have something else in mind: Arnold's view of the cultural situation. If the findings of geology had made it impossible to believe in Christianity, why had not the findings of biology made it impossible for Arnold to believe in romantic love, a notion which pretty obviously flies in the face of biological fact? Conversely, if science had not denied the possibility of that gallantly absurd poetic creation, had one the right to conclude that science had really disposed of religion? The poem "Dover Beach" taken as the dramatization of a situation encountered has much to be said for it; taken as a guide through the wasteland, a good deal less. It dramatizes a cultural situation; it does not dispose of it.

Space does not allow here for a detailed account of the criticisms of Arnold's position that have been made in the twentieth century. I must limit myself to certain significant tendencies. The analysis of Arnold's confusion has served to rehabilitate poetry by relieving it of a burden that it ought not be asked to carry, and concomitantly, it has served to point to the possibility of—and to some minds, the necessity for—religion. Reconsiderations of the relation of poetry to science have raised afresh the problem of poetic truth. The differentiation of science and art has pointed to the limitation of science as the purveyor of all truth and has

suggested the possibility of other kinds of truth; or, remembering the ultimate oneness of truth, we may prefer to say that it has suggested the possibility of other modes for apprehending truth. Poetry is obviously not
related to fact as science is. (Arnold had rejoiced that poetry was not
"tied" to fact as religion unfortunately was.) One vigorous group of in-
quirers has come to realize that poetry is essentially metaphor, and along
with the rediscovery of metaphor—not as decoration, not as illustration,
but as an essential and irreplacable mode of apprehension—has come the
rehabilitation of symbolic and nonscientific modes of statement—including
"myth," though one hesitates more and more to use this overworked and
hard-pressed term.

Truth, Life, and Poetry

Much of the critical effort of the last forty-odd years has gone into exploring
the metaphorical and symbolic structure of poetry. The basic truth of a
work of art is conceived to be a truth of "coherence," not "referential"
truth in the sense that there is any direct pointing outside to a realm of
fact. In this view, the poem becomes a little world to be studied in its own
terms, and those terms have to be respected.

Literature retains its humanistic function, to be sure. The special kind of
mirror that it holds up to nature—though a distortion mirror, a lens, or
prism—can tell us a great deal about reality, including that portion of
reality that is ourselves. But the critical effort of our time for a good
many years has placed stress upon the special mode through which literature mediates truth and has discouraged the abstraction from any piece of
literature of ethical principles, messages, and preachments. Literature is
to be confused neither with science, philosophy, or religion: it embodies
its own principles and has its own peculiar function.

A natural and thoroughly predictable reaction to this critical emphasis
has now set in. It exclaims that poetry has been detached from life, as indeed, in some sense, it has. For the modern critical effort has been to
stress the fictionality of literature and to insist upon this special kind of
symbol of which it is constituted. What was an attempt to define and
defend the autonomy of literature is thus, with a certain plausibility, being denounced as an arid formalism. This, in substance, is the charge of
the reaction: criticism has dried up the vital juices of the poem, leaving
it a kind of brittle shell, quite emptied of life; a mere arabesque which
could be of interest only to a rather finicking and detached observer. The
critical reaction of the last few years now strives to reassociate literature
with life, to insist again on the art work as an expression of the artist's emo-

tions—even as a mere overflow of his passions—and to emphasize the prophetic role and the "poetry of power" which is to be associated with it.

The present reaction was predictable, but is it really necessary, and does it understand that which it denounces? There is no reason in the world why a work as carefully structured as *Macbeth* may not represent a tremendous personal utterance by Shakespeare. Quite possibly it does if we knew enough of Shakespeare's life to say, though—one almost says "fortunately"—we do not. It is quite evident that a work so intricately wrought as Milton's *Paradise Lost* has exerted a powerful influence, changing, for good or ill, the course of several generations of Protestantism, and changing it in ways which the author would have in part approved and in part surely disapproved. Literary works then are not only symbolic structures; they are usually personal expressions and they may often change history. To regard them as literarary structures does not deny them either their origins or their consequences.

Again, there is no necessary antagonism between "vision" and "technique" or between "sensibility" and "structure." But the vision of a great novel is mediated to us only through the technique. The mute and inglorious Milton remains a surmise, a conjectured potentiality that has not been realized. The speaking—and therefore, glorious—Milton's vision is realized for us in and through the literary structure of his poems. We surely have the right to study a work of art in any way that interests us or that makes sense of it. *Paradise Lost* can be studied as cosmology, psychology, ethical theory, theory of myth, and even as economics. But in proportion as we are studying literature—not just the life of a particular man or the background of a specific historic event—we will probably have to take into account literary modes and techniques and structures. After all, it is reasonable to think that the most important thing that a poet has contributed is his poems.

It is a pity that so much of this needs saying again. It ought to be obvious, but evidently it is not. I note that the prospectus for the present volume itself made the interesting comment that the theory of art for art's sake "while it has served to free the art of our time from subordination to a too rigid religious, political, or cultural dogmatism, nevertheless implies an aesthetic autonomy which does not fully exist." And in this general context the editor proceeds to quote with approval from Gilbert Highet's statement that literature "deals with people, and people are moral agents: therefore it is impossible to write about human thoughts and human actions without, consciously or unconsciously, raising moral

103

problems and answering them." [1] Of course it is impossible to write about human beings without raising moral problems. Who had ever thought otherwise? Morals have to do with human behavior and, as Allen Tate put it long ago, concrete moral problems are the subject matter of the arts. I am less sure that literature "answers" problems: it certainly need not issue in ethical generalizations. But in any case, a novel does differ from a treatise on morals; and if it does, is not the difference important? (If it is unimportant, then we would save ourselves trouble by dropping the term literature altogether: we should simply talk about the various "discussions" of human beings.)

There is every temptation to do just this—to say that the specifically literary aspect of literature is the least important part of it, that life is indeed a seamless garment, and to agree with Leslie Fielder's remark: "Literary criticism is always becoming 'something else,' for the simple reason that literature is always 'something else.'" The present volume cites Denis de Rougemont's comment upon the inadequacy of the term "beauty" in any serious discussion of literature—a sentiment which many of us heartily share. Should we go further then and also dispense with the term "literature"?

Yet in spite of the reaction (and because of its very vigor) one has to say that the fictionality of literature is a matter of first importance, that literature, in spite of its intimate relations with life, is not life and needs to be distinguished from life, and that all literature is finally symbolic, or, I should prefer to say with Robert Frost, metaphoric. Literature is indeed always "something else" but primarily through its symbolic dimension— because it is always about something other than itself. Literature makes its comment about that something other through its own grasp on concrete particulars, or, to put it in another way, we may say that literature conveys us into the universal only through the narrow door of the particular.

The practical importance of keeping a distinction between literature and life is easily illustrated. Let me instance the present state of Faulkner criticism (since I have had to read most of it during the last six months). By and large, honorable exceptions noted, present-day Faulkner criticism shows exactly what happens when the critic neglects the fictionality of the work or abuses it. Thus, Faulkner's novels and stories are treated as sociological descriptions of life in north Mississippi, or they are turned into moralized allegories in a display of unabashed "symbol-mongering." There is no reason why these two misapprehensions should not occur together,

---

[1] *The Classical Tradition* (New York: Oxford University Press, 1949), p. 445.

and most often they do. For the excessive literalization which converts the fictional into factual events and thus yields "sociology" is the counterpart of a misguided yearning for universal meanings that produces the symbol-mongering and turns every thirty-three-year-old character into a type of Christ and every murder into a crucifixion. But such faults are mutually related failures to understand how fiction renders its meanings.

Some knowledge of how life is actually lived (and has been lived) in Mississippi would have prevented the writing of some nonsense. But an awareness of how fiction "works" would have helped even more. Faulkner, to be sure, has much to tell us about life in Mississippi and in the South generally. He is indeed concerned with human beings and human values. But his novels are neither case studies nor moral treatises: they are works of art and have to be read as such.

Myth and Symbol in Literature and Religion

Literature and religion are indeed close together in their areas of interest. Both use symbols, symbols of a kind quite different from those employed by the physicist or the mathematician, being value-structured, "mythic," and in some way keyed to human response. But they have differences, too, and those differences are important ones.

Literature always involves an as-if. The literary mode is par excellence that in which we learn what it feels like to be in a certain situation. Literature has always been, therefore, the prime instrument for understanding other men and other cultures and other value systems. One need not confine it to that function. Through literature, men discover themselves, the further reaches of their personalities, the dark and hidden places of their own beings. But religion always involves, it seems to me, some kind of commitment, something deeper than any as-if. It is notorious that when religions lose their hold on their adherents, they tend to turn into a kind of poetry, no longer exerting an absolute claim or demanding certain actions by way of response, but grading off into a series of possibilities for contemplation with which we refresh our imaginations or enlarge our spirits, or in which we simply indulge.[2] The transmutation of Santayana's religion into poetry

---

[2] Compare Croce on this subject:
But the distinction of art from philosophy . . . brings with it other distinctions, among which that of art from myth occupies the foremost place. For myth, to him who believes it, presents itself as the revelation and knowledge of reality as opposed to unreality,—a reality that drives away other beliefs as illusory or false. It can become art only for him who no longer believes in it and avails himself of mythology as a metaphor, of the austere world of the gods as of a beautiful world, of God as of an image of sublimity.
Benedetto Croce, *The Essence of Aesthetic* (London, 1921), p. 18.

is perhaps one of the most celebrated and interesting of such cases in our day. (I do not mean to oversimplify Santayana's experience: his religion as "poetry" evidently meant a great deal to him and perhaps not merely as "art," though here we are dealing with a highly sophisticated personality who had other resources upon which to draw.)

Something of this sort is happening today on an ever-larger scale: on the part of our more sensitive poets and men of letters, the conversion of Christianity into a sort of poetry. Christian terms and symbols are appropriated for what they can contribute to particular literary works, but in the process, usually transformed and transvalued, their meaning reshaped to the author's own end. The process is not new, and it testifies to the abiding strength of the Christian heritage: the symbols retain enough potency to be worth appropriating. But the tendency is not pro-Christian. In attitude it is at best neutral and in total effect, disintegrative. The Christian need not be alarmed; he ought to be highly interested; but he should not entertain any illusions about what is going on.

For Christians, the problem is to prevent our religion from turning into mere literature, a fairy tale with ethical implications. But this problem, I suggest, is closely related to another, which is the topic of my essay: how to prevent our literature from turning into a religion. (Arnold's position obviously gives us a kind of fusion of the two tendencies.) It is interesting to use this general context for relating the two most powerful critical tendencies of the present day. The first, the resurgent romanticism typified in its most violent and "anti-intellectual" form by Shapiro's *In Defense of Ignorance*, but well represented at every other level, is bitterly hostile to emphasis on "form" of any kind. It fears or despises intellectual analysis of the arts. It celebrates ardor and enthusiasm. Skeptical of the autonomy of art, it tends to coalesce art and "life"—whether in the dithyrambic outcry or in the directly moralized judgment. (Shapiro illustrates how easily dithyrambist and moralist may combine.) Poetry displaces religion or takes over its functions.

The second, the "myth" criticism, typified most brilliantly and humanely by Northrop Frye, sorts and classifies the archetypal patterns which all literary works (and all religions?) exemplify. As a kind of "social science" of literature, it plays down value judgments of individual works, is tolerant where the new romanticism is intolerant, and by contrast is dry, detached, and "intellectual." But like the new romanticism, it is primarily concerned with the origins and genesis of a work of literature—not its achieved form as such—and like the new romanticists, the "myth" critics tend to work from a naturalistic base. The myth is psychologized: all literary symbolism (and presumably religious symbolism too) becomes a function of the basic postures of the human psyche.

Both tendencies move us away from the work of art into "something else," and thus, whatever their incidental merits, deflect us from the prime critical task. But I have no space to argue that matter here. Instead of that argument, let me conclude with this observation: that a Christian concern for literature has little to expect from either tendency. In my considered opinion it is better served by a theory which is jealous of the autonomy of literature, which holds that literature mediates its truth indirectly and that poetry expresses its values, not directly, but through metaphor and symbol.

XI

Poetry and Religion

AMOS N. WILDER

No clear line can be drawn between poetry and religion, if only because religion properly involves the whole of life and the total man. The relationship is therefore a more subtle one and all the more interesting. Art has its staple in our actual human makeup, and must therefore hold some kinds of transcendence and mysticism in suspicion. Yeats insists that the stuff of poetry is our human drama, "man's blood-sodden heart," "the lion and the honeycomb," the riot and fecundity of life. These may be transfigured in art but not left behind. Yet Dante for one knew how to raise his pinnacle of religious vision by basing it on the heart and the flesh.

Faith and the Autonomy of Poetry

Certain special factors in our time draw our attention to the question of the mutual relations of poetry and religion. We are today acutely aware of the long-standing divorce between religion and the arts generally. Since the Romantic period we can observe the detachment of many of the more significant poets from the religious traditions. More recently this can be noted in the cases of Hart Crane, the imagists, Joyce, Yeats, Pound, and the earlier Eliot and Auden. One thinks also of Allen Tate's two series of "Sonnets at Christmas" as symptomatic; of Eliot's "Hippopotamus," of Wallace Stevens' "Sunday Morning," or of Yeats' gentle rejection of the faith addressed to the Baron Von Hügel.

Relevant to our problem also is the concern for the autonomy of poetry which has been so prominent in recent criticism. No doubt the prior occasion for this has been political or ideological pressure upon the artist; the official or popular expectation that the poet should be mobilized to defend the state or the *status quo*, to curse the enemy like Balaam, or to offer his talent as a weapon for one or another "ism." Such expectations represent a misguided homage to the mythmaker and derive from a true recognition of the social significance of the arts. But in the naïve form in which they are espoused they falsify the integrity of the artist. In the Hebrew-Christian perspective they represent a new form of what the Bible calls "false prophecy," either a "bought" oracle or an assurance of peace where there is no peace.

But insistence on the autonomy of poetry, reaching even to the demand for a "pure poetry," is motivated also by a properly aesthetic concern. So long as the works of the imagination are conceived of in an indiscriminate way as inspiring, idealistic, and didactic, the true canons of the art are blurred. Poetry best serves society and its moral traditions by following its own genius and genus. While in earlier phases of man's social development art and ritual, imagination and faith, are indistinguishable in their cultural expression, in a period like ours science, religion, and art become specialized activities and rightly develop and defend their own rationales.

If the plea for the autonomy of art has highlighted the issue of religion and poetry today, conversely the contemporary theological revival has had the same effect. Neoorthodoxy in whatever terms we understand it has powerfully challenged "cultural religion" and has set a great question mark against the aesthetic dimension of life. We have here a modern phase of the Old Testament prophetic challenge to idolatry and of the early Christian war on the pagan imagination and its natural mythology. This challenge forces the arts, poetry included, to clarify their own role. Of great interest in Auden's later work is the way in which he comes to terms with this problem of the artist who is also a Christian. The poet must no longer confuse his role with that of the intoxicated seer or "healer." He must not, as a magician, usurp the place of saint or apostle. On the other hand, the true aesthetic function of play with its essential freedom is thus restored to him.

Defining the Terms: Poetry and Religion

It is evident already that the dialectic with which we are occupied depends very much upon the way in which we define our two terms. We shall content ourselves with a very matter of fact characterization of poetry, that of rhythmic utterance. One aspect of it in all cultures is the high level of absorption in the import of words, an intensity of concentration which carries with it not only rhythm but various other patterns and subtleties; all of which together provide a potent vehicle for the celebration of various facets of reality. But we must also keep in mind the plastic and mythopoetic features which characterize poetry and which it has in common with primary religious discourse in its cultic and chant aspects.

The one thing to avoid in any working definition of religion is too loose a conception such as would exclude any real dialectic with poetry. There are many still for whom the adjectives "religious" or "spiritual" connote merely any psychic enhancement or intensity of subjective experience, any kind of aesthetic pantheism or cosmic emotion. We should not, indeed, dissociate the religious consciousness, as something *sui generis*, from man's experience of nature, but distinctions should be made. It is best to recognize, moreover, that religion in the singular is an abstraction. It appears actually always in inseparable relation with particular social-cultural constellations. In any case religion has to do with the primal springs of life, with the level at which man is made and unmade, a level at which creation and transformation involve not only the self but society and the world.

The two useful approaches, phenomenological and psychological, point toward an understanding of religion as a celebration of the mysterious sources of human potency, security, orientation, and obligation. In defining religion in this way it is immediately evident that any disjunction between it and the aesthetic life is difficult. On the phenomenological side the social enactments of our relations with the forces of life are carried out in ways that are also aesthetic: dance, chant, space-demarcations, and myth. On the psychological side the subjective experience is closely related to aesthetic sensibility. If we may speak of the moment of religious apprehension in terms of epiphany—a moment which is not a mere response but a creative mimesis—we see how close the two orders are to each other.

Genesis, Structure, and Belief in Contemporary Poetry

Turning to certain crucial aspects of the relationship, we consider first the "genesis of the poem" and its religious analogue: poetic and religious "inspiration." It is a question today whether poet and critic are still willing to accept the classical view that the impulse to this art is to be understood in terms of inspiration in some sense. In older periods the afflatus in question could be ascribed to Apollo, the Muses, the gods, or to the "Wisdom and Spirit of the Universe." The modern poet suspects such quasi-religious categories. He is averse to such spiritualistic views of reality and such oracular views of his own function. He would rather adopt the modest role of craftsman than be etherialized into a medium of Beauty with a capital *B* or Spirit with a capital *S*. Thus we find William Carlos Williams saying: "There is a 'special' place which poems, as all works of art, must occupy, but it is quite definitely the same place where bricks or colored threads are handled." [1] This would seem to be a view of poetry-in-the-making which would remove it a long way from religious experience. Valery's discussion of the art, though not his poems, would afford another such view.

Nevertheless the classical view returns in new forms. Yeats may have given up one form of it in his later work but this also assumes visionary and auditory endowment. Figures as different as Hart Crane and Dylan Thomas can only be called dithyrambic poets and their work evidences a doctrine or assumption of transpersonal impulse. Thus Crane in his apostrophe "To Brooklyn Bridge" characterizes his art as well as the bridge:

> O harp and altar, of the fury fused,
> (How could mere toil align thy choiring strings!) [2]

Or Thomas:

> Light breaks on secret lots,
> On tips of thought where thoughts smell in the rain;
> When logics die,
> The secret of the soil grows through the eye. [3]

It is of great interest to see how modern poets reformulate the reality of inspiration under conditions where the older metaphysical and psychological assumptions for it are no longer available. We have exactly the same dilemma in contemporary theology. The meaning of the Holy Spirit has to be redefined where the older Platonic or Semitic or modern idealist world views are no longer meaningful.

Take a contemporary poet, John Wain. He offers us a brilliant satire upon mechanical or behavioristic conceptions of art in "Poem Feigned

[1] Cited by Hugh Kenner, "Dr. Williams Shaping His Axe," *The Hudson Review*, Spring, 1955, p. 149.
[2] "To Brooklyn Bridge," From: *The Collected Poems of Hart Crane*. By permission of Liveright Publishers, N.Y. Copyright © R 1961, Liveright Publishing Corp.
[3] *The World I Breathe* (Norfolk, Conn.: New Directions, 1939), p. 25.

to have been Written by an Electronic Brain." This alleged cerebral computer speaks up for itself and confutes its naturalistic engineers:

> You set me like a cactus to draw life
> From drought, in the white desert of your mind,
> Your speculative wilderness of charts;
> What went you to the wilderness to see?
> A matrix made of glass? An electric thought?
> Come quick! I snow down sheets of truth; I print
> The sleep of Socrates, the pain of Christ! [4]

Another example of the modern poet disabused of an older romantic aesthetic but who yet presupposes ulterior endowments is Wallace Stevens with his varying formulations of the imagination.

Modern criticism has also been much concerned with the "structure of the poem." This is one aspect of the insistence on the autonomy of poetry. In distinction from the way in which words are used in discursive prose, attention is given to the plastic and connotative use of language, to exploitation of its ambiguity as an asset not a liability, and to the rich constellation of meanings so attainable. Such communication is not more vague but more precise, and not less real but more concrete, than the discursive statement which proceeds by generalization and abstraction ("the spectral dance of bloodless categories"). Beyond the particular metaphors significance is also assigned to what structural fable or myth may be employed by the poet. By all such means many-layered allusion to potent symbolic legacies will be employed. Thus a poem has a fusing and palimpsest character corresponding to the human consciousness at its richest.

But analogies to this understanding of poetic structure in religious texts are not far to seek. The primary oracles of religion are poetic with respect both to rhythm and trope. In the biblical literature law and teaching (in the New Testament *didache* and *paraenesis*) rest back upon oracle and upon cultic recitation. The larger part of the Old Testament is poetry by the canons of the age. In the New Testament the records of the sayings of Jesus evidence in good part the underlying Aramaic poetic conventions.

The issue of "poetry and belief" offers a further area where our topic is illuminated. Modern criticism has rightly been concerned to dissociate

---

[4] From *A Word Carved on a Sill* by John Wain (London: Routledge & Kegan Paul, 1956), p. 14.

proper appreciation of poetry as an art from whatever explicit or even implicit didactic elements may be found in it, including such as may be religious. The conclusion of the long discussion is that faith or unfaith, one or another world view or social dogma, may properly find expression in poetry but not in the same way as in prose. (Where the two come closest together is in the particular genre of satire.) The body of Catholic faith in the *Divine Comedy* is something different from the anatomy of it in Aquinas. Mythopoetic statement of belief as found in poetry is different from doctrinal statement. *Paradise Lost* presents the faith of Milton in a different register and with a richer manual than the *De Doctrina Christiana*. But poetry does have a cognitive root and import. Moreover, the ideological element in poetry can be an essential aspect of the aesthetic achievement and it enters into the very structure.

Religion and Poetry: Distinction and Similarity

We have noted the renewed interest today in the relation of religion to poetry. Our tentative definitions have suggested the close relation of the two activities. We have seen, further, that under different aspects the art of poetry is one which has analogies with religious expression in genesis, in structure, even with respect to cognitive content. We must ask finally, however, what it is that distinguishes religion from poetry.

As soon as we pose this question we are reminded of a number of familiar answers as well as test cases. In Plato we find poetry sometimes disparaged as an enervating or disorderly element as over against the better counsels of philosophy and the kind of religion approved by it. The Aristotelian-Thomist tradition assigns poetry to the practical reason rather than to the contemplative. The eighteenth century in part similarly defined poetry in terms of a *techne*, and set a real gulf between it and religion. Samuel Johnson, in his *Life of Waller*, writes: "Contemplative piety, or the intercourse between God and the human soul, cannot be poetical." Poetry deals with the works of God, he observes, but not directly with God as prayer does. Where Matthew Arnold would see poetry as taking over the role of religion, Auden has insisted that the poet must not confuse his role with that of the seer. The most interesting case is that of G. M. Hopkins, who looked upon his gift with intense scruple as an interest that could distract him from his religious vocation. Yet much of his best work represents the religious life in its direct confrontation with God, in direct contradiction of the view of Samuel Johnson cited above.

In the last analysis religious expression and poetry have it in common

113

that they testify to reality, and by symbolic means. The final difference must be in what they report or reveal. Evidently it is here that we would find the peculiar existential concern of religious discourse. Revelation represents the initial moment or *arche* from which also the arts spring. But it would be mistaken to deny existential seriousness to poetry or art. It is true that poetry, in the innumerable forms and genres that it takes on in various cultures, has many roles that are largely unrelated to the religious life. We must also recognize, as the Thomist would put it, that the artist gives himself to the work in view where the believer presses on to communion with God. But such distinctions should not lead us to a denial of that initial "epiphany" or world-making moment which lies behind all significant poetry, particularly today when religious forms have lost much of their relevance for man's perennial need.

XII

The Existential Temper of the Modern Novel

COLIN WILSON

THERE ARE TWO OBVIOUS WAYS OF DEALING WITH THIS SUBJECT. ONE would be to write about a number of "existentialist novels," from Unamuno's *Marquis of Lumbria* to Dürrenmatt's *The Pledge*, with all the usual references to *Ulysses*, *La Nausée*, and so on. The other is to try to talk about "essentials" and hope that whoever reads this book is already familiar with his Dürrenmatt, Sartre, and Musil. The latter course appeals to me most.

What Is an Existential Novel?

First of all, what is the meaning of "existential" and what does it mean in connection with the novel? I myself have been using the word for years without having any nice, compact dictionary definition at the back of my mind. Let us admit that it is a word that has meaning only within a limited context. But it so happens that it has a great deal of relevance to the culture of the twentieth century. So although it may seem as superfluous to our great-grandchildren as phlogiston is to the modern chemist, we may as well get what use we can out of it. It means literally "connected with existence." This means nothing whatever, considered on its own. But consider it in relation to the philosophy of Schelling or Bertrand Russell, in relation to orthodox Christianity or the modern novel from Anderson to Mailer, and it immediately becomes an octopus of a word, a skeleton key to many locks, a spotlight with a hundred purposes.

115

When speaking about existentialism, it is impossible to avoid reference to Sartre's novel *La Nausée*, for the book is the end product of a process that has been developing for more than a century. This process can best be described by quoting three lines of W. B. Yeats:

> Shakespearian fish swam the sea, far away from land;
> Romantic fish swam in nets coming to the hand;
> What are all those fish that lie gasping on the strand? [1]

Shakespearian fish—the detached creation of the great writers, Shakespeare, Balzac, Trollope, a creation that takes its premises serenely for granted and creates in the way that a carpenter makes a table. The romantic fish turned to introspection and felt that art could not be "honest" unless it talked about the struggle of the individual. Zola and the realists declared that the novel should provide what religion was failing to provide —moral guidance, preaching. But finally came the devotees of art for art's sake, beginning with Rilke's novel *Malte*, culminating in *Ulysses* and *La Nausée*. *Ulysses* sacrificed everything to honesty—or almost everything—and its critics declared nervously that the novel was becoming a scientific catalogue. But although *Ulysses* contains details about the exact capacity of the Dublin reservoir, it was not this kind of "honesty" Joyce was concerned with. Joyce wanted to say, in effect: "How can we keep on talking about elopements and forged wills and the feminist problem when the texture of reality is so different from anything you will find in novels?" His revolt was not entirely original; in *Crime and Punishment* Dostoevski kept the rudiments of the conventional nineteenth-century plot—the wronged sister, the villainous landowner, etc.—but the thing one remembers about the novel is the smell of St. Petersburg's hot pavements, the dirty horsehair sofa on which Raskolnikov sleeps, the cracked windowpanes, the cobweb on the ceiling, the cup of cold tea, the smell of cooking. Dostoevski is concerned about the *texture* of everyday experience in a way that his contemporary Trollope was not, in a way that is familiar to readers of Joyce and Sartre.

But Dostoevski learned an important lesson. You must choose between "texture" and plot. You cannot have both. *The Idiot* was an uncomfortable compromise. There are certain chairs and tables and rooms in that book that we remember as clearly as Van Gogh's chair. But somehow the book is a failure, and it is a failure because the microscopic method can-

---

[1] W. B. Yeats, "Three Movements." Used by permission of The Macmillan Company, A. P. Watt & Son, The Macmillan Co. of Canada, and Mrs. W. B. Yeats.

not support a complicated plot. Dostoevski realized that complex plots were necessary to say what he had to say. So without a second thought, he abandoned the microscope. *The Devils* and *Karamazov* are told in the first person—which, of course, precludes the "movie-camera" method that is the essence of texture writing. The narrator has a story to get on with; he cannot linger around a room, creating "atmosphere."

I am speaking now of the *existential method* in the modern novel, the microscope that moves slowly over the surface of a chair or a wall, observes the sheen of color on the wing of a dead fly in a glass of water, etc. I am assuming that readers are familiar with *La Nausée* and its slimy gray stone and twisted tree roots and the other *objects* that dominate the book. This method has been carried to a strange limit by three young French novelists: Alain Robbe-Grillet, Michel Butor, and Nathalie Sarraute. Robbe-Grillet derives from Hemingway in ignoring emotions and concentrating on "the facts." Like Hemingway, he never tells the reader, "This character is in mental agony"; he prefers to record casual conversations, the appearance of a chair, and allow the reader to infer the agony. But he is infinitely less successful (artistically) than Hemingway, for the method demands strong, clear emotions that can make their own impact without the writer's help. Robbe-Grillet specializes in long, dull descriptions of physical objects; his attempt to keep the novel detached and scientific has simply emasculated it.

Michel Butor derives from Sartre, but in a different way; he is more concerned with self-analysis, and his *Passing Time* is written, like *La Nausée*, as a journal. Nathalie Sarraute is the most interesting and talented of the younger French writers. She is far closer to Henry James and Proust than to Joyce, and she writes about the oversensitive mind—close to insanity—agonizingly trapped in the present and in human relations. The main point about these three novelists is that they are all Yeats' fish "gasping on the strand," completely static, so preoccupied with the "texture" of the present that they forget that a book is meant to amuse and entertain.

The writer who seems to me to be by far the greatest in Europe at the moment—Friedrich Dürrenmatt—has no such disadvantage. He is refreshingly in control of his material. He has called himself "this lover of gruesome fables, this pen-pushing Protestant." His two novels, *A Dangerous Game* (*Die Panne*) and *The Pledge* (*Das Versprechen*), are perhaps the most important novels to appear since *La Nausée*. The style is clean and concise. His existentialism is closer to the Sartre of *L'Etre et le Néant*, a preoccupation with the destiny and psychology of man. Unlike Sartre, he

117

seems to have a broad streak of irrepressible optimism. Let me confess that, as far as I am concerned, this is his greatest recommendation.

Existentialism vis-à-vis Religion

Dürrenmatt brings this discussion to the next aspect of existential writing: I mean, existential defined vis-à-vis religion. In this sense, the first great existential drama of European literature was Faust. Existentialism in this sense means "the search for meaning." It is the ultimate failure of the Joyce school of writing (which includes Robbe-Grillet) that it uses an existential technique while completely ignoring the existential content. Joyce was in conscious revolt against his successful contemporaries: Shaw, Wells, Chesterton, Galsworthy, etc. Out of a schoolboyish desire to be "different," Joyce preferred Ben Jonson to Shakespeare and Aristotle to Plato. But he took this odd position further, and declared that logic meant more than ideas. Stephen had to be a formidable logician and intellectual, but Joyce couldn't allow him to seem a disciple of Yeats and A. E. by discussing ideas; so Stephen is made to advance a complicated and nonsensical theory about Shakespeare, displaying his erudition and logic, but steering well clear of general ideas.

Henry James—the other major branch of the gasping-fish business—also eschewed ideas, although this was mainly because fate had given Henry all the artistic sensibility and his brother all the capacity for thought. He was interested neither in religion nor in politics—and in sex only in a rather nervous and cautious manner.

So the two major forces on the modern novel defined its method and limits: endless interest in fine shades of psychological analysis and in the detailed description of physical actuality; a certain vague and melancholy interest in the problem of individual destiny (Roderick Hudson, Stephen Dedalus); but a horrified avoidance of religion and politics.

The next problem is the ten-thousand-dollar question. Can literature survive within these limits? Are the problems of meaning—of religion, sex, and politics—superfluous in the novel? Can the ascetic novelist do without them, as the religious ascetic does without sex and human relations? Or are they like food and drink—a variable but ultimately inescapable necessity? For a great many years, no one asked these questions, and the "existential method" reigned supreme in the novel. For subject matter, the new novelists followed the lead of Flaubert, and wrote about the "ordinary man." Observation was all that mattered. Take any character walking down Main Street, write about his misery and futility and about how he is condemned from the beginning. If he is lucky, this ordinary

118

man may reach the stature of tragedy, like Buchner's Woyzeck. But ask no questions about the meaning of his life and of life in general; concentrate on its social significance.

Sartre was one of the first to break away from this particular tyranny. He was, of course, an "intellectual," even though his favorite writers were Dos Passos and Faulkner. After *La Nausée* came the war which pitched him, whether he liked it or not, into all kinds of convictions and questions about human life. Sartre was a true pessimist, as confirmed in his world hatred as Graham Greene. But this attitude was of no use to a patriotic Frenchman. So the word "choice" found its way into the existentialist vocabulary, and the necessity for revolutionary action was emphasized. From the super-subtle Jamesian analyses of *Being and Nothingness*, with its inevitable pessimism, Sartre suddenly found himself committed to telling men they were free and that they ought to do something with their lives. An embarrassing position for the admirer of Faulkner, who suddenly found himself sounding like the H. G. Wells of *Mr. Polly*. Sartre did his best to tone down this Wellsian note by repeating that life is basically horrible (down to his latest play, *The Hermits of Altona*), but the note of optimism had been introduced. Worse still was the implication that the novelist can no longer be content to represent his hero's environment and sense of futility with strict realism. Again, Sartre tried to soften the blow by writing novels of unrelieved futility and sordidness, all expressed with an uncompromising experimentalism; still, the impression persisted that perhaps some kind of idealism—social or religious—should be a part of the novelist's equipment.

Religion and the Writer's Dilemma

This brings us to the crossroads for the modern novel, the latest dilemma. The novel of the eighteenth and nineteenth centuries—from Richardson to Trollope—had imposed a meaning on its material, and had done so without apology. Trollope broke off to have discussions with the reader, and in one novel even asked the reader's advice about how he ought to continue the story. The new novelists wanted to do away with all that. "The novelist is not God," they said. "The material should be allowed to speak for itself." Instead of being a storyteller, the novelist was now more like a tourist guide taking his readers around some underground cave, allowing his torch to rest on some interesting crystal structure, then on a stalactite. (Joyce somewhere or other refers to *Ulysses* as "Joyce's guide to the City of Dublin.") Opinions are lies; the "truth" about the world can best be expressed by allowing the world to speak for itself. But the result of this technique is to create a mindless universe of objects and of men who are always "acted upon."

This is the problem: on the one hand, the oversimplified moral universe of Richardson and Trollope; on the other, the more honest but ultimately static world of Sartre and Robbe-Grillet, a world as detached and dead as a moon landscape, in which man's life is meaningless.

Immediately, an obvious question presents itself. Does "meaning" involve some simple religious view of the Richardson-Trollope variety? Or are there other possibilities? Very frequently, the writers who seem to subscribe to the Joyce-existentialism are actually cheating. Faulkner, under the impressive facade of experimentalism, hides a juvenile romantic-sadism. Even Robbe-Grillet's technique seems to hide a completely romantic attitude and an embarrassment about asking the fundamental romantic question: What are we doing here?

I would argue that the distinction between the "didactic" novel (Wells, Mann, Hesse, etc.) and the existential novel of Joyce is a false one. All art asks the same question—"What is the meaning of human life?"—and implicitly answers it. Its "value premises" may be completely hidden and taken for granted, but they are present. The history of the experimental novel in the twentieth century proves that "technique" in itself defeats its own object: increased maturity. Hemingway and Joyce have nothing in common except their avoidance of "general ideas" and their technique of detachment. Both, after a magnificent beginning, went somehow to seed. The reason is the same in both cases: the questions asked and the values implied in their best work were never developed.

The problem is plain enough. The questions that lead to a development of values are moral or religious questions. But in view of the state of Christianity in our time, no writer wants to come up with a "religious answer." So before he gets to that stage, he simply stops asking the questions and contents himself with his old attitudes: stoicism, detachment, etc.

Existentialism means asking the questions. If the answer is unsatisfactory (as, for example, Mr. Eliot's "answer" is unsatisfactory for most of us), then the questions must be repeated and a finer analysis developed to deal with them. This, for me, is the meaning of the phrase "the existential temper of the modern novel." Literature has been lazy for half a century—has preferred to ignore the questions formulated in Goethe, in Melville, in Dostoevski and Nietzsche. If things are changing, it may mean a new vitality for literature in the second half of this century.

XIII

Camus: The Argument from the Absurd

STANLEY ROMAINE HOPPER

THE APPEAL TO THE ABSURD HAS APPEARED IN A VARIETY OF FORMS IN THE literature of our time—specifically so in the novels of Sartre and Camus, not to mention Kafka. The ironic consciousness also bears witness to it.

In Camus, it is the myth of Sisyphus which sums up the nature of the absurd. Like Sisyphus rolling the stone to the top of the hill only to be overborne by its burden, so man's long history of toil and daily tasks seems merely to return from day to day, from age to age, to the starting point: whence we begin again the absurd attempt to push the burden of consciousness over the hill of meaning.

Similarly, Simone de Beauvoir recounts the tale of Pyrrhus and Cinéas (as told by Plutarch). "First we shall conquer the Greeks," said Pyrrhus. "And after that?" asked Cinéas. "Then we shall win over Africa." "And after Africa?" "We shall pass into Asia and conquer Asia Minor and Arabia." "And after that?" "We will go to the Indies." "And after the Indies?" "Ah!" replied Pyrrhus, "then I shall rest." "Then," said Cinéas, "why don't you rest now?" [1]

In both instances the absurdity of human behavior—and thereby of the human condition—is made plain. Life itself is absurd if it comes to that, particularly when I consider that, do what I will, turn right, turn left,

---

[1] *Pyrrhus et Cinéas* (Paris: Gallimard, 1944), pp. 9-10.

push the stone or leave it alone, conquer Africa or take my ease now—whatever course I pursue, death awaits me sooner or later. "We all go into the dark," as Eliot says.

Nevertheless, the absurdity, while existentially omnipresent, is logically transparent. To detach myself from the condition and to stand outside the predicament, as it were, is a logical achievement, and poses the category of the absurd. But to do so breaks the line by which I am *attached to* the other and deprives me of my movement toward the other. If I do so I become exiled from the reality; I become a Stranger (*L'Étranger*), a wanderer, a stone pushing a stone, a thing among things, floating in a dreamlike indifference to feeling, to value, to concern, to fatality, to life or death. That is why we see in existentialist novels heroes—or at any rate protagonists—who are either sinking back into the daily round, the "quotidian indigence," or are moving dialectically to that nadir of contradiction from which they may be wakened into awareness of "responsibility" (destiny). Otherwise they lapse into thinghood—like Kafka's hero of *The Metamorphosis* who awakes one morning to discover he has turned into a cockroach. That Kafka himself is infected with this debilitation of the absurd is evident from his comment on himself: "What will be my fate as a writer is very simple. . . . I waver, continually fly to the summit of the mountain, but then fall back in a moment. Others waver too. . . . But I waver on the heights; it is not death, alas, but the eternal torments of the dying." [2] This is the Sisyphus movement reporting its own fatality.

Simone de Beauvoir, however, points out the illogic of this logical pose: man is not first of all a thing, but spontaneity which desires, loves, wills, and acts. He is possibility already projected toward the future; a possibility which actualizes itself precisely through recognizing what it is there where it commits itself. Pyrrhus was right, at any rate, to the extent that he recognized that every end is at the same time a fresh point of departure. This is the ambiguity of the human estate and the root of human freedom. Camus also, recognizing with Kafka that men today are estranged from reality and from themselves, seeks to take this condition as the fulcrum for his narratives and, without petitioning the *Deus ex machina*, to see in what sense the dialectic of the absurd contains within itself the power of its own transformation and how the report from the outside may be made prophetic of new meanings and fresh recognitions.

[2] *Diaries: 1914-1923*, ed. Max Brod, tr. Martin Greenberg and Hannah Arendt (New York: Schocken Books, 1949), p. 77.

The Absurd as Exile

What this fulcrum is Camus sets forth quite clearly in his essay on Kafka, who has so deeply influenced him—along with Kierkegaard, Dostoevski, and Pascal. "The final attempt of the surveyor (in *The Castle*)," he notes, "is to find God by traversing that which denies Him, to recognize Him, not according to our categories of goodness and beauty, but behind the empty and hideous faces of His indifference, His injustice and His hatred." And he notes how the existentialist novelists and philosophers, who begin by turning directly towards the absurd and its manifestations, come out "with this immense cry of hope." [3] Our failure to achieve honesty and candor (authenticity) in this regard has led us to project structures of regulation by which to "order" our lives. We have followed these out into the desert "of stones, fogs, and stagnant waters" (*The Fall*) where we find ourselves today.

The Stranger presents the plight of such an exile. Since the years had become unreal to him, events could make no difference—neither the deaths of others, nor a mother's love, nor the death of the priest's God, nor the way a man chooses to live. With a revolver in his hand, Mersault reflects: "It crossed my mind that one might fire, or not fire—and it would come to absolutely the same thing." Again, a little further on: "To stay, or to make a move—it came to much the same thing." [4] His mother dies, he has an affair with a girl the next day, he shoots a man in self-defense (and is absurdly condemned for murder), and the whole tragicomic pantomime is played out like a dream—until finally death, and the cross-questionings of the prison chaplain, trip him into passionate rebellion.

Then, I don't know how it was, but something seemed to break inside me, and I started yelling at the top of my voice . . . I'd taken him by the neckband of his cassock, and in a sort of ecstasy of joy and rage, I poured out on him all the thoughts that had been simmering in my brain. . . . And what did that mean? That, all the time, I'd been waiting for this present moment, for that dawn, tomorrow's or another day's, which was to justify me. Nothing had the least importance, and I knew quite well why. He, too, knew why. From the dark horizon of my future a sort of slow, persistent breeze had been blowing toward me, all my life long, from the years that were to come. And on its way that breeze *had leveled out all the ideas that people tried to foist on me* [italics mine] in the equally unreal years I then was living through.

[3] Albert Camus, *Le Mythe de Sisyphe* (Paris: Gallimard, 1942), pp. 183, 185.
[4] Albert Camus, *The Stranger*, tr. Stuart Gilbert (New York: Vintage Books), 1946, pp. 72, 73, 152.

The "dark wind" from the future seems to be the fate-laden awareness of ever-impending death indifferent to human hopes and values, thereby reducing all claims to an indifferent level. And then he fell asleep. But when he awoke, and "the stars were shining down on my face," a "marvelous peace of the sleepbound summer night flooded through [me] like a tide," and he understood, suddenly, his mother's sense of freedom at her life's end. "And I, too, felt ready to start life all over again. It was as if that great rush of anger had washed me clean, emptied me of hope, and, gazing up at the dark sky spangled with its signs and stars, for the first time, the first, I laid my heart open to the benign indifference of the universe." [5]

The aesthetic strategy of this conclusion is not unlike that of François Mauriac, whose narratives frequently end with the hero's turn into the open, with the new and emergent life implied by way of symbols drawn from nature or from psychological symbolization. Both writers, it should be recalled, have Pascal in common; and both are recipients of the Nobel award in literature.

But does the resemblance end here? Mauriac's report on the human condition presupposes the Christian dogma of original sin, whereas Camus says: "We all carry within us our places of exile, our crimes and our ravages. But our task is not to unleash them on the world; it is to fight them in ourselves and in others." [6] Yet in Camus there is a peculiar victory: as though Mauriac's dogmatic structure were inimical to the deepest authenticity, interposing, so to speak, a patterned orthodoxy between his reader and the truth; whereas Camus, reporting with a candid acceptance the wilderness turnings of contemporary man, emerges with a prophetic openness (albeit "an empty prophet for shabby times," an "Elijah without a messiah") preparing the way for the new name of God.

The Dark Night of the Absurd

This problem is at the root of all our deepest concerns today, and further, it is at the heart of and comprises the greatness of contemporary literature. Even Camus, when fascinated with Sisyphus' return to the stone, would find in this return a positive principle. He finds it in the fact that we know our condition, a consciousness to which we are led when the stone rolls down the mountain (when our distresses are too heavy to bear), and when we win our victories over the absurd in the respirations of the night. ("There is no sunshine without shadow, and we must com-

[5] *Ibid.*, pp. 153-54.
[6] Albert Camus, *The Rebel, An Essay on Man in Revolt,* foreword by Sir Herbert Read, tr. Anthony Bower (New York: Vintage Books, 1954), p. ix.

prehend the night.") And he adds (with an absurd leap of his metaphors) that "these are our nights of Gethsemane." Herein is betrayed what is *naturaliter* Christian in Camus: for the nights of Gethsemane forecast the bearing of another burden up another hill by another Man. It is significant that Camus' reflections on the human predicament move from *The Rebel* to *The Fall.*

In *The Rebel* Camus proclaims that the time of rebellion through which we are passing presents a radical change in the nature of revolt. We are experiencing a metaphysical revolt, "the revolt of man against the conditions of life, against creation itself." In it we are contesting the ends of man and of creation. But it is a compound protest, against the refusal of man to be what he is, against his handing over his need to become freely what he is to tyrants who will order his life for him by way of the mass extermination of those who stand in the way, against the failure of historical Christianity to give an answer to the problem of evil (postponing "to a point beyond the span of history the cure of evil and murder"), and against the temptation to reproduce the husks of thought instead of probing the dichotomies of our inner experience. "Even in Faulkner, a great writer of this generation, the interior monologue only reproduces the outer husks of thought."

One feels, nevertheless, that the purview of *The Rebel* is ambivalent. Camus recognizes that "The night on Golgotha is so important in the history of man only because, in its shadow, the divinity abandoned its traditional privileges and drank to the last drop, despair included, the agony of death." [7] It is the power of this event that seems secretly to inform the protest of the contemporary rebel, and permits Camus to assert that "at this moment when at last a man is born, it is time to forsake our age and its adolescent furies" and to recognize that "all of us, among the ruins, are preparing a renaissance beyond the limits of nihilism. But few of us know it." On the other hand, the real strength of Christianity was compromised long since by the church's having "placed the emphasis on history to the detriment of nature"—which increased the claims of temporal power, accelerated the dynamisms of history, and left the created orders as nothing more than open prey for actions aimed merely at transforming them.

These themes achieve their synthesis in *The Fall,* a work of fiction which will easily rank with the finest literary works of our time. The concatenation of the themes—the casual encounter of judge and client; the ironic progression from the heart of things, the city Amsterdam, the last

[7] *The Rebel,* p. 32.

circle of Dante's hell (the concentric canals resemble the circles of hell), through the limbo of neutral angels where we lack both the energy of good and of evil, to the ironic Dutch heaven of "the Last Judgment"; the theft of the painting of "The Last Judges"; the traumatic incident on the bridge where the Judge might have risked his life to save another, but didn't; the ironic emergence of Jean-Baptiste Clamance as the John the Baptist of the Gospel of our Fall; and the ironic denouement in which the reader, having been led to the point of an inverted revelation, is revealed to himself repeating once more his failure to risk his life for truth and true being instead of perennially knuckling to "a master, God being out of style"—and the integration of its plot (irony raised to the nth power of denial of the traditional view of the Cross): these proclaim the skill and relevance of its master craftmanship.

The reader will hardly gain from such a summary any adequate notion of the novel's movement. Yet it is plain that we are moving here on a far deeper and far richer terrain of implication than is to be found in most conventional novel writing. The reporting of the human condition has here passed over into negative prophecy—into a negative disclosure, that is, of the *nature* of our predicament.

This is apparent, first of all, in the pedagogical intent of the work of art. Camus' work—his concatenated plot—is no "icon," nor is it an "epiphany" in Joyce's sense of the term. It is, as De Rougemont has remarked, "a trap, a calculated trap" in which to catch the reader. Jean-Baptiste explains himself: he begins by accusing himself, which leads his clients to accuse themselves. With the dialogue thus instituted he constructs "a portrait which is the image of all and of no one. A mask, in short, rather like those carnival masks which are both lifelike and stylized." When the portrait is finished, he holds it out to his client, saying, "This, alas, is what I am!" And then he remarks, by way of explanation, "But at the same time the portrait I hold out to my contemporaries becomes a mirror." [8] This is an ironic denouement, leading the reader into the abyss of his own antinomies (his inner contradictions), derivative from and attached to the antinomies of his age.

But the antinomies of our age, as herein revealed, derive from the absence of God and from the ironic disclosure that we are all of us somehow implicated in the crime. *The Fall* is an explication of our guilt: "Every man testifies to the guilt of all the others." The loss of Eden consists in thrusting intermediaries between life and ourselves. Religions generally

[8] *The Fall* (New York: Alfred A. Knopf, 1957), p. 140.

have misunderstood this. They have converted their own proclamations into systems of mediation, thereby compounding the Fall and driving the wedge between life and ourselves that much deeper. Religion fabricates (like art) another world in which the self escapes by abdication of its task—the recovery of its own integrity in the open *telos* of its calling. Its way is the way that is *beyond irony*, beyond the irony even of its own masks, let alone the complex carnival of artificial (not to say artifactual) grins and grimaces which compose patterns of posture and approval behind which the great majority of men play out the artificial roles imposed upon them. *The Waste Land* also ends, as Philip Wheelwright has recently noted, with a succession of masks, prominent amongst which is Hieronymo's cry, in which he confesses to play-acting. Upon which Wheelwright comments: "But the confession of playacting is itself a bit of playacting, and therefore should not be taken with unguarded assurance. The relation of the poet-protagonist to his masks, as of the doer to his situations, is never fully resolved" (in this poem).[9] Such are the involutions of our predicament, from which the poet-protagonist of *The Fall* is not exempt either.

Beyond the Absurd

To go beyond irony is not easy. Yet when irony has reached the postulation of its own existential antinomies, it can no longer maintain its position of prophetic negation outside the predicament. It must bring to a close its "career as a false prophet crying in the wilderness and refusing to come forth" in order to avoid becoming a clown of itself. It may choose the way of the priest or of the icon or of dogma (but for Camus these also are the ways in which we drive the wedge betwixt ourselves and reality); or it may choose the journey into the depth of its own antinomies, into humility, into the mysteries of reconciliation.

Most of our ironists (Huxley, Orwell, Mann, Sartre, Camus, Kafka, Auden, Eliot, etc.) actually effect some blend or amalgam of these possible alternatives, once the precarious cerebral perch outside the predicament has become untenable; and each must be pursued with thoroughness and care before one ventures to say, "Thou ailest here, and here," and also because we know that even in our deepest journeyings we are followed by the shadow of our own ambivalences. The principle that is here invoked is the principle of Pascal: the defective or excessive aim evokes its own contraries and, followed far enough, the extremes will meet. It is instruc-

---

[9] Philip Wheelwright, *The Burning Fountain*, op. cit., pp. 342-43.

tive to see how this is true in Camus who refuses dogma and in Auden who espouses it.

Both Camus and Auden are centrally influenced by Pascal and Kierke-gaard and Kafka. Both are driven upon the Fall, and both report the absurd dimension in the human lot and probe the mystery of murder. For both, the Christ symbol emerges where the contradictions meet. For Camus, "Historical Christianity postpones to a point beyond the span of history the cure of evil and murder, which are nevertheless experienced within the span of history." [10] Therein historical Christianity has erred, has betrayed, indeed, the meaning of the plain event: "Believe me," his protagonist argues in *The Fall*,

religions are on the wrong track the moment they moralize and fulminate commandments. God is not needed to create guilt or to punish. Our fellow men suffice, aided by ourselves. . . . God's sole usefulness would be to guarantee innocence, and I am inclined to see religion as a huge laundering venture—as it was once but briefly, for exactly three years, and it wasn't called religion. . . . People naturally tried to get some help from his death. After all, it was a stroke of genius to tell us: "You're not a very pretty sight, that's certain! Well, we won't go into the details! We'll just liquidate it all at once, on the cross!" But too many people now climb onto the cross merely to be seen from a greater distance, even if they have to trample somewhat on the one who has been there so long. . . . They have hoisted him onto a judge's bench, in the secret of their hearts, and they smite, they judge above all, they judge in his name. He spoke softly to the adulteress: "Neither do I condemn thee!" but that doesn't matter; they condemn without absolving anyone. In the name of the Lord, here is what you deserve. Lord? He, my friend, didn't expect so much. He simply wanted to be loved, nothing more. Of course, there are those who love him, even among Christians. But they are not numerous.

Then follows the crucial irony:

He had foreseen that too; he had a sense of humor. Peter, you know, the coward, Peter denied him: "I know not the man . . . I know not what thou sayest . . . etc." Really, he went too far! And my friend makes a play on words: "Thou art Peter, and upon this rock I will build my church." Irony could go no further, don't you think? But no, they still triumph! "You see, he had said it." He had said it indeed.[11]

Thus Camus protests against the irony of two millennia in which the historical church has imposed a supernatural pattern upon the open social

[10] *The Rebel*, p. 303.
[11] *The Fall*, pp. 110-16, *passim*.

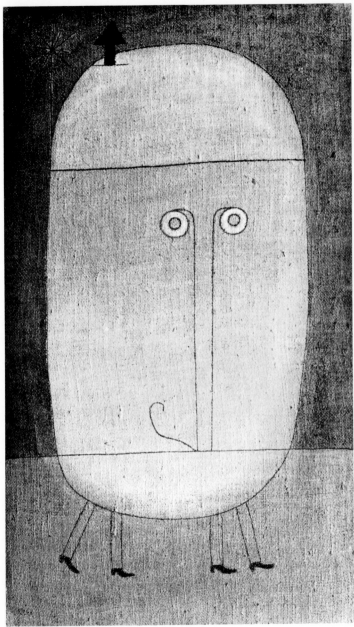

Paul Klee, *Mask of Fear*, 1932
Oil on burlap, 39½″ x 22½″
Collection Dr. and Mrs. Allan Roos

Georges Rouault, *The Old Clown*, 1917
Oil on canvas, 41¼″ x 29½″
Collection Mr. Stavros Niarchos

Pablo Picasso, *Guernica*, 1937
Oil on canvas, 11' 5½" x 25' 5¾"
On extended loan to the Museum of Modern Art, New York, from the artist

Graham Sutherland, *Crucifixion*, 1947
Oil, 40″ x 47⅞″

Jackson Pollock, *Cathedral*, 1947
Oil and mixed media on canvas
Dallas Museum of Fine Arts
Gift of Bernard Reis

Alfred Manessier, *For the Feast of Christ the King*, 1952
Oil on canvas, 80″ x 60″
Collection G. David Thompson

Clark Fitz-Gerald, *The Brothers*
Collection of the artist

Henry Moore, *Madonna and Child*, 1943-44
Hornton stone, 59″ high
Collection Church of St. Matthew, Northampton

Theodore Roszak, *Anguish,* 1947
Steel and brass, brazed, 10½″ high

Seymour Lipton, *Sanctuary,* 1953
Nickel-silver over steel, 29¼″ high
Collection Museum of Modern Art, New York
Blanchette Rockefeller Fund

Le Corbusier, *Notre Dame du Haut* at Ronchamp, France

Marcel Breuer & Associates, *St. John's Abbey*,
Collegeville, Minnesota

Eero Saarinen & Associates, *Concordia Senior College Chapel,*
Fort Wayne, Indiana

William Wenzler, *St. Edmund's Episcopal Church,*
Elm Grove, Wisconsin

Alden B. Dow, *St. John's Lutheran Church,*
Midland, Michigan

José Limón Dancers, *Missa Brevis*

murder of the innocent man ("He was not superhuman, you can take my word for it"). Thus we not only deprive the event of its existential virtue, but, by placing it within the context of our own projected system, we protect ourselves against the recognition of our own complicity and procreate the murder of each upon all precisely where our *unreal aims* collide. There innocence, openness, and hope are crucified.

Auden's poem "Vespers" [12] states the same. Yet it is less a proclamation, less an argument. It is more like a report. Its "shock of recognition" reaches far more deeply into that abyss of the inner antinomies, there to work the aesthetic mysteries of purification and self-identification. It begins with: "the hill overlooking our city [which] has always been known as Adam's Grave"—and already our *polis*, the human community, is set between the Adam symbol and the hill (which suggests Golgotha, the place of the skull). It is the hour of twilight, between Sun and Moon, when

> all must wear their own faces
> . . . .
> And it is now that our two paths cross.

The two paths which the poet now describes are false paths, leading away from reality rather than into it. They are labeled "Arcadian" and "Utopian," and typify between them all the escapist patterns of humankind —given the primary evasion of the Fall itself. The poet represents these unrealistic patterns as opposites, yet both are running from reality. Since the fundamental denial of reality is not acknowledged, each projects his enmity upon the other:

> You can see, then, why, between my Eden and his New
> Jerusalem, no treaty is negotiable. [13]

"My Eden" would represent our attempts to achieve the idyllic bliss of the garden of innocence through bypassing the Fall, and his "New Jerusalem" would attempt the utopian reconciliations by ignoring or leaping over the Cross. These are antitypes in the practical world. Harmless though they are when held as escapist flights of fancy, their hostilities mount when translated into fact. Eventually they collide in manifold destructive forms, the ultimate summation of which is murder. The poem implies that the point of absolute collision is the Cross. So the opposites are fascinatingly

---

[12] Copyright 1952 by W. H. Auden. Reprinted from the *Shield of Achilles*, by W. H. Auden, by permission of Random House, Inc., and Faber and Faber Ltd.
[13] *Ibid*, p. 78.

catalogued in the poem, gathering both momentum and implication until we reach the resolution.

Was it (as it must look to any god of cross-roads) simply a fortuitous inter-section of life-paths, loyal to different fibs,
or also a rendezvous between accomplices who, in spite of themselves, cannot resist meeting
to remind the other (do both, at bottom, desire truth?) of that half of their secret which he would most like to forget,
forcing us both, for a fraction of a second, to remember our victim (but for him I could forget the blood, but for me he could forget the innocence)
on whose immolation (call him Abel, Remus, whom you will, it is one Sin Offering) arcadias, utopias, our dear old bag of a democracy, are alike founded:
For without a cement of blood (it must be human, it must be innocent) no secular wall will safely stand.[14]

Thus the argument from the absurd, which begins in Camus and moves toward murder, is here recapitulated in terms which force the reader upon the central Christian event (though it is not mentioned) by the fortuitous but inevitable encounter of existential opposites. Without the central sacrifice, both Eden and the New Jerusalem are wish-projections which deceive the soul and then avenge themselves on others or turn in destruc-tively upon the self; but with the sacrifice, both Eden and the New Jeru-salem are one.

The Dimension of Depth

It may be objected, and justly so, that this solution is at once too logical and too arbitrary, that the transition from irony to dogma is an intellectual achievement; and that (as in a witticism or poetic conceit) it is the intel-lectual part that makes the identifying leap: and consequently we remain on the outside of the human predicament. Just as irony and wit and the metaphysical conceit represent the oversophistication of the aesthetic sense, does not substantialist theology represent the oversophistication of the his-torical manifestation of the Christ as reported in the Scriptures? Does not Auden's alliance between the two deprive his verse of that miraculous prop-erty of Rilke's lines, which move, as on running springs, into eternity? Does not the scaffolding of dogma, which supports his probing paradoxes, mask the deeper desire of his perceiving mind to unite with the deeper ground of Being whereby the rhetorical *coincidentia oppositorum* might be lived and translated into fact? These are questions which, of course, we may not

[14] *Ibid*, pp. 79-80.

answer; but they will serve to dramatize the remaining perspective on the literature of our time. Carl Jung has written:

Poets are the first in their time to divine the darkly moving, mysterious currents, and to express them according to the limits of their capacity in more or less speaking symbols. They make known, like true prophets, the deep motions of the collective unconscious, "the will of God" . . . which, in the course of time, must inevitably come to the surface as a general phenomenon.

Here is that dimension of depth which, under the circumstance of the universal impoverishment of symbols through which our culture is passing, must become the pathway of our knowing. The artist has been thrown back upon himself; he "cannot express himself without confessing." Theologians, too, are beginning to recognize the need to renew their symbols from within and to explore that dimensionless land that lies "in the height and in the depth, in the length and in the breadth of the spirit." It is here that art and religion may meet, retrieve the deeper meanings, and transform each other.

DRAMA, MOTION PICTURE, AND TELEVISION

XIV

Contemporary Drama in the Catholic Tradition

E. MARTIN BROWNE

IT MAY SEEM APPROPRIATE THAT I SHOULD BE BEGINNING THIS ESSAY ON the feast of Corpus Christi, for that was the day on which most of the medieval mystery plays were usually performed. But in fact the contemporary drama in the Catholic tradition is not much indebted to the mysteries; it is a new creation of our own century. It is conditioned by the history of the theatre, particularly its intellectual development in the last eighty years, and also by the fact that since the Reformation the Catholic tradition has run in more streams than one. Both theatrically and religiously it is very much alive today. Its individual practitioners are highly diversified, but the tradition is quite distinctive in its main features; and perhaps the best way of appreciating this drama may be to attempt a definition of these features and then to notice how they are shown in the work of a few outstanding writers.

The Catholic Tradition

The Catholic tradition is based on the belief that human life and history are a part of God's plan. In the mystery plays, this plan is clearly laid out from Creation to Judgment with the Incarnation of Jesus Christ as its climax. The only modern work which sets forth this biblical version of the play is Dorothy Sayers' radio series, *The Man Born to Be King*, a life

132

of Christ by an Anglican playwright-theologian. While she domesticates the apostolic band and involves the Passion in local politics, she keeps us aware throughout of the divine purpose overruling all the circumstances of time. The name of Pontius Pilate, under whose authority the Crucifixion took place, is sounded in every tongue forever: the petty tyrant of one moment has become the instrument of eternity. But the cosmic and eternal values implicit in the concept of God's plan dominate, as we shall see, all the works of writers in the Catholic tradition on quite unbiblical subjects. One is most widely and acutely aware of these values, perhaps, in such a work as Paul Claudel's *The Satin Slipper*, where the destinies of a few individuals are set against a panorama of history; but even in the more apparently intimate work of T. S. Eliot and Graham Greene they are always present.

This is true chiefly in two respects. First, in respect to man's relationship to God. Man is seen as he is, without illusion, without sentimentality, because he is being so seen by God. No view of man is so realistic as the Catholic view, for it starts, not with reasons why he is as he is, but with the facts of his sinful nature.

It is God who sees man as he is: it is also God who is determined to have him for his own. The "Hound of Heaven" concept is central. God's love desires and demands to have the soul which he made for himself: he is the inexorable pursuer, and is inescapable by any man who is truly alive at all.

With this conception goes the parallel idea that the grace of God is given in proportion to man's nothingness; therefore, it is when he has sunk to the lowest depth that God's power may most completely transform him.

The other aspect of God's plan is the social, the interaction between man and man. "No man liveth to himself": his life must issue in its effect on others, and at the very beginning of Christian history stands the foundation of the church, the society of Christians, which is the Body of Christ in the world. It is only in this society that the individual Christian comes fully into his Christian life. There is interaction between the church and the world. In the medieval conception the two were ultimately one, and indeed the political and economic structure of society was based on Christian premises. Today, they are separate but interacting forces.

"The things that are seen are temporal, but the things which are not seen are eternal," says Paul. The world is temporary; the church, however much it has involved itself—and indeed often should involve itself—in things of this world, has its eyes on the everlasting. It is both in and out of time: the "great cloud of witnesses" from beyond are as much a part

133

of the church as we on earth who run this temporal race. We can draw upon their strength as we strive to see our way step by step through the maze of this age, to meet the judgment and hope for the salvation of the age to come.

All this leads to the seminal idea of vicariousness. "Bear ye one another's burdens," says the practical apostle to the members of the early church. As the church grows, a mystical doctrine is developed from this beginning. The sanctity of one may benefit others unknown, far off in place and time. The prayers of dedicated folk may be a fertilizing store of strength for their fellows. Sufferings offered to God and gladly borne for him may be accepted on behalf of others. Some are elect, called of God to sanctity and suffering. If God never lets go of any soul, he also chooses and uses some souls as the yeast which is to leaven the spiritual community.

Three Writers: Paul Claudel

Of the three writers, above mentioned, in whose work I propose to study these ideas, one is a French Roman Catholic, one an Anglican, the third an English Roman Catholic. They are of three different generations, yet all three may truly be called contemporary. Paul Claudel, who died in 1955 at the age of 87, received his greatest acclaim as a dramatist since World War II, just when T. S. Eliot, in his sixties, broke into the theatres of Shaftesbury Avenue and Broadway, and Graham Greene, in his fifties, was successfully adding the role of playwright to that of novelist.

Are we perhaps to surmise that this simultaneous acceptance of three playwrights in the Catholic tradition, the original interpretation put on it by each seeming apposite to the movement, means that the tradition itself has something to offer that meets a contemporary need?

As examples of Claudel's genius we may profitably concentrate on the *Two Dramas* admirably introduced and translated by Wallace Fowlie (Henry Regnery, 1960). Both written in the prime of the poet's youth, these plays did not reach their final form until he rewrote them for productions made in the last years of his life. Thus they enshrine the life-work of his mind, which had cherished both for fifty years.

Break of Noon is the best translation so far found for an untranslatable title. *Partage de Midi* carries the image of a watershed, the ridge of a mountain from which water must flow down one side or the other. The moment of break, decisive in the lives of four people who comprise the play's entire cast, occurs on the deck of a ship in Oriental waters. The characters, seen under the unrelenting light of a tropical sun, are three men and a woman. The layout is, on the surface, a conventional one: Ysé, the seductive wife and mistress; de Ciz, the complaisant husband; Amalric, the earthy lover; and Mesa, the prim virgin whose self-involvement challenges the woman to break through it. But under the surface lies the eternal truth, the relationship of these souls to God's plan. Mesa has tested a religious vocation and been refused as temperamentally unsuitable: he has in fact never been taken out of himself. It needs the attraction of Ysé to make him prefer someone else to himself:

YSÉ: And that's what you don't like, Mesa, to pay dearly for something. We pretend to give everything while all the time deep down within us we are determined to keep everything for ourselves. That is how once you offered yourself to God, so wrapped up and tightly closed that I can't imagine how the good Lord would have gone about opening you. He would have broken the nails of His fingers. It's ugly, mon petit Mesa, to be avaricious. Ugly to be the self-centered egoist that you were.

MESA: At least you were very successful in getting what God failed to get.

YSÉ: Did I really succeed? Did I really teach you what it means to belong to someone else? [1]

Mesa has no illusions about this love. "I marry you not piously but in wickedness": [2] sin is committed in the act of his salvation. "Is it possible that you are happiness? No. You are what is in the place of happiness." [3] Mesa is "a man who is caught"—by whom? By more than Ysé. "Someone took aim at us together on the boat," [4] says Ysé. A new cupid, with arrows of fire. Ysé too is chosen: "Woman was made by God, and no matter how bad she may be she serves for some use. She too can be a cross. A great cross." [5]

God plans to take and turn the soul to himself, and he can use "even sins" (the epigram of The Satin Slipper) to cut a channel for his grace.

Besides these familiar notes, another is struck which we have not heard before: the note of personal identity. "Your real name. The real name which is yours and which only I know." [6] What am I? Who am I? The questions raised in every mind by the advent of psychology take on another aspect in the Catholic tradition. I have to face myself as I am: but I know that God knows what I am, and who I am is his child. It is God who speaks through

---

[1] Paul Claudel, Two Dramas, tr. Wallace Fowlie (Chicago: Henry Regnery Company, 1960), pp. 137-8.
[2] Ibid., p. 90.
[3] Ibid.
[4] Ibid., p. 96.
[5] Ibid., p. 138.
[6] Ibid., p. 139.

Ysé: "Your name is so inseparable from me that you would have to take it from me by force." [7]

If *Break of Noon* is the drama of the individual soul, *The Tidings Brought to Mary* is the drama of the soul in the church. Set in the time of Joan of Arc, it is concerned with a family of farmers who "have to feed and watch over" the nuns of the enclosed order of Monsanvierge which stands on the hill above them. The influence of the holy community is constantly breaking in upon the drama of violent passions which passes below. The protagonists are two sisters, Violaine and Mara: the name of the younger means in Hebrew "bitter," and she is bitterly jealous of the elder. Spying upon Violaine as in spontaneous charity she kisses a leper on the mouth, Mara succeeds in turning this so to account that she wrests from Violaine her farm and her betrothed. Violaine becomes a leper, taking upon herself the disease of the man she succored: Mara's child dies: she takes the dead body to her sister's lazar-hut on Christmas Eve, and as they read the midnight Mass the child is restored to life—with Violaine's blue eyes. This final inflammation of Mara's jealousy causes her to murder her sister.

The violence of the story is typical of Claudel's hard, uncompromising characterization, born of his own upbringing in the hard soil of the very region where this play is set. But the human characters are only the foreground of the picture. Behind them we see the great panorama of the church of which they in all their humanity are part; and the form of the drama is liturgical, a reflection of the worship of the church. This is most clearly visible in the resurrection scene, where the Mass of the Nativity provides the very words of the miracle. Most of the key scenes are cast in the symmetrical form of liturgy, and the play begins and ends with the Angelus of the title: "The Angel of God announced to Mary, and she conceived by the Holy Spirit." The voice of the church is constantly heard throughout the play. "I am not alone. A great people rejoices and departs with me." [8] So says the father of the two sisters as he leaves home for a pilgrimage. And Violaine's leper is Pierre de Craon, the great architect of churches, which he describes in vivid detail in the Prologue. He teaches the Christian view of building: "The Pagan artist did everything with the outside, and we do everything with the inside, like bees, as the soul does for the body. Nothing is inert. Everything lives, everything is an act of thanksgiving." [9]

But the most significant aspect of the church shown in this play is

[7] *Ibid.*
[8] *Ibid.*, p. 194.
[9] *Ibid.*, p. 250.

that of election. Violaine is the chosen soul. At first a young girl pure in heart, she becomes the vessel of grace, refined by suffering, for the succor of those about her. It is through her that the child is reborn; and this second birth is a symbol of the birth of the Savior and of the rebirth of humanity through the sacrifice of the second Adam. Thus Claudel dramatizes in Violaine the role of the elect, the saints, in the society of the church and in the redemption of the world, with which it is inextricably linked. As Wallace Fowlie tells in his introduction, Claudel

came to realise the absolute necessity existing between Mara and Violaine, and the need which each sister has for the other. Mara's faith in God, a violent and almost brutal faith, serves an important function in the play, that of revealing the sanctity of Violaine. The relationship between the sisters makes *L'Annonce* into a human and a supernatural drama at the same time.[10]

T. S. Eliot

In Eliot's drama this theme of election is at first the dominant one. *Murder in the Cathedral*, his first full-length play, deals with Thomas Becket as a man whom God has chosen and molded as in a furnace for his purposes. Becket's historic choice of road on being made archbishop is far behind him when the play begins. He has completely dedicated himself to the cause of the church and has passed through a long period of purgation and discipline at Pontigny during his exile from England. He returns to England knowing martyrdom to be probable and near. His position as the elect is enormously reinforced by the chorus of the "scrubbers and sweepers of Canterbury," [11] the ordinary women to whom he is lord, leader, and spiritual director, and who feel as Christians the full responsibility for the crime of his killing. As in classic Greek tragedy, the story is treated as giving the reason for a rite, the centuries-long pilgrimage to Becket's shrine:

> Let our thanks ascend
> To God, who has given us another Saint in Canterbury. . .
> Blessed Thomas, pray for us.[12]

This play was written for a church building and is highly liturgical. Eliot deliberately refused many invitations to repeat its great success and turned away from the historical and liturgical to the contemporary and

---

[10] *Ibid.*, p. 150.
[11] From *Murder in the Cathedral* by T. S. Eliot. Copyright, 1935, by Harcourt, Brace & World, Inc. Used by permission of Harcourt, Brace & World and Faber and Faber Ltd.
[12] *Ibid.*

the theatrical. But in the next play, *The Family Reunion*, the election theme remained paramount. This play, like all its successors, used a Greek drama as springboard; but in each case Eliot's version of the story is completely different because of his Christian attitude. The original here is Aeschylus' *Oresteia*. The hero's sin, which is in the original an actual murder, is in Eliot's play one of intention, not commission; and his salvation is not by the judgment of his peers but by the recognition of the nature of the "Hounds of Heaven" which are apparently pursuing him. In turning to accept them he finds that they are really his guides to the new life:

> It is love and terror
> Of what waits and wants me, and will not let me fall. . .
> I must follow the bright angels." [13]

This elect soul, however, does not help anyone else in the play. Harry Monchensey is seen, not after his purgation like Becket, but during the process of conversion. We are free to imagine that, after the play's action is concluded, his "care over lives of humble people" and the rest of his anticipated service will bear fruit, but we have no evidence. In contrast to the transformation wrought in the chorus of *Murder in the Cathedral*, who pass from fear and guilt to penitence and thanksgiving, the modern characters surrounding Harry receive no such benefits—a measure, perhaps, of the damage wrought by the fragmentation of modern society.

Eliot's next play came after the long interval caused by World War II. *The Cocktail Party* appears to be conventional comedy until, very soon, we discover the strange relationship between the three "guardians" and the other four characters. This group of three are under supernatural orders to help the others find their way to their own salvation. The play, in fact, is an exhibition of how grace works in the ordinary soul; here, for the first time, the focus of the play is a pair of ordinary people. The guardians are saved from smugness by their eccentricities and by their sense of their own inadequacy, particularly by the knowledge that they often "do not know what they are saying," and that their words are given to them from beyond. But their penetration into the characters of Edward and Lavinia is the means by which Eliot reveals the truth and by which a new start is possible:

[13] From *The Family Reunion*, copyright, 1939, by T. S. Eliot. Reprinted by permission of Harcourt, Brace & World, Inc. and Faber and Faber Ltd.

And now, when they are stripped naked to their souls
And can choose, whether to put on proper costumes
Or huddle quickly into new disguises,
They have, for the first time, somewhere to start from.[14]

Over against these two we have another elect soul, but this time we are taken beyond the moment of conversion. Celia, Edward's ex-mistress, has been searching for

something that I wanted—
No, not wanted—something I aspired to—
Something that I desperately wanted to exist.[15]

Under the direction of Reilly, the psychiatrist-guardian, she finds the way to it, the "unknown" way which

requires faith—
The kind of faith that issues from despair.[16]

It leads her to a horrible death while she is on missionary service. The others at first naturally react against the suffering and the waste, as they see it. But when Reilly convinces them that

That way, which she accepted, led to this death.
And if that is not a happy death, what death is happy? [17]

they begin to see a new vision of the meaning of life. It is for this that Celia has in fact died: her suffering, accepted in so positive a spirit, has a saving power over the lives of others. There may be faults in the presentation of the result; but Eliot has, in taking us so far, made a definite advance on. *The Family Reunion.*

Celia is the last of Eliot's elect characters. In the two following plays he is more and more concerned with the ordinary souls and increasingly aware of the social, and particularly the family, aspect of their lives. The concept of God as Father has always led Christians to stress the importance of the family, and the church is seen as the great family of the heavenly Father. At the end of *The Confidential Clerk*, when the young Colby has

---

[14] From *The Cocktail Party*, copyright, 1950, by T. S. Eliot. Reprinted by permission of Harcourt, Brace & World, Inc. and Faber and Faber Ltd.
[15] *Ibid.*
[16] *Ibid.*
[17] *Ibid.*

been taken under the wing of his predecessor Eggerson, there is left on the stage a family reunited through its experience and learning to live together. In *The Elder Statesman* we have for the first time scenes of romantic love, and the main theme of purgation through confession is set in the family— the hero, Lord Claverton, confesses to his daughter and her fiancé.

In this play the sins are deliberately made small to concentrate attention on the state of the sinner. And, as with Harry, as with Edward and Lavinia, as with Sir Claude Mulhammer in *The Confidential Clerk*, the heart of his trouble is a failure to love. As this understanding grows in the successive plays, so the poet's compassion towards his characters increases, and we feel them to come nearer to ourselves.

Graham Greene

Claudel and Eliot are poets turned dramatists, and had to master the problems of construction. Graham Greene was already a past master of narrative and suspense before he wrote his first play. He has always been close to base humanity in his studies of degradation and despair. Because of a certain morbidity in these, and because he was savagely critical of Catholic practice, some have thought that he has abandoned the tradition itself. Nothing could be further from the truth.

The Living Room, his first and perhaps still his most profound play, will serve us well as we try to appreciate his relationship to the tradition. In one aspect it is a study of morbid psychology. The house in which the action passes is owned by three elderly Catholics: a brother, once a parish priest but for the past twenty years crippled into inactivity by a motor accident, and his two maiden sisters. The elder is getting senile, the younger is vigorous, narrow, and bigoted. They have a morbid fear of death and will not sleep in a room where anyone may have died. So they shut up much of the house, and the living room is what used to be the night nursery.

To them comes a newly orphaned niece of twenty. She is in love with a man old enough to be her father, a professor of psychology who is her legal guardian, and they have already slept together. The atmosphere of the house drives her more and more to depend on him; the aunt finds it all out; and finally, after appealing in vain to the priest for help, Rose commits suicide, torn to pieces between her natural affections and the demands of her faith.

This is the end of the last scene but one. Next morning, the priest and the psychologist meet in a mourning discussion. She has dropped "like a stone into a pond," they agree in despair. But the priest knows that it is just at the moment of despair that God steps in—and so he does. The senile old lady enters with a pile of bedding. She has made up her mind to sleep in the room where Rose died. "There'd be no better room for me to fall asleep in forever." [18] Suddenly, the walls of her sister's hard heart break down, and she cries like a child. The mortal sin that is Rose's suicide has been the means of her redemption. Here is the grace of God working at the moment of despair—indeed, because of despair, of which Rose has been capable. Man's worthlessness has been God's opportunity—so long as the soul is alive. And we, in the audience, have witnessed Rose's death and know with what spirit she went to it.

The same theme recurs in *The Power and the Glory*, adapted from one of Greene's best novels. It is the story of a "whiskey priest" in revolutionary Mexico. The man is degraded, but he cannot escape his priesthood and must in the end die a martyr's death. Greene is concerned to leave him as little human dignity as possible, just in order to show the compulsion of God upon him. And in *The Potting Shed*, where a real miracle apparently happens and is tracked down through the play as if in a detective story, we see again the degraded priest; and to him is added the nephew who has been a dead soul since the moment when the miracle occurred and is brought alive again by finding that it did. The rescue at the last ditch is what Greene specializes in; and it illuminates very clearly an aspect of the Catholic tradition. Between *Quem Quaeritis*, the first Christian play, and *The Living Room* lies the whole development of the theatre, the whole growth of structure and characterization intensified by modern psychological knowledge. But in its presentation of the working of grace, *The Living Room* belongs to the same tradition as that Passion and Resurrection drama, written nine centuries ago.

[18] Graham Greene, *The Living Room*.

XV

Thesis for a Playwright Still in Hiding

TOM F. DRIVER

THE CHRISTIAN DRAMA MOVEMENT—IF WE ARE TO CALL A VAST AMOUNT OF activity a movement—is at a critical juncture. Its crisis is a Protestant one.

Protestantism is never put to more severe tests than when it sets out to speak relevantly to and through the artistic forms of culture. "The Protestant principle," writes Tillich, "implies a judgment about the human situation, namely, that it is basically distorted." [1] Although Protestantism has at its center the principle of protest, the arts function primarily as celebration. Therefore Protestantism has been more effective at voicing critical judgments (which does not necessarily mean acting upon them) than at expressing the body of the faith in works of the imagination. A recent report prepared by a commercial firm for a major Protestant denomination says bluntly: "It is not yet clear that Protestantism can become the foundation of a lasting culture."

Here is the reason the contemporary movement in Christian drama continues to stand under the shadow of the English and French writers. If we are asked who have been the leading writers of Christian drama in recent years, we think of T. S. Eliot, Christopher Fry, Graham Greene, Charles Williams, John Masefield, James Bridie, Dorothy Sayers, R. H. Ward, Henri Ghéon, Paul Claudel, André Obey, Gabriel Marcel, Ronald

[1] The Protestant Era (Chicago: University of Chicago Press, 1948), p. 165.

142

Duncan, perhaps others. The only American who could be put in the same class with this group is Thornton Wilder, who is both theologically and dramatically unique. Most of those in this list are, if not Roman Catholic, inheritors of the Catholic tradition as it survives in the English churches. The task of building upon and reinterpreting the cultural forms has been easier for them than for writers from the typically Protestant countries, where the religious tradition has been subjected to much more radical criticism and revision.

The Task of the Protestant Playwright

Now the Protestant playwright (and here I begin to think of that exasperatingly reticent American Protestant dramatist whose work we are so eagerly awaiting) has before him an almost impossible task. He must affirm the very tradition, the very faith, the very law, over against which he would stand in protest. He is not quite so fortunate in this regard as the reformer Luther, let us say, who had a known adversary in Rome against which he could assert wholeheartedly his radical critique. Nor is he as fortunate as the apostle Paul, who could make his stand quite clear against the Judaizers. No, the contemporary Protestant dramatist faces a world that is basically secular. Even when he addresses an audience of churchgoers, most often he confronts persons whose awareness of the great Christian tradition is vague. He must therefore teach them the law in the same breath that he proclaims to them the freedom from the law. He must make them religious and redeem them from religiosity in the same moment. In short, he must speak with a Yes and a No. He must, as they say, become dialectical.

There is only one good contemporary Christian play which seems to me to fulfill this requirement. That is Günter Rutenborn's *The Sign of Jonah.*[2] It has the genuinely Protestant dialectic throughout. It stands in affirmation of the biblical prophetic tradition. It is also in affirmation of man, his aspirations, and his institutions. Yet at the same time it stands radically over against these. Something within it looks with jaundiced eye at every figure, terrestrial or celestial, modern or biblical, who appears. It is this stance which gives the play its form. The double attitude of affirmation and negation results in the continual breaking of the dramatic action, a getting "out of it," so to speak. It produces an ambiguity as to whether we

---

[2] My praise for this play is based on appreciation of the translation by Bernhard Ohse and Gerhard Elston, (Chicago: Lutheran Student Association of America, 1954), now unfortunately not available. A much inferior version translated by George White is available from Thomas Nelson and Sons.

Editor's Note: For a critique of the relative merits of these translations, see Mr. Driver's review, "Metaphor into Simile," *The Christian Century,* October 26, 1960, pp. 1250-51.

are in Nineveh or Babylon or Berlin or Chicago or at the Last Judgment, and as to whether we are the accusing or the accused. At the same time that the author is showing us that we stand within the tradition of the chosen people and cannot choose otherwise, he is also showing us that we have no place to stand. We are reminded of that doubleness of attitude in Amos:

> You only have I known
>   of all the families of the earth;
> therefore I will punish you
>   for all your iniquities.

Adoption and rejection are part of the same divine work; mercy and judgment reach us together.

The Dialectic in Secular Drama

It is surely because of this dialectic at the heart of Protestantism that many Protestants find so much to interest them in those secular playwrights who think and write dialectically. The influence of Pirandello, for instance, is apparent in *The Sign of Jonah*. Pirandello looked upon truth and illusion with the same bifocal vision with which Pastor Ruterborn looks upon guilt and innocence.

Bertolt Brecht attracts us for a similar reason. He has a way of turning our conventional notions of goodness and propriety upside down, not merely to shock us—although he does that—but to make us think twice about the traditions of virtue that we have received. As in Pirandello, this dialectic gives him a positive-negative attitude toward the stage itself. The audience is constantly being swept away by the action on the stage, then forcibly reminded of its presence in the theatre. One's total self and the self which would like to be "lost in the play" are brought into dialogue, even as in Protestant worship the total self and the "worshiping self" ideally are made to confront each other. Liturgy and sermon stand together, yet in tension.

In America, the leading practitioner of dialectical theatre is Tennessee Williams. He is, of course, a far cry from Pirandello or Brecht. Yet he deals in irony and contrast more consistently and successfully than most of his American confreres. His is a kind of theatre essentially less psychological and basically more concerned with truth and morals than that, say, of Arthur Miller or William Inge, with whom he is often compared. Williams has, from the first, shown a strong desire to step outside the play he is writing and to warn his audience by one device or another that he is say-ing something more than what he appears to be saying. This is why Tom in *The Glass Menagerie* went to the side of the stage and established his own direct relation with the audience. This is why in play after play Wil-liams worked at the device of making his seemingly colloquial speech as-sume the multiple dimensions of poetry, so that the language itself could speak in obbligato over its own major voice. It is because of this that, in *Camino Real*, Williams was able to write of a world of despair in which something conquers despair, or, in *Cat on a Hot Tin Roof*, a world of men-dacity in which truth can assert itself. We thought for so long that Tennes-see Williams was simply giving us "life as it is" or depicting the sordid side of "the human situation" that we became blinded to the fact that he was all along speaking of dimensions of life which stand over against the merely natural, the merely sordid, or the merely defeatist. Every Williams play is a critique of the life it represents—not a critique in terms of social or moral reform, which would be merely to meet things on the same plane where they already lie—but a critique as if from another plane, as if life somehow transcends itself. Such critique is much more valuable than that of the obvious moral reformer.

No one will suppose, I hope, that I am suggesting Pirandello, Brecht, or Williams to be Christian dramatists. Pirandello embraced Fascism; Brecht was a Marxist; and Williams, when he is not bitter, is a secular romantic. What I am suggesting is that such playwrights as these will right-ly command the interest, and to some extent the imitation, of the Protestant American playwright whom we are expecting. The reason is that these playwrights point the way to a kind of poetic theatre which could embrace the Protestant dialectic.

Christian drama has learned very quickly that it cannot be prose drama. In England and France it tended to become poetic in a sense closely allied with the tradition of form and symbol which we call Catholic, broad-ly conceived. There is, however, another avenue for the poetic. It is the dialectic, in which the tradition is affirmed and denied at the same time. This is a "poetry" (whether it uses verse or not, who cares?) in which the stage bursts out of its still-remaining bonds of naturalism and confronts man both with his grandeur and with his misery so that he may know himself. Indeed, he must be forced to meet himself. Too long he has been meeting merely characters upon a stage.

It is only as I see myself that I may know that I am seen by the ultimate eye.

XVI

The Gospel in So-Called Secular Drama

EDWARD C. HOBBS

"GOD IS ABLE FROM THESE STONES TO RAISE UP CHILDREN TO ABRAHAM."
"If these disciples were silent, the very stones would cry out!"

—LUKE 3:8; 19:40

In these days when our own lips are silent or sentimental, when often
the only gospel preached by so-called Christians is a mere recitation by rote
of formulas we do not even comprehend, much less agonize over—in such
days as these, might God be ready to raise up stones to praise him, stones
to preach the good news that it may be heard among men? In our firm
conviction that God needs us most desperately, it is unthinkable that he is
so truly the Almighty, the King of Eternity, that he needs us not at all—that
even stones will do for his purposes. Yet we are witnessing mere stones—
outsiders to our organizations, nonmembers of our clubs, nonusers of our
religious labels, even militant opponents of our pretensions—who testify
to the message we so grievously neglect save in formulas, and bear this
testimony in a language we understand all too well. We need not ponder
whether or not they are "Christians" (even in our churches, it is rumored,
only God knows the heart, and it is not up to us to judge), but only whether
there is a word here given to us, to which we must pay heed lest we neglect
God's judgment and grace toward us.

146

The Self-Understanding We Are Offered

It is only too easy, in considering any work of art, to mistake the *object matter* for the *subject matter*. By the object matter we mean the *apparent* or *outward* matter of the work—the cast of characters, we might say. By the subject matter we mean the *true* or *inward* matter of the work. No doubt at times these two coincide, at least to some degree, perhaps more often in earlier days than now. Perhaps they so seldom coincide today because we are unwilling or unable to face the true subject matter of life unless it be symbolized or disguised—much as in the life subject matter of our dreams, where our real concerns at last come out in the open, but not without disguises, lest we be overwhelmed with what we see.

Plainly, we might have various combinations of these two. In works where the outward matter (the object matter) is Christian (such as that which deals with biblical characters or religious topics), we might find some whose true subject matter is also Christian, and others whose subject matter is actually non-Christian. Contrast, for example, one of Rouault's paintings of Christ with one of Sallman's. Merely painting a culture-hero with a (blond) beard and writing the word "Christ" beneath do not make a Christian painting—the real subject still shows through (which of course accounts for the wide sale of the Sallman pictures).

Again, in works where the outward matter is not religious in any way, we might find some whose true subject matter is not Christian, and others whose true subject matter is (despite outward appearance) Christian. Here we might contrast a Rouault clown with a clown by Norman Rockwell—the latter makes no claim to be more than a member of a circus troupe, and is just that; while the Rouault clowns penetrate to a level of meaning where we are confronted with the truth about ourselves, the truth of revelation.

The object matter of an art work might be almost anything. The subject matter is almost invariably—at least in "serious" art, by which term I do not mean to disparage unserious art, but only to distinguish it—some *self-understanding* or another. That is to say, any serious art work presents us some particular understanding of our human existence in the world as a possibility for our choosing. By self-understanding we do not mean coming to understand oneself, via self-help books or psychoanalysis, but rather that basic or radical attitude or approach in terms of which one understands oneself *in relation to* whatever happens to him and to whatever kind of existence is his own. The term might be equated with *mode of being in the world.* It is understanding and responding to one's existence in some particular way, an understanding-and-response which results in all the subsequent choices one makes. Or, to put it another way, we make our choices, ultimately, on the basis of some fundamental way we choose to be in the world—on the basis of a "self-understanding."

The purpose of any serious art, then, is to offer us some self-understanding —to offer it to us for our consideration, and presumably to influence us to assume the self-understanding so offered. This is the true subject matter of any art work.

But a great variety of self-understandings are available to the artist, corresponding to the great variety of ways men choose to relate themselves to their existence, and the great variety of gods which men serve. For a god is that which a man actually serves with his whole heart, that which he trusts to give meaning to his existence; which means that a self-understanding is faith in the god whom one trusts. And, similarly, from the Christian viewpoint, just as all gods save the God and Father of our Lord Jesus Christ are idols, false gods, so all self-understandings save that one which is faith in this same God and Father are false.

Should the gospel be preached, then—the good news that we can understand and respond to our existence in this special way because it comes to us as the gift of this special God who is the great King above all gods, and who is our Father—it will be found in the self-understanding offered by the art work, not in the apparent matter or object matter. We will not confuse the package with the product, the map with the terrain. It will not be the work which protests "Lord, Lord!" but only the one which offers to do the will of the Father, which will be seen as proclaiming the possibility of faith. We will not seek to forbid those who follow not with us; we will rejoice that the reality may be proclaimed even without our favorite words for that reality.

Of course, we will also realize that many other "gospels" are preached in art works, too; the task of "hearing" is one of coming to terms with just what self-understanding is being offered. But we will not try to settle this question by seeing the cast of characters or looking at the labels used in the work—the use or nonuse of religious words and names, for example, decides nothing for us. The average TV Western or crime show, for example, will certainly be found to offer another faith than the Christian one; but this does not preclude a Western from preaching the gospel.

A Motion Picture: Death and Resurrection

We visit the motion-picture theatre and see a drama about a dope fiend, a man with an arm of gold—and we suddenly realize that without ever mentioning Jesus or God (except in a curse), without mentioning the church (except that we hear church bells ring while a card game is in progress), without using words such as sin or hell or salvation, we have been shown the whole gospel. We have seen a man who rejected life, who thereby became enslaved to his past, condemned to repeating it and justifying it, a man who could not be released from his past by a hospital treatment any more than a white dog can become a black dog by the application of shoe polish. We have seen this man struggle to become a good man, to have a new life under a new name with a new kind of job; but it was no good, for the same old self-understanding remained. He was a junkie trying to straighten up—but he was a junkie. Then death intervened—a death which forced him to see his own end, in an electric chair or in a noose. How shall a man escape death? But—he *is* dead, isn't he? The answer is: to die to everything he ever has been, good intentions and all—without a doctor's help, all alone, through the waters of death, buried in a closety tomb, cold, cold, limp—dead. Then the resurrection occurs: the first morning of his life. The window of suicide the night before becomes the window of the sun's new life; the coming of police no longer threatens the junkie, for the junkie is dead. A new man, who can leave his crippled wife if need be—how callous *that* seems to us junkies!—goes out to meet life, even if it means jail and the electric chair, for at least he is now alive, which he was not before.

What is this about, if not salvation from the old which passes away—the new creation's appearance, the possibility of wholeness of life for one who repents and dies to what is past? And yet the play is about dope addiction, not sin; and salvation comes through a prostitute, not a twinkly-eyed priest who tells a good joke and then compliments God here and there. But who can deny that here is a situation which reveals to us *the* situation? This isn't my situation, I say, for I am not a dope addict; and the dope addict in the story says that he certainly isn't like that lush, that habitual drunk. But then a harlot tells him (and me) that everyone is a habitual something; with that fellow it just happens to be liquor. And so the gospel tells me. Yet, where are our favorite words? Where is the bragging on Jesus? Where is the broad compliment to God and the good word for religion?

Maybe it wasn't even written by a Christian (God knows!). Certainly many religious groups condemned the picture—as well they might. This man apparently consorts with harlots and sinners. Algren's religion or lack of it was not broadcast to viewers of the picture. But things are worse in other examples. Jean-Paul Sartre is an atheist—he says so. He doesn't believe in the God proclaimed to him by the church he knows. (Neither did the prophets of Israel believe in such a god.) He thinks Christianity (as he knows it) is a delusion (and perhaps it is?). What might such a man say to us?

A Play: The Way of Salvation from Hell

No Exit takes place in a Victorian living room, called hell. Three people who are dead—that is, people whose pasts are unchangeable, irrevocable, unlike your past and mine, which can of course be changed—these people unlike you and me, are dead. Each of them tries to change the past, pretend it wasn't what it really was, that they weren't the kind of people they really were. Each of them confesses to terrible sin—except they don't confess to what they really were. The coward confesses he was cruel, but he was only cowardly. The cruel, merciless, ruthless baby-killer confesses she was a coward, but nothing could be further from the truth. The love-hungry lesbian, starved for pity and affection and help, confesses she is so heartless that she needs no pity or love; but she is dying for want of love, even perverted love. A lot of confessing—but it isn't about what really lies in the past; it would alter the past, which cannot be altered (at least for these dead people!). So, they are all in hell. The door does not open; they cannot escape. Then, as the play moves on, each of them is shown most frightfully what he or she really has been and is, and each has the opportunity of coming to terms with his past, of confessing the reality of it and turning away from it responsibly. Then the door opens! They can leave. But none does. The coward explains that he must remain to convince one of the women that he was not a coward, and he will stay an eternity, if necessary, to prove it. Since he was actually a coward, such a proof will take eternity; he will spend eternity in hell, denying the truth about himself, refusing the possibility of leaving hell if he would only admit that the past was what it was and accept the new possibility outside the door.

The fact that the play does not have a happy ending only makes it more true, not less; most people, before and since the time of Jesus, prefer to stay in hell—even after the door opens. In every part of the Bible, the narratives show most people rejecting the revelation of themselves and the possibility of life. If all three characters in this play marched out the door, it would scarcely be very typical of the world we live in, though that would please us no end. But, in fact, the play is clear; hell has an exit, and it is the one we have been discussing—it is through confession and repentance, willingness to be responsible for the past (and leave it behind), to accept the present and be open to the future. Hell's doors stand open!

The conquest of hell! New life, if only we will! What a thing for an atheist to tell us! But we might as well face up to it—he tells us what he tells us. If what he tells us is the same as what the gospel in the New Testament tells us, then he is declaring the gospel to us—that is, he is offering us the same self-understanding as a possibility for life that the New Testament offers us. We can scarcely complain that the words are not the same as those used in the fourth century or the first; how many of us understand them anyway? Not we in the church; they drug us, just as Gothic architecture drugs us, into complacency. Can we complain that Sartre does not call himself Christian, when we who are Christians have told him appalling lies? Why are we so jealous of our prerogatives that we fear lest someone outside our group preach the gospel (Luke 9:49-50)? Let us be grateful instead, that the gospel is preached, whatever way (Phil. 1:18). Indeed, it may be that we shall only come really to know it through the plays written by some of these stones God seems to be raising up.

And let us not indulge in that sophomoric means of escape from the sharpness of the word we hear, which divides the "arts of the Fall" from the "arts of redemption"—reserving the latter for so-called "Christian" artists, while allowing that non-Christians may perhaps exhibit the sad case of man, his terrible fall, his hopelessness. This is perilously near blasphemous. For it suggests that the truth about the human situation can be told when God's provision for our salvation is left out; that an artist can present the human situation as "hopeless" and be telling the truth, which only requires the later addition of the way out of the mess. To present the human situation as hopeless, as having truly no exit (and here we should note the mistranslation of the title of Sartre's play, which is Huis Clos—scarcely No Exit, especially when we read the play itself), is to say something utterly contradictory to the gospel, for the gospel instead shows that the predicament is man-made and is always over against God's exit, which requires only turning away from our own hell and cage and sin and past and accepting the constantly renewed gift of God's grace and release. The predicament of man is Christianly described only when it is thus described; and to describe the predicament thus is to tell the whole story, salvation and all—even if the play ends with the rich young man turning away sorrowfully, or with three people deciding to stay in hell. The gospel tells a single story—it offers a single self-understanding, a single response to what God is doing toward us. To state any aspect of it is to imply the whole of it.

Wherefore, let us rejoice in the Lord; for whatever way, and for whatever cause, the gospel is preached! Not in all plays, and not in all pulpits—but here and there, it is preached. He who has ears to hear, let him hear.

XVII

The Image of Man: Criterion for a Religious Movie

MALCOLM BOYD

HOLLYWOOD'S CREATION OF MAN WAS A MOMENTOUS EVENT. SUDDENLY, THE stereotypes parted and the caricatures froze, and man leaped, full grown, from the brain of Selznick-Mayer-Zanuck-Warner-Goldwyn.

What was to be done with man? Almost immediately Hollywood felt, though one did not talk about it openly at first, that the man which it had created need to be redeemed. But how?

One placed man in an upper-upper-class Westchester-type house, gave him a Mercedes-Benz and an Imperial for the wife, a swimming pool, an excellent job in the city with a renowned law firm, and children who would soon be going off to Vassar and Yale, when, suddenly, without warning, he turned upon one, exclaimed that success had nearly destroyed his life, and bounded out the door (the set, an MGM masterpiece) crying for deliverance from success. He said he was searching for his own identity.

If ever anyone stood in need of redemption (restoration to conformist behavior and to the rules of the production code), Hollywood felt that man did. But how was Hollywood to redeem this brainchild?

At last it began to appear that there might be a way out. Write the script and direct it to satisfy man. Avoid, at any cost, arguments on the set. Just do it all the way man wanted it, then cut hell out of the pictures in the cutting room. Man would be very angry at the first sneak preview, go off and get drunk and mutter all kinds of imprecations against the front office. But in the morning he would sober up and start the new picture because, he thought, next time things would be different. This method actually seemed to work out.

Then one day man up and walked out. Six months later he turned up in a foreign film. The jig was up, the system ruined. The old movies were still turned out. But the public, which had switched to driving Volks-wagens, now began going in droves to foreign movies. Brigitte Bardot became almost as well known as Marilyn Monroe. Anyone with his eyes open could have seen what was coming when Simone Signoret won the Oscar away from Elizabeth Taylor, Katharine Hepburn, Audrey Hepburn, and Doris Day. Man—actor and audience—had indeed deflected to the foreign movie.

Even the church got involved. A number of theologians began to say that a religious movie, The Ten Commandments, was not religious at all, and that an extremely evil movie, Baby Doll, possessed real religious significance. These theologians began talking about a "doctrine of man" in the movies, claiming they found such a doctrine implicitly revealed in movies where it was not explicitly intended. Moreover, the theologians began to discern symbols of God in some of the movies which, they said, state accurately man's "existential situation." They must merely have enjoyed seeing dirty pictures, for they flocked to all the wrong movies and became more and more insulting about biblical pictures like Solomon and Sheba, The Ten Commandments, David and Bathsheba, and Samson and Delilah.[1]

The theologians felt that Tennessee Williams, for example, was saying some very important things both about man and about God. They thought some of his plays, The Glass Menagerie and A Streetcar Named Desire, stated accurately and poignantly man's condition. They perceived in other works, Camino Real, Cat on a Hot Tin Roof, and Sweet Bird of Youth, a definite awareness that there can be an exit from hell and redemption in loving someone other than oneself. Williams seemed to see that real hope follows the acceptance of oneself and one's actual condition in a moment of honesty with oneself.

Ironically, Williams, along with other rebel spokesmen of our time, has failed to realize how much he has in common with the theologians. They, like the playwrights, novelists, and scenarists, are much aware of the need

---

[1] I have discussed the biblical movies, especially The Ten Commandments, in my Christ and Celebrity Gods (Greenwich, Conn.: The Seabury Press, 1958).

to grasp the meaning of "the human condition" and to speak to man where he really is. They, too, are critical of nominal Christianity, watered-down theology, sentimentalized ethics, reductionist social morality, and pragmatic "faith" lacking commitment or depth. The theologians, also, are probing the meaning of sin, hell, heaven, judgment, love, and hope. And they, like the secular writers, are iconoclasts, tearing down man's false idols and judging his happy endings born of fantasy.

The Image of Man in Selected Films

It was Elia Kazan who said art is nothing if not personal. "It can't be homogenized. By its nature, it must disturb, stir up, enlighten, and offend." [2] Since the movies have seldom been art in this sense, man has had only sporadic success in his attempts to find himself via this medium. There have been, however, a few great movies which represent the fulfillment of the motion picture's promise as an art medium.

In Orson Welles's classic film *Citizen Kane*, we perceive the development of a partial knowledge of the self and the rejection of self-assurance. In my *Crisis in Communication*, I said of it:

The mystery of *this* "person," this Citizen Kane, was to be fought, rationalized, acknowledged briefly in broken and illogical (to observers) moments of desperation, and finally wrestled with upon an ornate and gaudy death-bed. This is meaningful symbolism (a sleigh in some snow, somewhere, or a name of absolutely private meaning like the "Rosebud" of *Citizen Kane*) in every man's life. Do we accept, even seek, or do we reject the symbolism in our own lives? Is our own person to be accepted, as having been created in the image of God and planted on earth in a certain time and at a certain place; or is our own person to be seen as wholly self-developed? Will we "break" ourselves and "make" ourselves in our own or Satan's image, or will we dig in both earthly and heavenly soil for the roots that may tell us who we are? [3]

The films showing the greatest integrity of artistic craftsmanship, like those of the French New Wave, are made outside the Hollywood star, production, and financial system.

A writer for the London *Times*, discussing the New Wave, made a general observation about the films coming from the creative talents identifiable with *la nouvelle vague*: "The human individual is paramount." This marks

---

[2] Quoted by Budd Schulberg, "The Writer and Hollywood," *Harper's Magazine*, October, 1959, p. 136.

[3] From *Crisis in Communication* by Malcolm Boyd. Copyright © 1957 by Malcolm Boyd. Reprinted by permission of Doubleday and Company, Inc.

a very un-French refusal to generalize, an insistence on the uniqueness of each moment in the existence of each individual. From the extreme of Marcel Hanoun's superbly economical, minutely observed television film *Une Simple Histoire*, which details without comment or imported "dramatization" a few monotonous days in a woman's life, through such varied views of life as the rapt sensuality of Louis Malle's *Les Amants*, the compassionate and completely unsentimental chronicle of childhood in Francois Truffaut's *Les Quatre Cents Coups*, and Franju's ruthless picture of asylum life in *Tête Contre les Murs*, this concern for the uniqueness of all experience comes first. The individual is reinstated in the centre of his universe; if not conventionally "humane," they are in this deeper sense humanists.[4]

Alain Resnais' *Hiroshima, Mon Amour* is that movie love story which is, at last, a love story. Two persons, a man and a woman, share intensely an experience which sears the soul. The woman, a Frenchwoman, and the man, a Japanese, make love in a rebuilt hotel in the city which first knew the meaning of an atomic bombing. Each has, in a different sense, experienced the agony of forgiveness. Each bears wounds and shelters hurts deeply imbedded in the spirit. Neither can remain simply a "one" but must discover himself or herself as an individual with a corporate sense of identity. The Frenchwoman's life must remain always unknown unless one understands its relationship to a French provincial village where she loved and came to embrace the dead body of a young German soldier. And one has only a surface view of the Japanese's life unless one comprehends at its deepest level the meaning for him of Hiroshima.

In Claude Chabrol's *The Cousins*, we identify with the lostness, the hurt, the unnerving agony of a country-bred young man who comes to Paris to stay with his cousin while he is engaged in law studies. The city cousin is also a law student; he is a sophisticate, a sensualist, essentially amoral. The cousin from the country is literally destroyed by the corrosive, resolute force of evil which asserts itself upon his life as relentlessly as ocean waves pounding the beach.

Another outstanding French film of the New Wave is Jean-Luc Godard's *Breathless* (*A Bout de Souffle*), which concerns a young thug, his romance, betrayal and death. His last word, as he lies dying in the street, is, "It's lousy." A critic has offered this comment about the memorable quality of the film:

There is a lack of continuity about everything: the dialogue, the dramatic movement, the action. Whence a startling effect of logical incoherence, a dis-

---

[4] "Thirty Years of French Cinema—II," *Times* (London), June 30, 1960, p. 6. Used by permission.

location of thought, a perpetual dance of discordant images. The film's great originality lies in this perception from multiple viewpoints constantly broken off and taken up again. Godard has realized that we take in the outside world in gulps, that the eye and the ear never achieve continuity in seeing and hearing, that, on the contrary, the peaks of visual and auditory sensation are like saw teeth, and that consequently the camera must see things in an irregular way, in a series of apparently disorderly glimpses. This is a film of tension, of impulses created by half-glances piled one upon the other, of the accumulation of brush strokes essential to the portrayal of each situation.[5]

The English cinema has given us a few film masterpieces such as *Brief Encounter*. Recently, from England came another first-rate film, *Room at the Top*. It concerns a young Englishman on the make for success. He is restless to break out of the confines of class stratification and to attain a place for himself "at the top." He has an affair with a Frenchwoman who loves him deeply. He loves her, too, but denies his feelings as well as his commitment to her in love by pursuing and marrying the boss's daughter who will secure for him a place "at the top." The film portrays the Frenchwoman's suicide and the utter emptiness of the young man as he carries his bride across the threshold of success. He is unforgettably revealed to us as an emotionally and spiritually lost person.

From Italy have come several cinematic works of art including *Open City*, *Paisan*, *Bicycle Thief*, *Umberto D.*, and *La Strada*. In *Umberto D.*, Vittorio de Sica gives us a story about an old man and his dog. The man tries to exist amid desperate economic conditions. For a while he shares a place to live with a young woman who is pregnant but does not know which of the two young lovers she has taken is her baby's father. De Sica describes the meaning of the film, saying:

It seeks to put on the screen the drama of man's inability to communicate with his fellow man. . . . When everything is at a dead end, when there is no more hope of getting help from anybody, it is just then that Umberto could have found a way out. By taking the girl out of this house, being a father to her. Two or three, together might solve their problems.

Nothing of this sort happened. Human beings have this primitive, perennial, ancient fault of not understanding one another, of not communicating with each other.

This is the story of "Umberto D.," that is to say, of a man like ourselves.[6]

[5] Paule de Beaumont, "Sous les Toits de Paris," *Réalités*, July, 1960, pp. 7-8, tr. Malcolm Boyd.
[6] Vittorio de Sica, "Analyzing 'Umberto,'" *The New York Times*, October 30, 1955, sec. 2, p. 5.

Frederico Fellini's *La Dolce Vita* is a memorable piece of cinematic art of great sociological and theological significance. In this film Fellini portrays the decadence of the contemporary Roman aristocracy and, in effect, gives us a damning picture of all contemporary aristocracy. For it is not the fleshly orgies which Fellini presents in his film tableau but the decadence of the will which constitutes the real orgies, sexual and spiritual. A decadence of the will characterizes our aristocracies—intellectual and social—far more than we have thus far permitted ourselves to admit.

Grigori Chukhrai, in his Soviet film *Ballad of a Soldier*, tells of a young Soviet soldier, a kind of Everyman, who sets out upon a trip home from the war front only to be delayed and frustrated by the press of human needs and the unpredictability of daily life. He reaches home, with only a few moments left to him before he must return to the front. He says to his mother, "I have only a few moments. Let's talk." But they are silent, understanding that communication is more deeply feeling and experiencing than talking. When the soldier breaks away from his mother's embrace, he returns to the front to die. The film poses the question: Why must the innocent suffer and the young die?

Satyajit Ray has given us a triology of films from India, *Pather Panchali*, *Aparajito*, and *The World of Apu*. In the last of the three, a young Indian student suddenly and sharply awakens to life when he marries, only to be plunged into a lasting and black despair when his bride dies in childbirth. She has left a son, but Apu rejects him, going away and working as a laborer. He has destroyed the manuscript of the book which had at one time represented the meaning of his life. Years later Apu returns to find his son an unruly, wild boy who yearns in his heart for his father. A strong redemptive element enters into the film when the boy and the father accept each other, just before the threatening moment of final rejection.

Christian Interpretation of the Movie

The movie has slowly been coming of age as an art medium, thanks to a select number of films which bear various national export labels and creative imprints as diversified as Griffith, Chaplin, Eisenstein, and Bergman. A film costing upwards of ten million dollars makes a world impact simply on its merit as a juggernaut. Yet an inexpensive documentary, *The Quiet One*, takes precedence, without argument, over such films. It belongs in the roster of cinematic classics. The star system, by virtue of the industry of press-agentry and the deliberate stimulation of the celebrity cult, guarantees star impact from Sioux City to Stalingrad. Yet the introspective, haunting old man in Bergman's *Wild Strawberries*, altogether without virtue of the

157

star system, enters immediately into the relatively limited roll call of unforgettable screen characterizations.

Christian interpretation of the movie was inevitable, though a long time aborning. The incredible naïveté of gullible clerics, thankfully taking Hollywood publicity handouts and using them in the pulpit as gospel, thus praising vulgar, hackneyed, fleshpot variations on biblical themes belonging to the best "dirty-picture" tradition, seems now to be giving way to a bit of judgment. At the same time, one notices a growing awareness by the same clerics that the movie is an art medium often possessing stunning religious insights when not clothed in the traditionally recognizable and acceptable raiment of righteousness.

Surely, living in this age, we have come to experience within ourselves and our society enough filth of spirit and rebellion against the will of God to dispel forever the "myth" of the goodness of man. It is precisely man's growing awareness of himself, is it not, which has matured the art form of the cinema and, at the same time, engendered Christian criticism of it? Is it possible that man, now that he has begun to see himself as human, will become increasingly interested in his creator and redeemer? If so, the now realistic and revelatory "art of the Fall" may give way to that toward which it is always pointing, the "art of redemption."

XVIII

Television: The Quest for a New Art Form

PAMELA ILOTT

THE QUESTION OF WHAT CONSTITUTES AN ART FORM BELONGS MORE APPROPRI-
ately elsewhere in this volume. The question here is: Can art be utilitarian;
at what stage does mass production of a masterpiece debase it? Does the
fact that American television is intrinsically a mass medium or that it has
its roots in commerce prohibit its developing as a new art form? When primitive man drew bison on the walls of his cave to evoke sympathetic magic,
did the simple desire for better hunting, more food, completely cancel out
the artistic merit of his self-expression in vivid line and color? Western
drama derived from Greek and from Christian liturgical origins was not,
and is not, art for art's sake; the commercial theatre spawned Shakespeare
as well as *Ladies' Night in a Turkish Bath*. Film, perhaps the closest parallel,
began merely as the exploitation of novelty; its evolution brought story
lines and visual artistry and later enhanced them with sound. Gradually,
from the profusion of slapstick and melodrama emerged the occasional film
with power and sensitivity worthy to be called a new art.

The evolution of television is at the same time more rapid and more confused. It is well past the stage when the first novelty, that of immediacy, gave
it its attraction. Apart from news events and historic occasions such as the
presidential inauguration or a U.N. debate, or the simulated intimacy of a
"personality" show, the public prefers the more elaborate settings, the

higher polish of a well-rehearsed, even prerecorded, program. This would appear to make television dependent upon a visual art developed by film.

Were one to examine most programs acclaimed as "artistic successes"—judged in terms of traditional criteria of sight and sound, they must be admitted derivative, and not all the nice distinction of zoomar closeups or special effects could justify a claim as a new art form. Nor, in over a decade of television, can one single out the creative spirits as in the fields of music, painting, or literature—only personalities. The names associated with "artistic" television prove to be merely the impressarios who have adapted existing material. Though much credit is due them for their good taste, this is not true creativity: the unknown executive who gave them the opportunity to experiment may be the more truly adventurous spirit.

The Problems

Is television then merely a pastiche of older arts? Not necessarily. Just as the film, embracing traditions of both theatre and photography—itself owing something to painting—must be judged by new standards of its own aspirations, so television must create its own yardstick of artistic achievement, that nebulous but powerful guerdon independent of either box-office success or publicity campaigns.

In what direction does it lie? No one knows yet: it is still a quest. Herein lies both the challenge and the frustration of a television producer—and, more terrible yet, the responsibility. For he is not only creating a new form but also the standards by which it must be judged. And though such has been the growth of all art, the gradual evolution over centuries lessened the individual awareness of it. The accelerated pace of the twentieth century gives an enormous sense of urgency to the television industry. The very admission of the term "industry" by the makers and leaders of television reflects another hurdle in its evolution as an art, the need of a vast production machine—a machine not even of the producer's making, infinitely more complex than the selected team of artists and craftsmen engaged in mounting a stage play or the elite group of key people who, in effect, create a film.

A modest half-hour television program directly involves at least eighty people, not counting performers. At no time is it possible for one lonely genius to venture forth with the tools of his craft and produce a unique work of art. The act of creation for him is intricately enmeshed with other people. Without reducing them to mere automatons, he is inevitably bound to delegate artistic responsibility; were he competent and willing to undertake every technical job involved, union rules would prohibit it.

His idea is modified, sometimes enhanced, more often limited, but always adulterated in proportion to the imagination and skill of the rest of his production team. At every stage of artistic development he is dependent not only upon his own power to communicate but upon his skill in helping other men be articulate.

First there is the writer engaged in scripting a basic idea, then a director whose interpretation of the script may not be apparent until studio rehearsal. The director's own manipulation, which can turn a delicate fantasy into an improbable melodrama or, be it admitted, as often put flesh on an unpromising skeleton, is in turn conditioned by the skill or tractability of his actors, the inventiveness of the set designer, or the competence of lighting technicians. And in the final stage of the creative act, the broadcast itself, the whole effect, for a live program, can be ruined in an instant by a mechanical failure of light switches or microphones or even the unpredictable moment when a stagehand nonchalantly strolls across the set.

So the television producer must work with tools at the same time more cumbersome and more volatile than brush or chisel.

A more severe handicap under existing conditions is the production schedule demanded by any industry. Even producers who do not have to meet the conditions of a weekly program are limited by the massive cost involved in spending as long as they may feel they need to create a wholly satisfying work. The voracious public appetite for television programs constantly demands to be fed whether the aspic has set or not. As with the nation's food, so with its arts, the trend is to "package," to offer a formula and ingredients which, when blended, will achieve a predictable, familiar, acceptable taste and texture with the least possible trouble to prepare or consume. Mass production can achieve neither memorable meals nor television art.

The Possibilities

Leaving aside, then, the bulk of television diet, the Hollywood-produced situation comedies, the scaled-down Western films and crime movies, or the cheerful contests inherited from radio, what is television? Wherein lies its quest for a new art form?

Television above all is communication. Nothing short of personal confrontation has the impact and urgency of the new medium. Khrushchev invades the living room to challenge us face to face; conversely, the viewer is transported to Cape Canaveral to peer anxiously over the shoulder of an astronaut as he climbs into his space capsule. Is it then only good reporting?

161

Television is illumination. It allows a man to present ideas not only with the persuasion of looks and gestures but with all the supporting devices of animated charts and superimposed visual images more flexibly, more vividly than in a classroom. Is it then but a cultural adjunct?

Television is a window on the world. It brings temple dancers from Bali or a string quartet from Boston into a ranch house in Wyoming. It involves forty million people in simultaneous laughter or suspense. Is it then merely entertainment?

It is all of these, and in each aspect it is possible in the broad sense to raise the level of performance to an art. For each calls for a degree of judgment and commitment to a purpose that goes far beyond mere skill.

A judicious blending of images and sounds can convey an idea more vividly, more excitingly than any novel; selective camera work can capture a microcosm that eludes a poem. It is not enough to read the poem aloud or to dramatize the novel; this is only translation and as inadequate as changing one language literally into another.

The challenge is not merely to make participation in current events possible but also meaningful with an urgency and clarity beyond the scope of newspapers or illustrated magazines. It is the challenge to make an art, not a craft, out of the practice of communications. Television must not merely reflect existing images of beauty; it must devise new ways of conveying the same emotions, the same impulse for loveliness or passionate concern. The elements are not new, but neither are the basic pigments which register serenity or drama on a canvas. It is a matter of selection and arrangement and above all of having something to say.

The Pioneers

So far, it seems, television has produced only its pioneers—producers who have experimented with what television can do—who plumbed its shallows and probed towards its heights. It has proved a superb medium for drama, combining the theatrical presence of a live performance with the flexibility and the subtlety possible in the closeup technique of film.

Television is able to bring characters literally into the room; they do not have to be exaggerated to reach the back row of a theatre or be spread across a wide screen. Interior conflicts can be shown in believable privacy; courtroom dramas can be duels between men, not gladiatorial spectaculars. The flexibility of the television camera lets it gently, almost tenderly, explore intimate scenes of the human condition—a shy, newlywed couple rattling around in a bare apartment. The blending of little telltale gestures of awkwardness or disappointment that made the characters real people would have seemed glaring intercuts on a big screen: the delicacy of the emotion, accepted so sympathetically in the intimacy of home viewing, would have provoked embarrassed titters in the self-consciously public atmosphere of a movie house.

You can watch a man think on television: freed from the "larger-than-life image" of film and stage, it becomes the ideal medium for the drama of ideas, of relationships, the very meat of human experience.

These possibilities, this flexibility, early produced a remarkable crop of writers and directors—Paddy Chayefsky, Tad Mosel, Horton Foote, Reginald Rose, Ernie Kinnoy—Delbert Mann, Sidney Lumet, Frank Shaffner. These are but a sampling of the perceptive and energetic imaginations that were challenged by the dimensions of a new form. Their work was but a promise of what could be in a newly stimulated creative atmosphere. If it does not succumb to the temptation to overedit tape, to hanker for the broader stage of "all outdoors" associated with film, television can fulfill its early promise and develop an entirely new drama.

Television can bring an added dimension to music, heightening mood by judicious setting and lighting, assuring an accoustical balance uniformly impossible in most concert halls, enhancing the audience's knowledge of a work by revealing a conductor's most subtle expression. And if the true concertgoer rejects the slim barrier of a television screen, how many amateur musicians have derived a new dimension of pleasure from being able to join the orchestra in the privacy of their own homes.

Experiments are being made in modern forms of oratorio that free the singers from the rigid stance that made an angelic chorus appear to emanate from an army drill team. Opera is freed from artificial asides that had to be bellowed across the footlights. Forms of ballet choreographed to the whisper of an interior voice, a subtler music, have already evolved.

Challenged by the demands of television for paintings that breathed with life, André Girard developed a completely new technique of "painting on light" that is already influencing film.

The art of public conversation as opposed to rhetorical debate is developing with a scope unimaginable since the days of Socrates. Leonard Bernstein has developed an enormously stimulating modern counterpart of the illustrated lecture, pioneered on *Omnibus*. Agnes de Mille has opened the doors of contemporary dance to a public who would never have ventured to knock, let alone walk in, save from the comfort and secrecy of their own armchairs. On such programs as *Camera Three*, the process of actual creation is glimpsed—a poet reaches for the expressive word, the mime improvises on a fleeting mood, a camera's sharp eye guides us through the labyrinthine wit of a cartoonist.

Thus many separate art forms evolve within the framework of television. Does the totality then become an art form in itself? This remains to be seen, for in the racking equation of potential and achievement the whole is not necessarily as great as the sum of its parts. The dimensions of television as an art will not come from the individual producers, talented, creative, dedicated as they are, but from the men who determine the aims and uses of this fantastically powerful medium.

Prophets and Pulpits

The Christian must consider television both as a reflection of our condition and as a potential means of influencing change. If it reflects a cruder image than that presented by the playwright or sculptor today, the image is nonetheless valid; television gives us a vast, sprawling reflection unrefined by the prism of an individual artist. As yet television but rarely commits that act of judgment that distinguishes a snapshot from a portrait; it is still intoxicated by its "mass" scope. As long as the public demanded that entertainment pour from their sets with the ready accessibility of tap water, the clear springs of thoughtful programming were lost in the spate of the commonplace. As the novelty wears off there is hope that people are becoming more selective: the emergence of public affairs programming as something more than a token of civic-mindedness offers a stimulus to the mind—even to the heart—of the mass society that else appears so doomed. A documentary on the plight of migrant workers found its way into more homes in one night than twenty editions of *Grapes of Wrath*; a concerto of George Antheil's reached an audience of young people who never dreamed anything but movie themes emerged from California. Two million people had their first glimpse of Segovia or explored Newport Synagogue with Robert Frost; after a religious ballet the Met's choreographer, John Butler, was inundated with queries from student groups across the country eager to imitate the articulate movement and simple lines especially devised for television.

It may be years before television can claim to be a separate art form, encumbered as it is with bulk and with mercantile commitments; and it should be charitably remembered, in passing, that American television was developed by, not ravished by, commercial interests. Yet, plainly, it need not await the accolade to serve the ends of renewing and reinvigorating the human imagination for which Nathan A. Scott, Jr., so eloquently pleads.

This purpose is already the guiding force in most of television's religious programs. Here, at hand, is common ground for theologians and artists, a chance to test the new vocabulary the church must develop to speak to the new condition of man. How are we to convey the modern concept of a hair shirt? With what visual device do we replace the hell flames that licked at medieval man or the rose petals that rained down on him from his church roof on Whitsunday morning? Who will bring samples of the world around us into a new kind of pulpit and proclaim the heresies of our day to more listeners than St. Paul reached in a lifetime? Who will translate the Bible into literally living words and scour the byways of our lazy minds with the challenge of the gospel?

The church must not await the evolution of television into a worthier art. Cedar and sandalwood adorned Solomon's temple, but the wheels that bore them there were doubtless of humble plane.

MUSIC AND DANCE

XIX

Mid-Century Man and His Music: A Christian View

GEORGE W. POOL

ANY ATTEMPTED STATEMENT OF A CHRISTIAN VIEW OF MAN AND HIS MUSIC must begin with the presupposition that the arts are primarily a source of revelation. Revelation yields insight into the nature of God, the nature of man, and the God-man relationship. The details of this relationship become known through the impact of the divine self-revelation and human response to it.

Diametrically opposed to the view which sees art as revelation-activity is another view too often held by the church both in its past and in the present. It is the view which sees art primarily as propaganda or as a means of "communication." Certain ideas are held which are esteemed right and proper, and art is made the vehicle for spreading them, making them appear more interesting and acceptable. The use of the term "communication" implies that art is merely another means for saying something which may be equally well said in other ways.

Art conceived as revelation is a continual, renewing activity. The artist cannot relive his past, but he must struggle with it, formulate some understanding of it, and finally make peace with it through a synthesis of those conflicting elements which he finds in his own inner experience.

The first half of the twentieth century has been one of disillusionment, of experimentation, and of growing frustration. It has been a time of sud-

166

den, irregular, and unpredictable change. This is the condition felt by all men generally—a condition of "uprootedness" or "alienation."

Twentieth-century man's "uprootedness" is not simply spiritual; rather, for most of the major musicians of our time, it has been a hard actuality of experience. Stravinsky, a Russian with the vast inheritance of Russian folk and peasant music; Bartók, with the rich Magyar folk tradition; and, in a less marked way, Hindemith—each has been geographically uprooted at least once. Similarly, each has been cast into a bifurcated spiritual tradition, into a musical world with its massive sophisticated tradition dominated by Germany. Yet each also brings with him a firm commitment to his own unsophisticated folk habitat. Each has sought "new wine," new modes of expression; and each has sought to emancipate his own musical individuality amid the vast and impressive musical monuments of the past. Each has been caught up in the tension between the isolation of his own folk culture and the European musical tradition. Thus, the early part of the century appears musically grotesque and often flaunts a snobbism which appears bent solely on shocking the ear.

Folk themes and melodies, with their limited but highly individualized rhythms in strange groupings, have been obliquely related to historic musical forms in negative and positive ways. Bartók's interest in Hungarian folk songs, his early advocacy of the piano as a percussive instrument, along with Dvorak's interest in the distinctive material of Indian and Negro music are exemplifications of this tendency toward new expressions.

To illustrate, I proceed now to a brief examination of the roles played by Hindemith, Bartók, and Stravinsky in the musical world of the twentieth century.

Hindemith

Paul Hindemith (1895—) inherited the massive musical tradition of Germany, especially that of German romanticism; yet he has always been more profoundly affected by that period of musical activity known as the classical than by Wagner and the late romantics. Early in his creative career Hindemith became aware that new wine cannot be contained in old skins; that if one desires successfully to emulate those traits which he esteems in compositions of another period, he must create within a tonal scheme as revelant to the world of the twentieth century as Bach's was to his. The immediate fruition of this realization was the reluctant but determined suppression of all personal feeling. It was a return to a nonhumanistic frame of reference, a rejection of personal concern for one's own feelings and preoccupation with the psychological realities of one's own ego. This stage of Hindemith is analogous to the ritualistic and primitive stages of Stravinsky and Bartók.

The music of this early period had important and direct bearing on the "serious" music he wrote during the 1920's. From jazz he had absorbed the penetrating sonorities and their continuous driving rhythms. These qualities he synthesized into neobaroque techniques, thus enlarging the tonal and emotional world of the baroques. *Konzertmusik* for brass and piano reflects no attempt to realize the tension between line and harmonic structure as does Bach. Rather, much of the musical interest comes in the oblique way the parts clash against each other, yielding a scintillating harmonic and rhythmic effect. Yet in the gradual growth which inevitably took place in Hindemith's craftsmanship, he sought more and more to create lines which imply their own harmonic structure.

In the early instrumental solos the technique emulates the method of Bach, as in the *Concerto for Viola*, but the tonal universe is vastly expanded; the strong tendency toward independence of line suggests a reference to bitonality, but it is never established as a dogma.

It was the purpose of Hindemith to provide for our contemporary world a basic tonal system for composition just as Rameau provided one for the eighteenth century. Hindemith's system is really a theory of tonality, the delineation of a tonal world, and not a method of composition. The *Ludus Tonalis* is a series of fugues and interludes for piano, and its plan follows the form set by the classical writers. Through these very effective pieces Hindemith sought to give practical embodiment to his theory of tonality in much the same spirit that Bach, in writing the famous forty-eight, demonstrated equal temperament. In *Mathis der Maler* this new tonal world is disciplined, chastened, and brought into close continuation of the tradition of Bach, Schutz, and the sixteenth-century polyphonists. Appropriately, the theme of the opera is that the artist, as the representative of truly creative tradition, is indeed the unacknowledged legislator of the world.

Bartók

The Hungarian national culture had for Bartók (1881-1945) a profound meaning. It imparted to him a strong desire for independence and a longing to blend the East and the West. His professional creed, as stated by him, was to learn from Debussy the importance of harmonic possibilities, from Beethoven the meaning of progressive form, and from Bach the significance of counterpoint. His life is search and work developed from his effort to make a living synthesis of these three masters.

The *Fifth Quartet* is the best example of Bartók's handling of his material in light of his conception of himself as a creative artist. The first movement in sonata form has its subject split in definite groupings; first the irregular percussive figure, then a trill and glissando which is suggestive of Magyar song. The developments involve sharp tonal conflict and, in the recapitulation, the material appears inverted and reverted. The thematic material is gathered together and ends in a close stretto, albeit not in an unambiguous tonal center.

The second movement is a chorale modally harmonized by evanescent wisps of sounds. The temper of the whole wistful section is otherworldly. At no time are we made to feel there is consonance of sound; there is no resting place. The categories of time and space are destroyed.

The third movement is a bright scherzo and trio on classical lines. It is rustic and sensuous and is suggestive of unself-conscious folk gaiety. This folk quality is in part evoked by the repetitious simulation of the bagpipe drone.

The fourth movement is reminiscent of the second, unearthly whirrings, wisps of sound funneling upward into the thin air. There is a constant tendency for the themes to disintegrate, again suggestive of breaking through the normal categories.

The last movement is a tribute to Beethoven, with its high degree of contrapuntal organization and its formal development. In his effort to create a living synthesis of the work of the past, with his own tonal system, flavored as it is by his own personal experience, Bartók seeks for the unity of paradise, rather than a unity in which paradise is attained.

Stravinsky

Stravinsky (1882—) as a Russian was never dominated by late romantic chromaticism or the symphonic principle. Yet we find in his earliest work a tendency to integrate traditional materials in untraditional ways. As a Russian, preoccupation with personal feeling was comparatively extraneous. He was prone to think of his music in terms of ritual and liturgy. Primitive ritual with its folk incantation, its insistently repeated modal patterns of dynamic and incantatory character, opens the way for constructing a tonal world which is at once impersonal and very moving. Harmonic streams proceeding independently flow along side by side, creating a bitonality which is incidental to the linear movement of the music. Harmony itself becomes percussive, and instrumentation is exploited for its nervous and incantatory impact. The music of Rite of Spring is orgiastic like the primitive ritual it re-creates.

In traditional musical form both harmony and melody are progressive.

169

When rhythmic patterns are devoid of melodic movement or harmonic context, chaos may reign, but the music does not seem to progress from one point to another. Therefore, every moment of music exists in and for itself. There is no "becoming," and the musical qualities are dependent on the trancelike vertical effect which they evoke. A disintegration of time, or at best a liberation from the consciousness of time, can take place in this setting. In the texture of the music there is constant clash with linear flow which produces a percussive effect since no equilibrium exists between melodic accent and tonal direction. Consequently, the resulting harmony is considered a "posture." The music is not suggestive of movement from one position to the next but of single position, of the frozen "pose" at a given moment. This balletistic effect is continuous in Stravinsky's music.

The Symphony of Psalms (1930) centers around fundamental consonances of the octave, fourth and fifth. In this respect it is reminiscent of medieval music. Its texture is also medieval in that what happens between points of concord depends on linear and rhythmic rather than harmonic considerations. The Symphony of Psalms only superficially resembles a baroque oratorio. It is much closer to the motet style of Machaut. The spirit of the Old Testament is re-created in a remarkable way in the setting of these three psalms of David. The alternating dramatic atmosphere of struggle and passivity are not illuminated by grace, and the concluding alleluias are suggestive of resignation rather than triumph and redemption. The emotional tone of the music suggests the image of human frailty bowed beneath the everlasting burden of its own humanness. The alternation of this tragic outlook with a trancelike contemplation of the firmament is kept alive through incantatory prayer mingled with reverential awe.

The imperious gestures, flashing rhythmic figures, violent scale passages, and heaped-up glissandos suggest the depths of travail of humanity and the longing for miracle. Following this development, the forlorn alleluia of the first section is taken up again timidly, rises to retrospection, and wearies itself away to an undulating melodic line. This rising and falling of the music gives the effect of insubstantial contemplation, of a dynamic polarization, "A flock of birds forever in flight." It is an adumbration of the consciousness of man in the twentieth century.

XX

Jazz as a Christian Expression

ELWYN A. WIENANDT

ONLY IN THE PAST FEW YEARS HAS ANY ATTEMPT BEEN MADE CONSCIOUSLY to introduce jazz style into places of worship in the form of either functional or supplementary music. These intrusions into the hitherto relatively serene precincts of the church have caused a furor out of proportion to their numerical occurrences, but there is no doubt that continuing efforts in that direction will be made. It is inevitable that an evaluation of the relationship between the jazz idiom and the purpose of church music should be undertaken in this decade, for, while jazz cannot, any more than any other musical style, be said to have come of age, it has increasingly made its presence felt upon a larger public than in the past. This is due, in part, to its ever-expanding areas of presentation in the form of recordings, critical evaluations, television, radio, and other communications media.

Definitions: Jazz and Church Music

Unfortunately, along with the expanding operational field of jazz has come a looseness of terminology brought about through limited experience on the part of its new public, or by the lack of a continuing tradition, that remains with us because of the absence of a single definition that can be accepted by the producers and consumers of jazz alike. Any consideration

171

of jazz in connection with religious activities must depend upon definitions of both jazz and church music that can be used as bases for evaluation, even though such definitions may leave a portion of the problem unanswered for either the jazzman or the churchman.

The confusion over what constitutes jazz is not confined to the layman, for there is small agreement on the part of performers, as well, about the ingredients of jazz style. The musician whose experience with music has been confined to the church or concert hall is even less equipped to deal with the problem, for he tends to use the word in a pejorative sense that equates it with commercial popular music, regardless of its function, style, or backgrounds. To those of us who lack both knowledge and sympathy with jazz, there is a tendency to use the word in connection with all music that is not art music—"longhair" music, for want of another term—or folk music. A definition is sorely needed and, among the many that have been offered, one recently provided by Leroy Ostransky furnishes the best working basis for our purpose:

Jazz is the comprehensive name for a variety of specific musical styles generally characterized by attempts at creative improvisation on a given theme (melodic or harmonic), over a foundation of complex, steadily flowing rhythm (melodic or percussive) and European harmonies; although the various styles of jazz may on occasion overlap, a style is distinguished from other styles by a preponderance of those specific qualities peculiar to each style.[1]

If this seems an attempt to beat the problem to death with words, it is certainly a long step forward from those efforts that describe jazz merely as "swing," "beat," or even from those definitions that confine the style to certain prescribed rhythmic or melodic patterns.

On a par with the foregoing is the degree of confusion among laymen and churchmen alike, when they consider as church music any whose text refers to the Deity, or all instrumental music that sounds complex but nonprogrammatic, especially if it is performed on the organ. We urgently need some area on which to focus our aim in connection with church music, but the possibility of our achieving any agreement on its proper style is limited by the needs and habits of denominationalism, as well as by a general lack of agreement over what the proper function of this music is to be, regardless of the church in which we find it. Whether it is to excite the listener or soothe him, to convey a sense of something beautiful or merely fill an awkward pause in the service—these are matters that

[1] Leroy Ostransky, *The Anatomy of Jazz* (Seattle: University of Washington Press, 1960), p. 45.

are not clear in the minds of regular churchgoers and that are certainly not held in common agreement by church musicians.

It is possible that our entire approach is too much tempered by an attitude that demands a compartment for each type of music, a separate function for each musical style.

If it is true, as I believe it to be, [writes Davison] that the partition of music into categories such as dance music, church music, school music, and yet others is justified not by anything intrinsic in the music itself, but because these names connect themselves with music through suggestion, association, or the circumstances surrounding performance, or through the employment of music jointly with language in some form, then it may be said that church music is only music set off by a manufactured title from the remainder of the art, possessed of no special capacities or limitations, and subject to the same laws and the same analytical processes, both technical and psychological, as all the rest of music.[2]

Nevertheless, we speak of church music as if it were a separate musical style with unique ethical qualities, capable of arousing ideas and attitudes that other music cannot encompass. Actually, there has never been a time in Christian history when a musical style used in the church was not also current in secular life or, at the very least, was not closely related to existing secular styles and devices. Although plainsong would appear to represent an exception to that pattern, we have evidence, even in our limited knowledge of artistic life outside the church in the early Middle Ages, that a parallel musical style served secular activity as well. We have come to accept as church music any that conveys suitable text, if it does not provide strong, direct associations with nonchurch activity, while our requirements for instrumental music remain equally vague, permitting such widely separated treatments as simple variations or elaborations of hymn tunes, or abstract polyphonic compositions that have no more connection with the church than the fact that they are not about anything and do not seem out of place. Yet, at the same time, we often expect our church music to take on what Davison calls "the character of a doctrinal protagonist."

Purpose of Church Music

What is it that we want church music to do for us, and is it supplying what we need? We have reached a point where roughly one-third of the Sunday-morning service is given to music, whether it be vocal music in the form of hymns, responses, and anthems, or instrumental music prior to the service

[2] Archibald T. Davison, Church Music: Illusion and Reality (Cambridge, Mass.: Harvard University Press, 1952), p. 5.

173

proper; music to fill awkward pauses, or a few phrases to permit the seating of latecomers. For such a relatively large, and proportionately important, part of our service we have achieved no great degree of agreement concerning what is proper and desirable. The demands placed upon congregations by the ruling bodies of the several denominations are often couched in generalities that are subject to a number of interpretations and often culminate in endless debate. Presbyterians are warned that "in singing the praises of God, we are to sing in the spirit of worship, with understanding in our hearts," and that "hymns should have the note of praise, or be in accord with the spirit of the sermon." [3] No matters of musical style or artistic taste are considered in the volume from which the quotation is taken; the implication is inescapable that decisions of appropriateness will be based on current values, if they need be made at all. Canon 24 of the Protestant Episcopal Church states, in part, that "it shall be the duty of every Minister to see that music is used in his congregation as an offering for the glory of God and as a help to the people in their worship in accordance with the Book of Common Prayer. . . . It shall be his duty to suppress all light and unseemly music and all irreverance [sic] in the rendition thereof." [4] Here the restrictions are more completely spelled out. (It is interesting to note that some of the recent appearances of the jazz idiom have been in the Episcopal service rather than in the comparatively unrestrictive Presbyterian.) It is fruitless to search other denominational rules for specific comments about the purpose of church music. The criteria are subjective and functional, depending upon the habits, tastes, and degree of progressiveness on the part of clergy and members of each group.

Whether any one of the jazz styles can serve the church's need successfully depends upon what each of the many groups expects of its musical aids to worship. Even though there is a general lack of common ground in the specific rules of procedure beyond the admonitions that all be done with a due consideration of good order, certain aims and standards have evolved, although the interpretation of how these are to be achieved varies from group to group. There is a common body of vocal music found throughout the churches of Protestantism. Congregational music, in the form of a fairly stabilized group of hymns, leaves little room for the introduction of new idioms and styles; hymnbook compilers and congregations alike adhere to the established patterns, removing from currency those tunes that

[3] *The Book of Church Order of the Presbyterian Church in the United States* (rev. ed.; Richmond: Presbyterian Committee of Publication, 1938), p. 159.
[4] Cited by James A. Pike, "Clergy-Organist Relationships—Law or Tact," *American Guild of Organists Quarterly*, July, 1958, p. 83.

reflect regionalism and the styles that reflect earlier experiments, such as the presently less desirable gospel songs. The other vocal music employs a group of more or less trained musicians who provide their skills for, rather than with, the congregation. Their contributions are usually in the form of responses and anthems, the first following prayers that create an attitude of quiet reverence, the second appearing as a piece of special music—in reality, a little concert piece—or as something to fill in the time taken up by the offering. In one instance, what is expected is a quiet musical affirmation of the prayer's content; in the other, the musicians are required to provide a piece of music that will heighten the significance of the moment.

Instrumental music is less subject to the restrictions of habit and acquired taste than is its vocal counterpart. Because it does not convey specific ideas, does not even create similar responses in the listeners, it is less often suspect as the means of conveying undesirable ideas into the service. Many an outworn love song or operatic aria has made its way into Sunday services under the convenient title of Prelude or Offertory without causing the slightest comment, merely because its originally secular function was apparent to no one who heard it. I suggest that earlier secular associations cause no harm in themselves, especially when the original function of the music has been lost. Many of our hymnals are continuing examples of the affection in which their editors hold some of the familiar tunes that have come to us from the concert hall and operatic stage. These contrafacta, in which a secular text has been replaced by a sacred one (or one applied where no text existed in the original), represent the continuation of a tradition that was already strong in the thirteenth century. In almost every case, the original function or text is unknown not only to the congregation, but to most of the musicians and clergy as well. It is not that I espouse the principle of our not being harmed by what we do not know; rather, I am convinced that music which does not endanger the dignity of the service through association with an undesirable secularism is capable of being used in church, subject to local and denominational standards. There are several conditions that must be met by any music that is appropriate. "Intrinsic in worship," says Davison, "are awe, detachment, exaltation, inner peace, contemplation, reverence, a sense of God's mercy, and, by no means least, mystery. To all of these the best sacred music gives eloquent voice." [5]

Jazz in the Church

Of the several identifiable styles that have appeared in our church music during this century, jazz is the least prominent and the least important,

[5] Davison, op. cit., pp. 75-76.

175

although its mere presence has caused it to be invested with a significance out of proportion to its quantity. It is because of its seemingly complete difference from the corpus of church music that it has received an unusual amount of publicity and unfavorable comment, rather than because of its presence in great quantity.

Because of the dual role of the congregation in church music as listeners and participants, we must consider the probable reaction of such a group to the employment of jazz in its worship. He who feels that the response would be one of immediate acceptance is probably caught up in the widespread confusion about the difference between the styles of the commercial popular music idiom and those found in actual jazz. The popular music that is most widely heard in our time lacks both the rhythmic complexity and the melodic or harmonic improvisation that mark the true styles of jazz. In fact, much of it contains less of the jazz element than does some of the church music that is in use in several denominations. To return to Ostransky, we see that "the jazz quality of a piece is determined by the manner in which it is played," [6] and not by the way in which it was written. Applying this criterion to church practice, we find that certain approaches to jazz style are made every time a pianist underlays the singing of a hymn with scale elaborations, arpeggiated figures, rhythmic, driving bass patterns, or any of the other devices employed in so-called evangelistic piano playing. What has been applied is a limited amount of "creative improvisation . . . over a foundation of complex, steadily flowing rhythm," as Ostransky has stated in his definition.

We may find musical situations of great dignity, serenity, and simplicity in those churches that confine the accompaniment of hymns to the printed version, permitting no kind of elaboration. On the other hand, there are churches in which the same hymns are sung with a combination of organ and piano, the latter providing rhythmic drive and excitement. If any are moved to argue that the churches using even these basic jazz elements, knowingly or not, have suffered a loss of dignity—a subjective comparison, at best—they are forced, also, to admit that the rhythmic impetus and tricky improvisation go along with a greater vigor in the rendition of the hymns. While we may, for one reason or another, have differing views about the means, we must acknowledge that the addition of the jazz element has produced the desired result of a vital congregational reaction in the matter of hymn singing. That the techniques involved are used less

[6] Ostransky, op. cit., p. 16.

skillfully than they would be in the hands of professional jazzmen does not bar the procedure from the classification of jazz; it merely places the performance on a different level of proficiency, something that has to do with skill and taste rather than with style.

Although we may accept the fact that isolated examples of the jazz style employed as instrumental pieces, anthems, and so on, would be offensive to the musically alert and startling to the rest of the congregation because they are so foreign to the generally acceptable bland mixture we now find suitable, we can see equally how it is possible to develop a service that is based entirely on current musical idioms. The same possibilities for musical variety and unity are available in such a service as are to be found in one whose music is taken entirely from, say, the eighteenth century. The conflict is, in great part, between what has been accepted in the past and what is offered without numerous precedents. Erik Routley, in writing about differences between good and bad music, says, "What is 'new' must be in controversy with what is 'old', and the real vice that lies behind this kind of composition is a fear of that controversy, a fear of 'newness'." [7] Jazz is such a new kind of composition in the precincts of the church; it is not *ipso facto* bad merely because it is new, either in its musical expression or in its presence in worship. No music is capable in itself of conveying absolute ideas, whether they be political, moral or dogmatic; it does, nevertheless, number among its functions the heightening of awareness, the inducement of reflection, the stimulation of imaginative comprehension, and the nurturing of objective ideals—all these in relation not to the music itself but to the area of religious ideas. When any kind of musical expression fails to convey these qualities in sum or in part, that music is open to valid criticism from all who are within its sphere of influence. Unless the adoption of a new musical style were intended to upset all current practices and standards, the inclusion of jazz would have to satisfy one or more of these functions or substitute others that are noticeably superior to them. Whether jazz style is able to stimulate any of the attitudes mentioned above depends upon its relative newness. The perception of such music with its many complexities requires serious attention and, for the inexperienced, can greatly detract from the purpose of worship. If the listener's attention is directed principally toward such matters as elaboration of melodic or harmonic patterns, or the complexities of rhythm, his thoughts are divorced from the proper area of religious meditation, whether the music in ques-

[7] Erik Routley, *Church Music and Theology*, No. 11 of "Studies in Ministry and Worship" (London: SCM Press, Ltd., 1959), p. 71.

tion be new or old. Proper attention focused on a Bach chorale fantasia that is played during the service could be equally as distracting to the listener as a composition in some current idiom, yet we have come to accept such an intrusion into the worship service without comment. Whatever style in music is to be presented, it must be done with the understanding that communication needs to be achieved between composer and listener. Music is not, as the old saw would have it, a universal language. Any form of communication must be equally clear to both the communicator and the auditor. Jazz is no more universally understood than is Arabic or Hindustani; our current church music is likewise incomprehensible to a majority of the world's people.

Even though a congregation might not flee the church premises because of the use of a strange musical style, it is certain that it gains nothing when the style is unable to communicate any spiritual values. Whether the style be that of Handel or Palestrina, or the idiom that of the hymnbook or the jazz combo, it is on its capacity to lend spiritual strength and vigor that it must be judged, and not on its strange newness.

XXI

Contemporary Dance in Christian Perspective

DORA CARGILLE SANDERS

CONTEMPORARY DANCE COMMUNICATES ITS GRAPPLINGS WITH THE HUMAN spirit with all the reinforced power of the other arts. With space for his canvas, the choreographer molds space as the sculptor, designs each moment as the architect, plans color as the painter, taps the emotions as the actor, and organizes rhythm and dynamics as the musician. Beauty of form, impact of color, excitement of motion, clarity of design, and stimulus of music all contribute to the intensity of revelation possible in the dance. The artist distinguishes himself from the technician by his ability to transcend the purely physical technique and craftmanship of the dance and penetrate the realm of deeper insights and spiritual truths.

The contemporary dance artist stands as a product of history with all of its resources at his command. He rediscovers the pure movement-response of the primitives as they translate basic emotional experiences into motion. He supports his philosophy with the Greek idea of harmony of body and soul. He redefines the art of pantomime so highly developed in Roman times. He absorbs the concepts of sacredness from the Oriental traditions in which man is one with his gods in the moments of dance. He borrows steps and figures from the vigorous folk forms of many peoples. He incorporates the rigorous disciplines of the ballet. And he searches endlessly for new forms of movement and expression as he accepts the challenge of freedom offered by the modern dance movement.

Origins of Modern Dance

The modern dance movement was inspired and spearheaded by Isadora Duncan at the turn of the century. Believing dance to be the very substance of life, she rebelled against the formality and virtuosity of the ballet technique which she found artificial and devoid of meaning. In free-flowing robes and bare feet, she experimented with a movement in harmony with nature that placed meaning and expression before form and mirrored the soul. Her art hit that universal note which renders personal emoting into artistic experience. She not only stimulated the modern rebellion but also inspired the foremost ballet artists in a revitalization of their own art.

The last sixty years have emerged as an era of exploration and invention, producing revolutionary concepts of movement, body training, and space. Such giants as Ted Shawn, Ruth St. Denis, Mary Wigman, Hanya Holm, Martha Graham, Doris Humphrey, and Charles Weidman have bequeathed to the present dance generation a legacy of technical innovations and dances as different from one another as the personalities of their creators.

As the Christian seeks an understanding and realization of self in relation to society and the world, so these modern dancers have made the *raison d'être* of their work the search for a new craftsmanship capable of expressing the meaning of life in dance terms. The fantasy and illusion of the fairy-tale idiom, in such works as *Swan Lake, Giselle,* and *Sleeping Beauty,* no longer seem valid expressions for a realistic, industrial age torn with fears and experiences of war.

The revolutionary impulses stirring in Germany after World War I found powerful expression in the work of Mary Wigman. Her concern with the philosophy of war, with death, and with the fate of man resulted in angular and distorted movements foreign to the classical curves. Her dynamic use of energy gave to her movement a power and strength not found in the lyric softness of older traditions. Gravity was a force not to be overcome with the illusion of lightness but to be grappled with as a means of giving weight and substance to movements expressive of man's struggles. Lying, kneeling, crouching, crawling, and falling, in contrast to the vertical elegance of the classical tradition, made possible the opening of new and relatively untouched dimensions of expression. With Hanya Holm, the influence of the German dance was transplanted to American soil where it matured under American influences.

With the marriage of Ruth St. Denis and Ted Shawn, the Denishawn school and performing group became the fountainhead of inspiration and education for American dance. Miss Ruth's Oriental interests and Ted Shawn's search in primitive sources for a virile American dance combined with ballet fundamentals to produce a universal dance formed and stimulated by international exchange. Doris Humphrey and Charles Weidman joined forces in a creative rebellion against the Denishawn school, while Martha Graham followed her own creative genius in another direction. From these explorations uniting the German and Denishawn influences evolved the principles and techniques which stand at the center of contemporary modern dance training.

Martha Graham discovered in the spine a powerful center of recoil and release movement not unlike the recoiling and striking action of a snake. Through his use of the spine the dancer is able to express introversion and withdrawal, like a giant sea anemone pulling in upon itself; or he can express the energy of extroversion or a motive shout of exaltation. The Graham technique (as demanding in its discipline as the ballet barre) has indeed developed the language necessary to expose the "inner recesses of the human heart."

Fall and rebound, precarious suspensions, dynamic changes, and assymetrical designs have become trademarks of the Humphrey-Weidman technique, growing out of the creators' investigation of the movement possibilities in the arc from the vertical stand to the prone fall. These principles took vivid shape in Doris Humphrey's Water Study, where the lovely successive flow, built on the rhythm of the breath, grew from a gentle swelling of the sea to the climactic breaking of the waves.

In her search for new impulses to motivate movement, Hanya Holm treats space as a living, moldable material. Her dancers have an electrical vibrance which charges space.

Modern Dance Themes

The themes which consumed the energy of these creators in the thirties provide a vivid picture of the era. Hanya Holm's sensitivity to the atmosphere in Germany was poignantly expressed in They Too Are Exiles and Tragic Exodus. With incisive humor she cut to the core of American materialism in The Metropolitan Daily where dance comments were made upon the "Want Ads," "Financial Section," "Society Section," "Comics," "Sports," and "Foreign News." Her most famous work, Trend, is explained as follows in the program note:

Trend is a picture of man's survival when the usages of living have lost their meaning and he has fallen into routine patterns of conformity. Though in this direction of decadence lie only catastrophe and ultimate annihilation there emerges out of the ordeal itself a recognition of the common purposes of men and the conscious unity of life.[1]

Charles Weidman's *Lynchtown* maneuvers a large group of dancers in twisted, frenzied forms, projecting the hysterical cruelty of a mob in action. In *Bargain Counter* mob character takes a no-less-revealing turn in his humorous treatment of the savagery of women in the bargain basement. Recently revived under the title *Atavisms*, these dances still speak uncomfortably to our time.

Doris Humphrey's concern with social problems is reflected in many of her dances. In *Trilogy*, *New Dance* deals with her concept of an ideal democracy where the individual develops in freedom and harmony with society; *Theatre Piece* treats the negative ruthlessness of selfishness and commercialism; and *With My Red Fires* unfolds the destructive force of possessive love.

In Martha Graham's ceaseless search to understand and externalize human nature, she probes literature, legend, primitive rites, the social scene, psychology, and philosophy. *Frontier, American Document*, and *American Provincials* reflect in an American dance her belief and faith in the American idea. In some of her most powerful works Martha Graham penetrates the passions and motivations of modern man while drawing from the heroic dimensions of the Greek drama. *Cave of the Heart* explores the Medea story with all the terrible destructiveness of jealousy unleashed to do its worst. In *Night Journey* the dance takes place in the heart of Jocasta in that terrible moment of reconciliation as, facing her ultimate destiny, she relives the circumstances of her life. As *Clytemnestra* she searches for understanding as she relives those circumstances of her life which wove the cycle of vengeance and murder into the pattern of love-in-hate and hate-in-love which destroyed her and affected all of Greece and Troy.

Against the background of an art form steeped in tradition, the moderns seek freedom. Expressiveness and meaning motivate the forms. Angles break the classical curves. Sharp explosions of energy puncture the lyric softness. Percussiveness interrupts the flow. Precarious assymmetry challenges the symmetrical security. New techniques are developed from parallel and turned-in positions of the body. The range of movement extends from the vertical to the floor. Herein lies the extremity of the rebellion.

[1] Margaret Lloyd, *Borzoi Book of Modern Dance* (New York: Alfred A. Knopf, 1949), p. 162.

182

The Contemporary Dance Scene

The contemporary picture is very different. The subtle interaction of one form upon the other defies analysis. Fokine and Nijinsky acknowledge the impetus given by Isadore Duncan in stimulating modern forms within the ballet idiom. Modern dancers have flocked *en masse* to the ballet *barre* in a rediscovery of fundamental principles and basic body disciplines. Ballet dancers study modern to develop freedom, expressiveness, and the range of movement necessary to meet the demands of contemporary choreographers who freely draw from both idioms. Such choreographers are Agnes de Mille and Jerome Robbins, whose works are often labeled modern ballet. Even the superficial comment that ballet dancers wear shoes and moderns do not is no longer true. Some modern touring companies use slippers, and sometimes ballet is done barefoot. Freely acknowledging their debt to both traditions, many dancers prefer the word "contemporary" because it permits them to draw freely from forms suitable to their purpose.

George Balanchine of the New York City Ballet, and a great master of the classical tradition, handles a subject such as the *Seven Deadly Sins* with such realism that his penetrating comments on each of the iniquities is far removed from the dream world of princes. In *Episode*, in which Martha Graham collaborated, Balanchine's inventiveness in new forms within the ballet style is so original that even "modern dancers" are shocked. Because of his preservation and revitalization of the classics, Balanchine has been labeled a neoclassicist. He brings to the dance world a rediscovery of the greatness of tradition. Who has not experienced a piercing of the veil of truth in the superb performance of Ulanova's *Juliet* or Margot Fonteyn's *Giselle?* All dispute bows here to the experience of a magic greatness. Anatole Bourman's description of *Le Spectre de la Rose* gives a glimpse into this experience of greatness in the performance of Nijinsky:

He was Krishna expressing the agelong mystery of life. He danced and the world shook with the power of his inspiration. His body was a delicately attuned instrument played upon the rhythms of the cosmos. He was harmony of sound and motion and beauty. His body swayed with invisible chords incarnating fleeting emotions. His feet pranced like winged spears, stabbing time with their immortal mastery until time died and it was an immortal who leaped and spun in hypnotic cadences. He was tenderness and understanding, yearning over his beloved when he permitted love to draw him to her side and take her hand.[2]

[2] Anatole Bourman, *The Tragedy of Nijinsky* (New York: McGraw-Hill Book Co., 1937), p. 185.

The current dance scene presents an abundance of material on explicit religious themes. As the spiritual grandparents of the modern dance, Ruth St. Denis and Ted Shawn continue to exert a powerful influence for the acceptance of dance as a direct religious expression. In the Temple of the Divine Dance in California, Miss Ruth has converted many skeptics to accepting dance as a valid form of worship even within the sanctuary. Still performing in her eighties, her spiritual radiance remains undimmed by her age. Ted Shawn, a theological student when he discovered the dance, has performed a complete service of worship with his famous men's group in the International Church in San Francisco. A concert work, *Doxology*, is said to have transformed a theatrical audience into a congregation through its statement of praise. Shawn believes that the laws of theatre can be applied to the canons of life and faith.

Margaret Fisk Taylor's teaching, lecturing, and group performances in churches have stimulated choreography designed for the sanctuary and the service of worship. Since the publication of her book, *The Art of the Rhythmic Choir*, movement choirs have sprung up throughout the country which focus upon dance as a meaningful part of worship experience for dancers and congregation alike. The simplicity and sincerity of their approach has gained them acceptance across all ecclesiastical boundaries. The nationwide growth and influence of the Rhythmic Choir Movement has culminated in the organization of The National Sacred Dance Guild.

Biblical materials continue to inspire dancers. In his *Traitor*, intended for concert stage, José Limon portrays the character of Judas, carrying it through the event of the betrayal. George Balanchine uses the *Prodigal Son* for the ballet stage. Margaret Fisk Taylor has choreographed the *Story of Job* for the chancel. Television's *Look Up and Live* and *Frontiers of Faith* series, which continuously explore dance resources, have included John Butler's *Adam and Eve* and *Saul and the Witch of Endor*.

The full concert stage makes possible the use of large group works with a company comparable to that of a symphony. Such a work is Doris Humphrey's *Passacaglia* which, with the aid of massive architectural designs and formal movement themes of nobility and grandeur, arrives at a statement of praise in complete harmony with the magnificence of Bach's music. Miss Humphrey, in this dance, makes a positive affirmation of the goodness of life in a generation preoccupied with degeneracy and negativism. Thanks to dance notation, this work survives its creator in the repertory of the Limon company.

José Limon was deeply moved by the courage and faith of people whom he saw in Europe calmly rebuilding their lives amidst devastation and the shadow of a bombed-out church. This scene provided the setting for his *Missa Brevis*. Using the complete Kodaly mass, *Missa Brevis* explores the feelings of these people as they participate in the worship experience of the mass.

The faith of Joan of Arc is recalled in Martha Graham's *Seraphic Dialogue* in which we relive with Joan her experiences as Joan the Maid, Joan the Warrior, Joan the Saint, and Joan the Martyr. In a more abstract vein is Matt Turney's performance of Robert Cohan's *Praises*—a suite of dances intended solely as the "unfolding of beautiful movement allowing the spirit to soar." Helen Tamiris' *Negro Spirituals* has caught the soul of the Negro people in the depth of their religious expression.

Dance exists in a moment of time and space. Yet it has a power to burn its way into the memory of man. Using the same transitory elements of time and space, God's penetration of history in his revelation of himself to Israel and in Christ has burned its way into the consciousness of mankind. God's redemption of man consists in his gift of integrity in the midst of brokenness. Dance may serve as a medium of response to this concern of the Creator for his creatures. The elements of time and space, united in the dance, may become the occasion for man's creative and living response to God, expressed as the search for life's meaning or as an invocation of praise.

PAINTING, SCULPTURE, AND ARCHITECTURE

XXII

The Catholic Imagination and the Painting of Our Time

CELIA HUBBARD

ANYONE WHO DISCUSSES THE RELATION OF CATHOLICISM AND CONTEMPORARY art enters into a debate which is charged with controversy and no little ignorance.

Since Catholics are very much like anybody else, in that they are human and individual, there is great diversity within the doctrinal unity of revelation. There are liberal Catholics and conservative Catholics, Democrats and Republicans, Catholics who are visually literate and aesthetically sensitive and those who are less so. The Catholic clergy have an official position and function in the church which is different from the layman's and which affects certain questions and decisions about art and its place in the service of the church, that is, in worship and teaching. To understand what is involved in a discussion of Catholicism and contemporary art some theological, historical, and philosophical orientation seems necessary.

Incarnational Theology

Theologically, belief and art are closely related in the church because of what H. A. Reinhold, interpreting Father Yves Congar, has called

the horizontal revelation of our own tradition, which is one of perfect and complete incarnation, of a visible Church, of symbolic sacrifice and sacraments,

186

of a God elevating and entering into His creation. This horizontal impact of the Incarnation came to its perfection in Jesus, complete man and complete God. And here lies the basis not only of the organized and visible Church, of the liturgy, of theology, but also of art, if only it is kept in mind at all times that we must remain within the realm of symbol and that art must in the religious sphere always carry the message of mystery and the shadow of an unseen and unseeable reality.[1]

One has only to review the iconoclastic heresies and controversies to see how strongly the Catholic church has defended her convictions about art.

Artistic Heritage

As for interest in art and the artist, the Catholic church has an unrivaled past. This interest has centered primarily in the need of the church for art in her worship, liturgical and devotional, as well as in her teaching.

In its earliest days, the Christian church confidently baptized existing pagan art for her own religious purposes. In the later and more Christianized cultures, one finds magnificent expressions of the inner essence of the Christian faith—especially in the art of the periods extending from the Byzantine to the Gothic. While marking a high point in art in the service of religion, late Gothic dates also the beginning of the decline of a truly sacral art, which sank to an unbelievably low level during the nineteenth century.

The church, traditionally, has always been contemporary, using the great artists of each period together with their "modern art" to express the living faith of Christianity.

This traditional harmony, however, between Catholicism and the artist has been severely affected by the weakening blows which the church has suffered during the period beginning with the Renaissance and continuing to the mid-twentieth century.

The self-consciousness of the Renaissance with its revival of the classical pagan past, followed by the rapid secularization of the arts increased by the Reformation and the French Revolution, prepared the way so that by the nineteenth century secularism had taken over almost completely and the arts had come to be more and more alienated from the mother church. Wounded by a divided Christendom, the Catholic church began to be preoccupied with her own survival and doctrinal content—thus tending to create a sort of siege-mentality disastrous to fruitful contact with

---

[1] H. A. Reinhold, "Art and the Liturgy," *Commonweal*, March 21, 1958, p. 631.

the contemporary culture. Counter-Reformation art, for all its brilliance and bombast, was somewhat artificial. The innumerably attempted revivals of every known style during the nineteenth century succeeded only in demonstrating the poverty of imagination and dynamism in religion as well as art during this time.

The Modern Art Revolution

The artist, becoming more and more disgusted with the mediocre state of affairs in art and society as a whole, revolted against academicism. He launched what is known as modern art by means of nothing less than a revolution which reinstated art as a creative activity and freed the artist to investigate his own world of artistic creation. Since this decisive time, art has achieved an unprecedented independence. What is the attitude of the church toward this autonomy of art which, since its aforementioned break with the patron church, up until fairly recent times has been almost completely unconcerned about religion?

The Catholic Philosophical Position

Believing that every genuine truth proceeds from the Holy Spirit, the church can never be the enemy of the true and the beautiful however alien their apparent source or however "secular" their uses.

The artist's first responsibility, insists Catholic philosopher Jacques Maritain, is to his work. "Art taken in itself tends to the good of the work, not to the good of man, and . . . its transcendent end is Beauty, an absolute which admits of no division." [2] In order to clarify this often confused relationship of art and morality, Maritain develops the idea further, explaining that artistic value and moral value belong to two different realms, artistic value relating to the work and moral value to the man. Even though the absolute toward which art is directed is a supreme good and an ultimate end in a given order—that of the creativity of the spirit —it is not, however, the absolutely ultimate end of man, which is God.

Obviously there is a never-ceasing conflict and tension between these two autonomous worlds, each sovereign in its own sphere—between the aesthetic interests of the artist and the moral interests of the community or the common good.

The fallacy of the idea of "art for the social community" is a result of the excess of the equally false theory of "art for art's sake." To avoid the danger of extremes in either direction it is necessary to realize what

[2] Jacques Maritain, The Responsibility of the Artist (New York: Charles Scribner's Sons, 1960), p. 25. Used by permission.

the common good actually consists of in regard to art and where art impoverishes itself when the artist operates as if he were only an artist and not first a man. This risks cutting art off from its indispensable element of poetic intuition when it rejects the existential world of things, and the food, fuel, and energy it receives from human life.

Art is essential to a true sense of the common good; it discloses "a vision of reality-beyond-reality, an experience of the secret meaning of things, an obscure insight into the universe of beauty, without which men could neither live nor live morally." [3]

With regard to the artist and his ultimate end as man, the only way of resolving the inner conflict of his art and his moral conscience is that which involves a purification in the very depths of the creative source in his soul. "When the love on which the perfection of human life depends, and which tends to the self-subsisting Absolute, is integrated in the creative source itself, it brings no division in creative activity, because it penetrates and activates everything, and the very love of an artist for the particular absolute he serves." [4]

The Sacral Potential of Modern Painting

With this brief background of history, theology, and philosophy the stage is now set to look at the question of contemporary painting in particular.

The freedom and the direction of his investigations have allowed the painter to develop a highly sensitive aesthetic of expressive forms. The technical and material austerity found in so much modern painting has many of the characteristics of the sacred art of the past: nonrepresentational, nonrational though highly intellectual, hieratic, and abstract.

Here we see an art which has all the traits for a sacral art, which seems in fact to be haunted by the sacred, but which is dedicated to the profane and is not informed necessarily by the spirit of religion.

With a marvelous asceticism of artistic creativity the artist has swept his house clean of the burdening clutter accumulated from the past and has thus freed his "spirit-of-creativity." He is, however, a man in search of a soul, and there is imminent danger, as the Gospel of Matthew, chapter twelve, warns, that the spirit will return to the empty, swept-out dwelling so neatly set in order with seven other spirits and that the last state will be worse than the first.

Now the Catholic is not disturbed by new art forms, whether in secular

[3] *Ibid.*, p. 85.
[4] *Ibid.*, p. 114.

painting or specifically religious work. The formal material aspects of modern art have the same sacral qualities and possibilities that have been present in all truly religious cultures. Distortion is an indispensable quality of an art which is intended to be hieratic and cosmic. Moreover, since the church serves sacramental mystery, a naturalistic and historicistic art would contradict its very spirit.

Dehumanization and Catholic Concern

All the newfound powers of expression which the artist has at his command appear as impressive and important advantages. It is only when we consider the content of contemporary painting that the Catholic will look at it perhaps with a more discerning and single eye.

There are painters today who seem more intent on expressing psychological values than the purely formal ones which so occupied the early moderns.

Art has always reflected its times, and modern man has been vividly expressed in modern art, more deeply penetrated, more forcefully portrayed in all the depths of his existential situation. If this dehumanized image of man disconcerts and upsets us with its revelation of anxiety, degradation, and evil, we should not blame this on art or the artist—who has done nothing to the image of man that man has not done already to himself. It is a salutary examination of conscience to be aware of these prevailing winds and to sense the seriousness of this crisis of modern man.

The progressive desupernaturalization begun with man's loss of faith in God has finally brought us to the dehumanized man of today, who has lost faith in man as well.

The Catholic regards unbelieving modern man with compassion and love, and understands the meaning of evil and the suffering of fallen man in a world which, however, has been redeemed by Christ. This does not alter the intensity of suffering or the apparent success of evil, but it eliminates the despair which results in the belief that God is dead and it negates the inevitable disillusionment of those who believe that man (or the state) is god. The dehumanization in art therefore reflects a situation which is surely not Christian. Thus there is a certain uneasiness in the relationship of Catholicism to this spirit in contemporary painting with its distortion of the meaning of man.

Artists' Concern with the Situation

Some painters feel that it is their role merely to observe and report the situation as it is. Max Picard, the outstanding Swiss philosopher, reminds us that "destruction cannot be overcome by destruction but only by something completely different. Orpheus did not conquer the infernal regions by making himself dark or even darker than the abyss and drawing Eurydice into that hollow of darkness. He overcame darkness by something completely different: by his song, his shining song." [5]

It is not enough for the artist to hold up a mirror or merely to register the confusion about him; to be truly human he must bring order into it. Such a painter is Alfred Manessier, who says:

I paint in response to my desire for harmony and unity, to a renewal of self, reconstructed step by step, towards this world lost from grace. But such painting is far removed from the public, because the public lives in a materialistic world and no longer has need of what I wish to express. This need for harmony and unity is as though asleep and we must watch for an awakening.

Sooner or later the world will once more feel this need. But I believe also that in order to understand our painting, it is necessary that Christianity recover its place in the life of the world; all will be saved if we recover the evangelical spirit, the spirit of childhood. It is natural for a child to feel the harmony between a certain blue and a certain yellow—at least in the first years of its life. But men of today are opposed to this feeling; they think only of business, of their cars, etc. . . . and they reject more and more the idea of eternity.[6]

Painters like Manessier and, earlier, Rouault, both contemporary, both involved in religious painting as deeply believing Catholics, bear witness to their concern with the universe of visible forms as well as the other universe of interior feeling and faith. These two artists combine formal means which are completely contemporary in development, Manessier abstract and Rouault expressionist, with a poetic intuition which has been purified at its deepest source by the spirit of truth, giving us some of the greatest religious painting of our time.

Spiritual Vacuum and Danger of the Demonic

The technical and material austerity of art today, the great sincerity it demands of artists, the honesty and open-mindedness it requires of its viewers prepares it for and attracts it to things Christian. This art is basically spiritual and needs only to be baptized and infused with a spirit that is holy. The responsibility which the Catholic feels toward con-

[5] Max Picard, "Atomisation in Art," *Cross Currents*, Winter, 1951, a translation from *Schweizer Rundschau*, July, 1950.

[6] Alfred Manessier, *The New Decade, 22 European Painters and Sculptors* (New York: The Museum of Modern Art, 1955), p. 26.

temporary painting and the post-Christian, pseudo-Christian culture that it portrays is one of helping it to rediscover its God and its salvation.

It is with a certain alarm that one discerns in some of the more recent contemporary painting a sort of satiety and boredom on the part of the artist with mere aesthetic enjoyment and even with expressing the image and predicament of modern man. The artist has begun to make of his painting a sort of object of cult-invoking quasi-magical powers, a kind of satanic dynamism. When "the ivory tower has become the cathedral of the world, the temple of Pythoness, the rock of Prometheus and the altar of supreme sacrifice," [7] then the Catholic feels that the time has come for all good Christians, Catholics and Protestants alike, to come to the aid of contemporary painting, lest in the absence of Christ it be filled with a spirit more deadly than the materialism it decries.

[7] Maritain, op. cit., p. 65.

XXIII

Art Beyond Celebration

ROGER ORTMAYER

SOMEHOW OR OTHER, INSISTS THE ARTIST,[1] "ART PLAYS AN UNKNOWING GAME with ultimate things, and yet achieves them." Whether or not he rationalizes what he is doing, the artist gives us glimpses, foretastes, talks in shorthand, tantalizes us, defeats our struggling wit. That is why, whenever we analyze or critically evaluate what he does, our claims are suspect; and, if dogmatically we assert them, of one thing alone we can be sure: the case is weak in direct ratio to its assertive strength.

It was Blake who insisted that art is a conversation with paradise. And paradise is something of the nature of creation itself, into which both heaven and hell have been married. Blake was a religious poet, which is as it should be, for if we are going to talk about painting we will have to do it, as much as possible, in the language of poetry. Which is why works on aesthetics seldom quote artists. Artists want to talk as artists and aestheticians want discourse after the manner of philosophy, and these are two different languages.

Art today requires that we join that order for which Paul Klee inscribed the banner: "Merrily dancing tears"—which is an analogy of the marriage of heaven and also parallel to the myth of creation and the fact of redemption.

[1] Paul Klee.

The ritual of our salvation demands that we, too, live and witness and suffer and die and again be born as little children, that is, as creatures of God. His new creation is for that sensational man for whom there is neither past nor future, but also for those of us who are men of the future for whom the nostalgic landscapes of the past are dear no longer. We do not wonder that the priest spoke of the Christ as the "perfecter of our faith, who for the joy that was set before him endured the cross, despising the shame" (Heb. 12:2).

A ritual is equivocal if treated as a saying. When the imagination atrophies, we want assertions, not presentations. In painting, formed by the succession of cause-and-effect images of linear presentation and the accompanying delusion of the immutability of the hierarchy of values represented by the mechanism of optics, we became so accommodated to the illusions of reality which naturalistic paintings purported to give that we were quite incapable of living with the new painting that tried to force us into a direct experience with the work of art.

The naturalistic image, dominant in the last four centuries of Western art, was a parallel to the quantitative, inductive alignment of language that made possible the fantastic technological development of our time. Just as the language itself, especially in the form of print, lent itself beautifully to segmented thinking, objective analysis, specialized investigation, so the parallel image of the painters let us assume the objective stance. The work of art was always out there, held at arm's length. Its values were clearly delineated. The eye knew where to look because line, color, and tone conformed to the hierarchy of values that optics suggested: things in their proper places according to the arrangement of linear perspective.

Just as the liturgical reforms in the shaping of worship have been based upon the assumption that the proper form of Christian worship is that which forces the communicant into involving his whole self in the re-presentation of the drama of salvation, so the painter has now asked for direct experience, not thinking about something. Just as Christian worship, properly, is not contemplation of some abstraction called God, so the encounter with paintings in our time is an act of confrontation, not of analysis. As the communicant is driven to his knees with the words: "Thou art the man!" so the work of art shakes down the guardrails that have kept us away from the experience of the work of art in itself.

The Celebration

Some time ago an artist friend gave me an etching from a series using biblical subject matter. It was titled: "II Kings 2:23-24." Expressionistic in style, but with a representative image, one could get a clue to the story, and I recalled one of the low ironic tales from the Old Testament: "He [Elisha] went up from there to Bethel; and while he was going up on the way, some small boys came out of the city and jeered at him, saying, 'Go up, you baldhead! Go up, you baldhead!' And he turned around, and when he saw them, he cursed them in the name of the Lord. And two she-bears came out of the woods and tore forty-two of the boys."

Why did the artist use this story? Are the ways of God toward men best celebrated by a tale so morally questionable and absurd even as legend? There certainly is nothing in the story that lends itself to what was once called edifying discourse. Some youngsters taunt a touchy old man about a physical defect and he reacts to their teasing with a curse and then— is it coincidence?—out come two bears and forty-two youngsters go on the casualty list. Critical exegesis has had a rather awkward time with this story. Perhaps, as with the folk meaning of Samson's might, there is strength in a good head of hair, and to be shorn of one's hair is a sign of debilitated strength. Perhaps it is that to mock God's servant because of his weakness is a mockery of the holy itself. In any case, the tale is not one designed for sturdy example nor ennobling reflection. It is an offense and an absurdity to rational justice.

Certainly one of the most fruitful ways of coming to terms with a work of art is to be enlivened by the penetration of the archetypal images it deals with, just as religious ceremony quickens our awareness of the prototypes in which faith finds meaning. When an artist pulls out such images to comment upon in the language of painting, he gives us clues as to what has been and currently is really happening. If he chooses his paradigm from the collection we know as Scripture, then he must have done it with a double significance—that of a general illumination of the human condition and a specific comment or celebration of a point of view.

Instead of giving us an illustration, what the artist does is to celebrate. In celebration he arouses the clusters of associations and analogies that stimulate the poetic imagination. When his celebration is identified with religious patterns, then his images have the accelerated power that comes from identification with rituals of salvation.

The print of the bald-headed prophet bedeviled by boys who are threatened by bears is not an illustration of a scriptural text. It is not about something else, even though it represents specific subject matter. Rather, it is a commemoration of the mystery of the holy which may choose to outrage even the moral.

195

When Rico Lebrun paints the bestial monuments of twentieth-century inhumanity, such as "Buchenwald Pit" and "Study for Dachau Chamber," it is to mark the time of the day, not to describe a horrifying story or to make a historical record. It is rather that he illuminates the persistent myth of death and resurrection, the transfiguration of the image shown through its disfigurement. This is celebration. "I believe," he has said, "that if an authentic, unprecedented image of man is to appear, it will only be through a complete acceptance of that obligation to sponsor, reveal and celebrate man's condition." [2]

The art that celebrates always challenges existential response and reaction to its forms. Its subject matter may be of historical events or remembered legends, but its themes are the condition of man in relation to his world and overworld. They thrust into the core of his being where he knows that something vital is at stake.

Such art requires an expressionistic style (I am not using the term in a technical sense) that the theme may properly take on its shape. The naturalistic illusion in painting is quite inadequate to its demands. Because it attempts not to describe but to show, it distorts the appearances that the inner vision may be thrust into view. To resort again to Paul Klee, whose celebrations of man's time and place have brought painful joy to twentieth-century man: "Art does not reproduce the visible; rather, it makes visible."

Such art is, of course, not the Sacrament. Heretical claims of this sort have been made, but they come from the common confusion of symbol with reality. But expressionistic art does celebrate, as does the representation of the Lord's Supper. It does so without the intensity, without the wholeness, and without the blessing by which the celebrant administers the bread and wine. It is, as authentic celebration, analogous to the Sacrament in the way in which the mysterious is given form.

Art Beyond Celebration

There has been a genre of painting, of decisive influence in post–World War II, which has attempted to probe beyond celebration. Its artists seem to have tried to speak of the thing in itself, to image being. The proclamatory mood of their work gives one the impression that here is a gospel parallel to the gospel.

The "actionist" painters do not provide a commentary. Their works

[2] Statement of the artist accompanying a showing of his paintings in the "New Images of Man" exhibition at the Museum of Modern Art, 1959.

of art are not *about* something. They seek rather to uncover something close to that of which the gospel speaks in other terms.

Their paintings are not propositions and they do not assert, even as they do not describe. They evoke upon contact. They illuminate rather than define. The landscape which they uncover is not one of which we say, "Ah! I recognize the high places and the low, the contours of familiarity where I have been and to which I return."

Their maps are not for pilgrimages. They are not guides to heaven and hell. They do not attempt to symbolize anything. They are images neither of ideas nor of opinions. They simply are.

The paintings of the "actionists" have some correspondence to music, but are quite without the disciplined and abstract contours of the musical image. They are a kind of madness.

Kandinsky opened the door. He sought to "express mystery in terms of mystery." His "symphonic" paintings were attempts to pry into the source of life. He admitted to the search for total being. But he was never quite able to drop the preconception. The form of the work continued to take on the shape of the idea and the search, just as it had the evocative power of celebration.

The actionists have gone on from Kandinsky and Klee and have tried to create ex *nihilo*. They have come to their canvases with nothing but the raw materials of painting, and even these accessories are often loaded with the accidental. Canvas and duco, sand and turpentine, air hoses and knives and sticks and plastics: these have been their tools and materials—and about anything else that might immediately be at hand, except preconception.

The problem of being and nonbeing is probably best left to the systematic philosophers. Nevertheless, such artists as Pollock have dared to probe as far as their own emotional and artistic limits would allow. When one tries to create ex *nihilo* what does he find? Being or nonbeing?

In any case the actionists have given us their paintings. Some are ominous and some are gay. Some are frenzied and seem rather spirited and delightful. Against the lowering power of Kline and the tempting strength of Soulages loom the enveloping and hovering squared clouds of Rothko that seem to pull us into the center where ideas and emotions and desires and fantasies are all swallowed up.

While technically it is a mistake to identify Rothko with the actionist painters, for instance, there is an identity in the point of view. With them he is relentlessly probing the meaning of the creative act and the creation of a work that *is*. His art is not something else; *it is painting*.

Space and time and idea and meaning are all equally irrelevant questions to be asked. Tragedy and irony and metaphor might be terms of association, but at best they are parallels and have little to do with the meaning of the paintings. The paintings just are.

The necessity of the paintings in this contemporary genre is in their own being. When we encounter them they are ambiguous, but never opaque. Their meaning is evasive, probably because we ask for the proposition, the assertion, or even the celebration. Recoiling from their threat, we often ridicule their formlessness and find much to scorn in their seemingly undisciplined structure and technical carelessness. Can these drippings be taken seriously? Is there anything permanent about this work?

This art must be taken seriously, and the question of permanence is an impertinent one.

We must treat these works seriously because they thrust us into the heart of the search for meaning. Does a work of art have to have any necessity outside itself? Long ago the claim that a work of art was an imitation of nature was challenged. As celebration the work of art was found to have an immediacy that imitation was always felt to lack. Now they ask us: Is anything outside the painting itself (other than the creative act of the artist and the few feeble materials of his craft) required?

For the orthodox, even to pose such a question is to make one suspect of some new form of heresy. That the works of art are with us is but a confirmation of idolatry. The iconoclasts have been roused with their cries to destroy.

Whatever may be the verdict of time, there is no question but that the discontinuities of these works force a study of the venerable continuities. This is why I said that the question of permanence is impertinent. Whenever a discontinuity pokes its nose into our tent, we try to ignore it by crying that it has no permanence. Permanence is not a criterion of relevance. We make no decision at this point. Those of whom we are the predecessors will do that.

Art in our time has reasserted, in part, its power to force man into something like existential self-recognition. It need no longer assume the succession of cause-and-effect, nor must its outlines be a reproduction of the contours of something "out there." It has reasserted itself by demanding direct experience. As symbol it partakes of the reality it illuminates. As celebration it stirs into life the depths of experience. As a work beyond celebration it has probed the edges of creativity itself. In all of this surge of life there are dangers, mistakes, and frauds. But there is power, too—the kind of power that feeds into true religion.

XXIV

A Sculptor Discusses Contemporary Religious Work

CLARK B. FITZ-GERALD

AN ARTIST HAS SEVERAL ROLES: HE MAY BE CRAFTSMAN, TRANSLATOR, INTER-
preter, prophet, or just a voice. He may be a mixture of these with the
added spice of his own uniqueness. All of these roles involve the primary
prerequisite, which is to think clearly, to analyze what is to be said,
and to say it simply and clearly in an order.

In this day—with so many people working in the various art fields
in so many different media—the emphasis which mass communications,
or a magazine such as Life, can give to an artist or an art form is frightening. A television program from the Metropolitan Museum or the Museum
of Modern Art and the critics' comments can exert the same influence.
All these influences make their impact upon our subconscious minds—
the degree, of course, varying with the individual. Hence, it is not easy
for an artist to maintain his integrity, even when he earnestly wishes to.
He must constantly be on his guard against the temptation to do something different simply for the sake of being unique. He alone can say
whether he is searching for truth or simply looking for attention. A
sculptor's personal integrity involves the same elements as that of any
other artist: a deep respect for materials and tools, and truth to his own
highest creative abilities.

Religion and Sculpture

Artists, like everyone else, change. An artist's small gods change as does
his concept of the great God. His understanding of love at forty is

199

different from his understanding of it at twenty. Similarly, an artist's understanding of religious sculpture may change. During the last five years I have made an effort to translate and interpret the Bible sculpturally in a way which relates it specifically to our own society in the 1960's. For me this restores to the Bible its original vitality. Sometimes its real meaning is obscured by its ancient, though beautiful, language.

There is something about the creative process that involves one not only with the problem at hand but also with God. I know that I am meant to work with my hands as well as my mind. This is the moment when I am closest to God.

As a sculptor, I find the less subtle stories of the Old Testament a more fruitful source of material than the New Testament. Its love, hate, fire, and general dynamics provide all the scope one could ask for. Its boldness of action seems easily related to the unique qualities of dimensional sculpture. This is a personal observation, and I'm sure another sculptor would feel differently.

Religious sculpture can be pigeonholed *ad infinitum*. I prefer to leave its definition and classification to the art historian. Religious sculpture must first of all be sculpture. The artist's basic concern must be for his craft. One would think this would be taken for granted. Yet we are surrounded with examples of "religious sculpture" where the whole focus is on "religious" while the "sculpture" is indefensible. Being a sculptor, I know there is no good religious sculpture which is not first of all good sculpture. A theologian might see this differently; this is one reason he is not a sculptor.

A good piece of sculpture is not necessarily religious sculpture. The word "religious" is one that has too many traditional overtones. It means different things to different people. It is the word we are using, however, so I had better explain what I mean by it. I believe purely religious sculpture can be made by one who has never heard of Christ, who has never entered a church. Thus organized religion is not a prerequisite for religious sculpture. For me its prerequisite is the portrayal of some aspect of the human spirit as it relates to other human spirits and to God. The archaic Greek Calf Bearer is religious, as is the primitive African carving of a sober, queenly mother with sucking child.

Symbolism and Sculpture for Our Time

The interpretation of his time is an artist's responsibility. Generally this responsibility is carried out intuitively rather than consciously. It seems the natural and logical thing for the content of contemporary sculpture to be bounced off the wall of our time.

As a sculptor, I desire the broadest possible scope of communication. Fortunately, in the field of contemporary religious sculpture there is little sectarianism; seldom are the Methodists interested in making a strictly Methodist statement or the Episcopalians a rigid Episcopalian statement. This is, I feel, to the great advantage of the church. It seems obvious that the survival of the church in today's world lies in unification. Hence, as a contemporary sculptor, I prefer to work within the framework of the unifying elements within the faiths rather than to emphasize their divergencies.

The visual symbol—of which sculpture and architecture are but two forms—has been frequently and effectively employed by the church. But Calvinism, Puritanism, and Victorianism have left us visually crippled. Fortunately we are beginning to see again the value of the visual symbol and to use it intelligently. The spoken word is not the only vehicle of communication for the church. A sensitive soul can be attracted and stimulated by things other than the preacher and the sermon. If Christ is risen, this fact should be so proclaimed in every aspect of the church. In other words, one should not feel that he is entering a tomb when he enters a church building. If the church professes to understand modern man and his needs, this understanding should be reflected in the symbolism used. Most traditional symbols have done their job too well. They are no longer applicable to our present-day lives, yet many of us resist seeing them changed. The church building with its adornments is a visual symbol of what the church—or better, the particular congregation—really is. Look at a few of these buildings and you quickly get a clue to the vitality, vigor, and awareness of the people it houses.

The church is, or should be, a living thing. Some of our period churches are beautiful. But as their decor is refurbished, communication with their congregations should not be sacrificed to a style of decoration. If the elements of a church, its visual symbols, do not speak to us today, they are of little value. To build a church today with anything but a contemporary attitude can only result in the work being stillborn. I'm fully aware of the pain caused by a new idea; every creative person has struggled with it. Yet if our churches are to have real meaning today they must go through this same struggle. Members of building committees should be picked with an eye to their willingness to cope with the pain of a new idea as well as with the rigors of a budget.

The Church and Contemporary Sculpture

In working for a specific church, the sculptor must look to the minister for an explanation of the dogma, the theology, and its liturgical use. The minister must further communicate to the sculptor the spirit of the church. It is only through thorough knowledge of these things that the sculptor can begin to think in terms of meaningful symbols.

The sculptor's work may be representational or abstract. Each of these is merely a means to an end and should not be thought of as a particular style but rather as a means of expression. Some ideas are abstract by their very nature and can best be expressed without reference to recognizable forms. Neither representational nor abstract work can be labeled traditional or modern. It is the context of the work, either implied or designated, that is important. Sculpture, wherever it is used, is more than an enriching element. It possesses the power—or is the medium of power—to demand, excite, challenge and repel. Unlike a sermon which must come a word at a time, a piece of sculpture can be grasped completely at a glance. For this reason its initial impact can leave an impression remembered throughout life.

Symbolism can be the heaviest millstone around a sculptor's neck, or it can be a high pinnacle from which to see new horizons. Tillich's plea for a new and meaningful interpretation of religious symbols should be the creed of contemporary artists. The fact that the Latin cross (3-3-3-5 relationship) has been seen in our churches for hundreds of years does not make it the only or the best design for a cross. The cross fitchée with its swordlike points, for example, conveys better the idea that Christianity is not passive but something to be dealt with! The immediacy felt before battle by the crusaders when they plunged the sword-cross into the ground for a battlefield service is echoed today in our turbulent times. We are a dynamic society. The focal point of our church should be a dynamic symbol. I am not suggesting that a cross fitchée should be seen in as great numbers as we see the Latin cross. Each church presents a unique designing problem, and every congregation has its own individuality. Such uniqueness and individuality can be expressed even in the design of a cross. A creative sculptor can design a cross or any other piece of sculpture so that it speaks of the church's glorious past and at the same time asserts a firm belief in the here and now.

In this time of automation and mechanical devices, we need to reassert those qualities of man that are his own, which cannot be duplicated by machinery. People must know that beauty and usefulness can be achieved through man's labor and passion. The exertion of our bodies in artistic discipline can produce profound insight into problems of the known and unknown. And what better place to expose ourselves to evidence of man's dignity than at the point of his creativity expressed in relation to and seen in our worship services? Here, if anywhere, he has an opportunity for quiet contemplation. Here he should be surrounded by objects that have been wrung from an individual's heart and hands for the specific purpose of aiding worship. The chancel area especially is intended to communicate a man-to-God and God-to-man relationship. The mass-produced, die-cast, extruded, or stamped is not appropriate in this situation. Of course we are all aware that mass production serves us well. But must it speak for man on God's altar?

The characteristics of contemporary religious sculpture are similar to those of contemporary sculpture in general. New combinations of metals and new techniques of working metal have literally reshaped sculpture. The welding process, which is a relatively young technique, has given sculpture a linear quality, forms defined by line rather than by weighty volumes. Many other forms of sculpture appear on the contemporary scene, but the use of the welding technique is prevalent enough to distinguish our contemporary sculpture from that of any other time. Casting has become so very expensive that welding seems the logical and economical answer for the sculptor of metal. Personally, I find that welding allows me to maintain—and it even fosters—spontaneity that would be impossible in the laborious casting process. Welding is different; I accept its limitations and do not try to make it something it is not. I have found it particularly valuable in interpreting some of the Bible stories where vigor of attitude is often important.

We have lived with abstraction in art for about fifty years. And we have become familiar with a great variety of cultures. These factors influence our use of the visual symbol. As our basic knowledge is broadened, we are able to communicate with greater subtlety. We are able to suggest without spelling out and thus to evoke meditation. I suspect that those who frequent our churches are more sympathetic to creative work by the sincere artist than our building committees realize.

Of considerable influence on contemporary sculpture, including religious sculpture, is the very great increase in the number of persons who experiment in the field. Some of the work produced is valid and sincere, but far too much is of the do-it-yourself-kit variety. Because more people today have more leisure, we are urged to turn to the arts as hobbies. I do not quarrel with this. I do quarrel, however, with the notion that good sculpture can be produced without tremendous study and concentration. Today

203

the number of pieces of sculpture that are made far outweigh the number of pieces that have lasting value.

By way of a footnote, we must be reminded that the art of communication is always dependent upon two basic factors. The message must be clear, but also the receiver must be listening and must understand the language of the sender. The artist is not always available to offer a ready explanation of his work. If his message is geared to the level of the average, it is perhaps so diluted that it is obvious and could better be left unsaid. A good piece of sculpture should have a tinge of prophecy about it; it may be a voice crying in the wilderness. Is it too much then for the sculptor to expect each one of us, each individual man, woman, and child, to exert some effort in developing the aesthetic aspect of our brain as diligently as we do its scientific and sociological side?

XXV

Contemporary Christian Architecture and Catholic Faith

ROBERT E. RAMBUSCH

THE SACRAMENTAL CHARACTER OF FORM, WORD, IMAGE, AND SOUND IS an integral part of being united to God. Man's relationship to his Creator is one of dependence and homage. Church architecture bears witness to the evolving concept of the relation of man's homage to God. Sacred architecture and art have shared the mainstream of creative activity within the Catholic church, expressing eternal truths in an idiom meaningful to contemporaneous man.

In the Judaeo-Christian tradition architecture and art consecrated for worship are inspired by faith, and express that faith, orienting man effectively to God. The form of the religious edifice, its art and artifacts, depend upon man's interpretation of the homage he owes his Creator. The church or temple is the site for religious worship and ought to be an authentic expression of the religious conviction as well as a reflection of the era in which it is built.

Forms of Worship and Forms of Architecture

There are two types of homage: one, a prescribed ritual or liturgy (Catholic, Orthodox, Episcopalian, and Lutheran); and two, a service centered around a sermon (the reformed Protestant groups). A building's structural form and interior design are derived from the type of homage to

205

be offered. The focal point of liturgical homage is the altar of sacrifice and the focal point of nonliturgical homage, the pulpit. In the first, the interior ordering is essentially related to dogma; in the second, the interior ordering is less so. The Jews of the Old Covenant, with their priests and sacrificial acts, belong to the rite or liturgical group. Today, the Jews are more concerned with a nonsacrificial concept of homage, with readings from Scripture, instruction, and song.

Sacrifice is the central liturgical act of the Old Covenant; Eurcharistic sacrifice is the central liturgical act of the New Covenant as celebrated in the Catholic church. The Old Covenant worship of expiation, sacrifice, and holocaust is a prefiguration of the New Covenant perfect worship of the Father by Christ. Homage of the Old Covenant is man's worship of God; homage of the New Covenant is man's participation with Christ in the worship of the Father. In the Old Testament, God is architect and designer of the tabernacle which is symbolic of the future church. In the New Testament, Christ is the reality of the present church. This reality is glorified and expressed in different architectural forms throughout history, each architectural style an interpretation of the mystery and presence of Christ in his worshiping church. In the Old Testament, the role of the priest and teacher-prophet are separate. In the New Testament, Christ is both priest and teacher, and commissions his apostles to continue the unified ministry of sacrament and of word.

Enlightened judgment demands knowledge of the accepted beliefs and traditions of the Catholic church in order to understand its resultant architecture. Dogma, tradition, Scripture, and liturgy are sources manifest in the different architectural styles. A sacramental system involves the members in the Christ-life of the church administered through a hierarchical priestly order. The church houses the communal celebration of the Eucharistic sacrifice, the presence of Christ in the sacred species enshrined in the tabernacle, the administration of sacraments (baptism, penance, and matrimony), and provides for private devotions of the faithful.

In early Christian times the site for worship was the catacomb, the home, and eventually the basilica or hall of public assemblage. The basilica's rectangular ground plan, considered in keeping with catechical and sacrificial needs of the community, was modified by the Christians for worship. An atrium or enclosed courtyard at the entrance served as a transition from the city of man to the vision of the city of God. The interior ordering was structured on hierarchial spatial principles. The celebrant and altar were surrounded by the choir, and the sanctuary was articulated by flanking ambos or raised lectern and pulpit. In the fourth century a great sense of liturgical participation existed on the part of the clergy and the faithful as indicated by the altar located towards the center of the church, e.g., the Domus Caritas in North Africa. The writings of Sts. Ambrose and Cyril gave insight into the active participation in the Mass of this time. Gradually the conscious involvement of the people in the sacred rites became less and less marked. This was reflected in the architectural ground plan. With the rise of monasticism, the choir of monks situated between the altar and the people spatially separated the laity from the altar—by now positioned at the far end of the church. Gothic architecture furthered this separation so that the ringing of bells was necessary during the Mass to alert the dispersed faithful to the time of sacred consecration. The rise of the orders of preachers introduced an architecture that gave greater emphasis to teaching, but the ministries of sacrament and teaching became visually distinct, if not rival, focal points of the interior. The pulpit was moved forward into the nave of the church from its traditional position near the sanctuary. The classically inspired Renaissance and emotionally charged baroque periods marked a low point in liturgical awareness and participation. Compensatory peripheral personal devotions of the faithful increased at this time.

The Scandal of Dead Forms

The scandal of the nineteenth and early twentieth centuries was the divorce of the church from talented architects. The church became less a patron of a vital Christian architecture and more a sponsor of lifeless Gothic imitations—monuments filled with stereotyped furnishings. As the nymphs and shepherd costumes were to Marie Antoinette and her courtiers more truly than they knew symbols of a false arcadia, so the eclectic Gothic flying buttresses and pseudocolonial steeples are to nostalgic clergy and laity alike indications of an anachronistic Christianity. Ontologically, the inability to accept what is leaves only the ability to accept what is not. A living faith will inevitably express itself in living forms. The true faith held timidly will express itself in tried formulas. Eclectic Gothic is not a valid alternative to contemporary architecture.

The religious climate of the United States is predominately Protestant and nonvisual. Except for creative colonial efforts in the East and the simple mission churches in the South and far West, Catholic initiative has been imitative. The great European immigratory waves of the nineteenth century brought Catholics of proletarian and peasant origin. The immigrants' visual frame of reference remained rooted in the sentimental art and architecture of their European homelands. The Italians transplanted the Renaissance exuberance; the Germans and Middle Europeans, unbridled romanticism. The Irish, coming from a Catholic nation with little religious visual culture, also reflected eclectic tastes. The character of church architecture was determined by the taste of the clerical patrons, also immigrants. The great period of expansion, financial betterment, and Catholic church building, occurring as it did at the end of the nineteenth century, was understandably sterile. The still-remaining neo-Gothic of this period has been unconsciously accepted as a traditional model, yet it represents canons of immigrant taste. We cannot conceivably settle for the facile solution which eclectic architecture offered to our immigrant forefathers and their clergy. If we continue to accept this architecture uncritically, we become victims of a historical anachronism and an evasion of reality. To the extent that this imitative architecture poses no question, its acceptance reflects an arrested spiritual and liturgical development. If the Christian's visual categories are determined by nineteenth-century eclecticism, he will find it difficult to accept good architectural forms expressive of the twentieth century. The Christian with nineteenth-century vision will often find contemporary architectural expression meaningless or repugnant precisely because he has been educated to accept eclectic styles as eternal forms expressing eternal truths. The Catholic with twenty-twenty vision demands a profound and living architecture to express the truths he believes to be alive. A third generation now counts America as its native land. The advances made in education should have freed the American Catholic community to turn its attention from the struggle for literacy to the pursuit of culture. The defensive apologetic attitudes of the immigrants are gradually giving way to a lively interest in theology and liturgy. It is from these considerations that a necessity for and expression of a living Christian architecture will grow and flower.

Liturgical and Architectural Renewal

The Old World evidences a greater interest in and acceptance of contemporary church architecture than the New World. The liturgical movement which eventually will affect church architecture has its roots in Europe. The encyclical letter *Motu Propio* (1903) on sacred music calls for active participation in the sacred mysteries. At the Conference of Malines (1909) Dom Lambert Beauduin set forth proposals which initiated the liturgical movement in Belgium. In Germany at the thousand-year-old Abbey of Maria Laach, Abbot Ildefons Herwegen and Dom Odo Casel (1914) led the way in the development of studies with the laity to induce greater lay insight and active involvement in the liturgy. In Austria, Pius Parsch introduced some reforms in the ancient church at Klosterneuberg, simplifying the interior appointments and spatial arrangement to allow for greater communal participation. Such groups influenced further scriptural and liturgical scholarship and initiated conversations among theologian, liturgist, and architect. These conversations led to the logical evolution of architectural forms and disposition of interior space to complement the requirements of the liturgy. Too often communal rites conformed to the limitations of an established architectural mold. The liturgy should inform and form the architecture.

Notre Dame de Raincy (1922) was the first Catholic church built of twentieth-century materials expressing spatially the communal sense of participation. Auguste Perret built this church of steel and exposed concrete, bringing the altar forward toward the assembled community in the nave. Other European architects evolved new and significant forms —their diversity in character underlined by their unity of purpose—to serve the liturgy. Among these pioneers were Karl Moser (St. Antony, Basel, 1927); Rudolph Schwarz (Corpus Christi, Aachen, 1930); Dominikus Böhm (St. Englebert, Cologne, 1932); and Fritz Metzger (St. Charles, Lucerne, 1933). The encyclical letter *Mediator Dei* (1947) articulated the theology of the Mystical Body of Christ and its relation to the enactment of the liturgy. No longer could the laity remain passive spectators. They, as members of the Mystical Body, must unite themselves actively with the head, Christ, in public worship rendered to the Father. Several liturgical commissions set forth succinct and informative directives compiled by groups of theologians, liturgists, and architects formulating criteria for a living sacred art and architecture.[1]

Too often the visual requirement that a church "look like a church" is the measure of clerical and public acceptance. This demand is easily met by less creative architects who copy the "looks" of familiar Gothic or colonial buildings. Some pastors suffer from an "edifice" complex, envisioning an impressive and costly structure that might seem more a monument to the patron than to God. The directives of liturgical commissions have re-established the primacy of what a church *is* over what a church *looks like*. The liturgical and theological function should determine the church's layout and visible forms.

Scripture describes the church as the temple of the living stones, the

---

[1] *Directives for the Building of a Church*, Catholic Bishops of Germany, 1946; *Diocesan Building Directives*, Superior, Wisconsin, 1957; *First Principles for Church Architecture*, French Centre de Pastorale, 1960.

house of God, the gate of heaven, the majestic court of God, and the tabernacle of God set among men. The church is the house of God wherein the people of God assemble. It is the vision of the heavenly Jerusalem; it is the symbol of the Mystical Body. Since the church is already a symbol it need not recall graphically another symbol. Certain romantic architects today delight in structuring the form of a church to suggest a cross, a fish, or some other symbolic silhouette. Appreciation of such iconographic architectural expressions is limited to airborne creatures, usually feathered. The function of the church requires that it be an assembly place for the community to participate in the celebration of the sacrifice of the Mass, to receive the sacraments, to hear the Word of God preached, to give homage to the divine Presence in the reserved Eucharistic species, and to allow for private and public devotional practices. Functional emphasis is essentially communal. The traditional iconographical symbols of the church bespeak this communal sense. Among these are the beehive, Peter's bark, building of stones cemented by love, and Noah's ark.

The heart and focal point of the whole church interior is the altar. The altar is the symbol of God's presence, and on the altar is the reality of God's presence. Here it is that Christ exercises his priesthood; here it is that man is sanctified; here it is that man encounters God. The church is an extension of the altar. Its architectural structure develops from the relationship of the altar to the assembled community. Architects have evolved different arrangements for the position of the altar in reference to the classic basilica (rectangular) form. Some have placed the choir or sacristy behind the altar, insuring that the altar is brought forward with the minimum spatial and psychological distance between the celebrant and participant. Other architects utilize the trapezoid (St. John's Abbey, Collegeville, Minnesota); the semicircle (Christ the King, Seattle); the ellipse (St. Columba's, Minnesota); and combinations of geometric figures. In theory the circular church with the altar in the center may seem ideal, but such a design is destructive of the hierarchical ordering of space. There is no democracy in true worship.

The contemporary altar is more simplified in form, as befits its sacrificial nature. It is disengaged from the rear sanctuary wall. Sacred space surrounds the freestanding altar, allowing for proper enactment of the altar consecration ceremony as well as permitting the situation of this throne of Christ in a dignified and uncluttered setting. Cathedrals, collegiate churches, abbeys, and parish churches, with the permission of the bishop, may have a permanent altar of reservation with tabernacle in the sanctuary or Blessed Sacrament chapel, as well as another altar of sacrifice. Instead of the usual fencelike altar rail, some contemporary churches allow for "stations," or small tables at which communion is distributed to the faithful as they move forward in procession to the sanctuary. These stations allow the faithful an unencumbered view of the altar (St. John's Abbey, Collegeville, Minnesota).

The position of the lectern, situated within the sanctuary, recalling that we are fed by the bread and the Bible, restores the unity of the ministries of sacrament and of Word in the liturgy. St. Thomas Aquinas points out that "the place of sacrifice is not distinct from the place of teaching." [2] As the Eucharist is the sacrament of fulfillment, baptism is the sacrament of initiation. Some architects and liturgists prefer to maintain a sacramental axis by situating the baptismal font by the entrance doors in line with the center aisle of the church. The Easter Vigil liturgy has emphasized further the importance of our birth in Christ and the need for font and baptistry to be articulated in significant architectural terms. Historically the baptistry was a separate building (St. John Lateran, Rome; cathedrals of Florence and Pisa). Architects today are continuing this distinctive location (St. Marie-Königin, Cologne; Resurrection Church, St. Louis) or creating a fitting setting within the entrance of the church.

Shrine altars, stations of the cross, and other aids to personal devotions are to be considered also in the ordering of the interior church space. Essentially the church should be designed from the altar outward. When the liturgical and theological function of the church is creatively solved, the architectural shell, which houses the sacred action and the community, will express logically a religious character. Certain contemporary materials and forms are fitting for use in the construction of the sacred edifice. Concrete and steel used with imagination and integrity are as fitting for God's house as traditional stone, wood, and brick. An inadequately designed church is an aesthetic deformation. It is destructive of the fulfillment of the worshiping community's active priestly role. Dynamic periods in the Catholic church's history have inspired a creative and living architecture; static periods, a correspondingly inferior one. We live in a dynamic epoch. Liturgical, scriptural, and theological realities are being epiphanized. These contemporary insights must be translated into a vital and significant church architecture. Man's union with God requires the support of the worshiping community. Man's attraction to God and the living church is enhanced by living architecture.

[2] *Summa Theologica.*

211

XXVI

The Matrix of Form in Church Architecture

JOSEPH SITTLER

I MUST BEGIN WITH A CONFESSION: THE ROAD FROM CHRISTIAN AFFIRMATION to appropriate forms is a more difficult and complex one than I had envisioned when I first began to think and to speak about church architecture. In those former days I entertained assumptions, had hopes, and made statements which further reflection causes me to retract, complicate, or radically modify.

Inaccuracy of the Term "Christian"

I became acutely aware of the unsatisfactory nature of our statement of the problem of faith and form when I observed that the adjective "Christian" is used in such a way as to suggest relationships which cannot be designated and to hold up promises which it cannot fulfill.

In the burgeoning field of religion and art there is a disposition to attach the adjective "Christian" to certain poems and plays (e.g., those by Eliot or Auden) and certain novels (e.g., those by Camus), and claim these as Christian in an assured sense. The moment one asks why a poem, a play, a novel, or a building is more Christian than another, he is really asking the general question, "Is there such a thing as Christian art?" Is it even possible to talk any longer as if the adjective "Christian" should be used to designate anything except so deep or non-negotiable a fact as God-relationship?

212

One of the graduate students at my university has suggested to me the usefulness of Aristotle's four categories of cause to crack open the problem. According to this analysis a thing is Christian if (a) its *efficient* cause is Christian, (b) its *material* cause is Christian, (c) its *final* cause is Christian, (d) its *formal* cause is Christian.

Efficient Cause: This would mean that a building is Christian if it is designed by a Christian. According to this understanding of causality it would be possible to argue that the pants I am wearing are Christian pants because they were made by a tailor who is a Christian. This category won't do, of course, because it does not answer the question—building or pants—in terms of the things being inquired about. The absurdity of this kind of argument is disclosed if we ask if a building or a pair of pants, made by a man usually pious and an announced Christian, were fashioned by him in a period of doubt or unbelief.

Material Cause: This would mean that the adjective "Christian" is proper if the subject matter has to do with Jesus, the apostles, the sacraments, and so on. A painting is Christian if its theme is an aspect of the Christian faith; architecture is Christian if it houses activities of the people who call themselves Christians; poetry is Christian if it talks about Jesus, worship, feelings generated by contemplation of Christian meanings. This is plainly a useless kind of designation because it ignores that content and form may be so related that the first is betrayed, or twisted, or trivialized by the second. Content can be banalized by such a tune for a lyric as to deform it. A madonna may be pure cheesecake. An image of Christ may be so little controlled by awe as to be a reduction, a distortion, or a plain hoax.

Final Cause: This would mean that anything is Christian if its final cause is believed to serve a Christian cause or purpose: to ornament a church, to further piety, to illumine faith, and so on. There is no reason why the furnace that keeps Christian worshipers warm may not be called a Christian furnace, or why a painting or poem well intentioned but aesthetically and religiously catastrophic may not be called Christian. This position acknowledges that an artist need not be a Christian to be capable of creating a work of art that somehow serves the Christian community and the Christian faith.

Formal Cause: This would mean that anything is Christian whose form (or essence) is somehow suggestive or evocative of the form of the Christian story. The artist's intention to serve the faith, or the artist's own existence in relation to that faith, would have nothing to do with the matter. Neither need the subject matter (the material cause) be Christian.

The criterion would be whether the form and movement and structure of the poem, play, building, have the form, movement, structure of the Christian story. Wherever and however this movement controls an artistic reading of human existence, then, it would be argued, one has Christian art.

This analysis, it seems to me, is sufficiently disordering to the mind to suggest that what may seem a radical suggestion is, in fact, the only rational one: that we drop the use of the adjective altogether when talking about art. We must drop it because it suggests too many, and contradictory, things. An adjective that covers so many things fails to specify anything.

When everything that has been done by Christians, for Christians, for the Christian cause, or having the same structure as the Christian story is in, then nothing is out. And a definition, by definition, has to define—that is, to set limits, to say what is within and what is without.

Art as Historical, Natural Activity

A second suggestion, following upon this first, is that the term "Christian" is incapable of being enclosed within purely historical categories. Its meaning, no matter who interprets that meaning, always appeals to transhistorical events, ideas, powers, or possibilities which constitute the particularity of the term but embarrass or infuriate the artist.

What is available to the artist is the actual historical affirmations, programs, liturgies, ways of worship, polity, educational and ethical procedures of particular churches. It is with this stuff that the artist must work and not with the uncapturable content of the term "Christian." The allusiveness of the big word "Christian" may actually be the deep spring of the artist's creative drive; but the forms he creates are derived from his immersion with the historically exhibited practices of existing communities that call themselves churches. This means that it would be more useful and meaningful and intelligible to call Milton a Puritan poet than to call him a Christian poet, better to call Chartres a Roman Catholic church than to call it a Christian church, better to call J. S. Bach a Lutheran artist than a Christian artist. For these adjectives, while not eliminating the Christian ground of historical formations of a peculiar force and clarity, use a historical adjective to designate a historical product.

What is being argued here is simply that the Incarnation is the only possible charter, guide, and animation for the work of the architect as he seeks to give form to faith. For he must dare and be free to do his own way the astounding thing that God did in his way in the thundering paradox of the "Word became flesh and dwelt among us."

214

If grace can become nature, then nature can ever after that embody, celebrate, and refract grace. Nature does not do this by trying to de-naturalize itself and become grace; it can do it by a kind of tender, free, exulting willingness to accept and use nature (now cleansed of demons!) to the glory of God and the amplest requirements of the human.

Now that grace has made nature the theatre of its gift, all of nature is free and able to offer its redeemed self as a kind of transparency to the reality of grace.

G. K. Chesterton has put this new way of living within nature in the following words:

For our Titanic purposes of faith and revolution, what we need is not the cold acceptance of the world as a compromise, but some way in which we can heartily hate and heartily love it. We do not want joy and anger to neutralize each other and produce a surly contentment; we want a fiercer delight and a fiercer discontent. We have to feel the universe at once as an ogre's castle, to be stormed, and yet our own cottage, to which we can return at evening.

No one doubts that an ordinary man can get on with the world: but we demand not strength enough to get on with it, but strength enough to get it on. Can he hate it enough to change it, and yet love it enough to think it worth changing? [1]

Art is a historical, natural activity. There is a sense in which all art is radically unphilosophical, and this fact is revealed by the impatience all artists feel when they fall into the interpretive hands of fashioners of general statements—philosophers or theologians.

And all art, on the other hand, aims at a universality which shall transcend the occasion of its work. What this surely adds up to is that the artistic way to the universal is by way of the particular; that what is most universal is achieved as a result of precise attention to and effort to articulate the particular. The way to make a thing significant is to make it precise; the path to excellence is the lowly path of artistic obedience to the historically particular. Bach wrote for a world beyond Leipzig because he was concerned to do a particular job for Leipzig, in Leipzig between 1734 and 1750. And if Mr. Saarinen's Christ Church in Minneapolis is called a fine church, that is because Mr. Saarinen was primarily concerned to build a place of worship and work for a particular congregation.

There is, it seems to me, a rhythm in all creative work; it is born in

[1] Reprinted by permission of Dodd, Mead & Company and The Bodley Head Ltd. from Orthodoxy by G. K. Chesterton. Copyright 1908 by Dodd, Mead & Company. P. 130.

generality, it takes on flesh and blood in particularity, and it so manages the particular as to suggest the abiding generality with which it became first aware. One has a feeling, let us say for humanity—its scope, possibility, variety, contrariness, pathos, and delight. But training in the humanities is a course of study which does not deal—cannot deal—with creativity, musicality, poeticality, aspiration, dread, or delight. It must deal with actual creation, actual musical and poetic and dramatic products, articulations by particular people of dread and anxiety and common boredom and delight.

Theology and Architecture

Architecture, as actual product, is to theology as an actual ethical decision is to the commandment of God to love the Lord and one's neighbor as oneself. What this means in terms of actual deeds for the neighbor will never be known in advance or in abstraction. The shape of the need determines and demands the shape of the deed. So it is with a building to enclose and celebrate the actuality of a community called a congregation. There is no simple and direct road to simplicity.

No theologian—nor anyone else operating with general categories—can tell the architect the precise deed appropriate to the need. This answer, or alternate answers, will be generated in the rich potential of the life of the imagination. Theological clarity may point, and ought to; it cannot designate. It must supply to the mind of the architect affirmations characteristic of the community, knowledge of cultic accents, peculiarities and practices; and it may even transmit in a general way the group's understanding of how its worship relates to the environing culture.

To attempt to do more is to confuse categories, to require that theology shall exude aesthetic norms. That it cannot do.

XXVII

Little World in Crisis: A Tragicomic Caricature

JIM CRANE

THE CARTOON IS AN EXTREMELY EFFECTIVE ART FORM PARADOXICALLY BE-
cause we seldom think of it as art at all. Its form is conventional; communication is immediate and direct; and there is no need for the critic
as intermediary. The cartoon is enjoyed by almost everyone and thought
about by almost no one. It is, I think, about as close to being genuine
visual folk art as we can come today. Publications of almost every size,
shape, quality of paper, and level of brow use some form of cartoon
regularly or on occasion. Cartoons are so familiar to us that we take
them completely for granted and seldom devote a line of type or a
moment of thought to what they are saying or how they say it. Our very
lack of self-consciousness about the cartoon allows it to speak to us directly
and personally, as ideally any art should.

The usual cartoon brings a chuckle or, at times, a hearty laugh; the
page is flipped and the cartoon forgotten, soon to be disposed of with
last month's magazines. Occasionally, however, a cartoon will break
through, will touch us in an unexpected place. The little drawing will
illuminate an idea or situation so poignantly, so concisely, that it stays with
us and we are reminded of it again and again. I remember a Lichty "Grin
and Bear It" showing a matron and her little boy at a toy counter. The
salesman is saying, "This is an educational toy to prepare the child for the
modern world. No matter how you put it together, it's wrong." The car-

217

toon is an old one, but I heard it quoted at a recent education conference.

The situation in this cartoon is funny enough if taken literally, but the real meaning is symbolic and points beyond the particular situation to the deep concern that most of us have about educating our children for a world in flux in which it seems that many problems have only a variety of "wrong" answers. Or it may echo the personal frustration resulting from our right-wrong, two-valued orientation in a world that offers us only an ironic multiplicity of problems with but partially adequate solutions.

The cartoon, in contrast to the comic strip, usually employs a single picture and caption. At times, as in this example from Lichty, the picture is simply an illustration of a verbal gag. But the best cartoon is usually a perfect matching of visual image and no more words than are necessary.

While, as a rule, we see single cartoons, it is best to see them in the context of a book of one man's work or to follow them, drawing by drawing, in the publications in which they appear. The individual cartoon, while it may amuse, delight, and occasionally disturb us, is itself a single segment of a world which the cartoonist creates and which possesses its own unique meaning. This meaning is the sharing of the artist's vision. The successful cartoon is much more than a funny picture and the authentic cartoonist more than a distorter of reality. An authentic comic artist has a point of view, a unique way of seeing the world, and an ability for communicating this vision so that we are given new insight into people and events.

The Seriousness of the Comic

While pompous sobriety is deadly to humor (and often the butt of it), the holding of some values with utter seriousness is indispensable to humor. If all is absurd, nothing is funny. Many people have forgotten this or never knew it. There are "sick" comedians and cartoonists who exploit the maudlin and macabre for its shock value. The majority of people, however, react against any humor of serious content or implication. Humor has become for them a diversion, entertainment, a way of escaping reality or the specter of potential and fearful realities. Authentic humor, as a sudden revelation of truth in the biblical sense, may carry with it overtones of pain and sadness as well as joy. Ben Shahn put it succinctly in a critical essay on the French comic artist André François: "Humor itself is not—never was—jocularity. Humor is a way of feeling about life, and when humor is great it is almost never without one of its opposite moods—tenderness, tragedy, concern for man's condition, recognition of man's frailties, and

218

At last, national security, just for the two
of us, Eve—speak to me Eve!

What do you mean, "Communicating with
me is difficult"?

what's wrong with the
artists of today

why are they sick?
why have they no spirit

can't they see
the beauty of nature?

of mountains
and sunsets?

of flowers

or mushroom clouds?

Mushroom
Cloud!

we've got enough to
worry about without
a bunch of silly artists

sympathy with his idealism." [1] The comic and the tragic are often different ways of looking at or feeling about the same reality. Humor is never lacking in a profound seriousness toward life, and those who would protect themselves from the possibility of the tragic by repressing its expression also eliminate the possibility of meaningful humor.

In my own work I have found the line between a comic statement and one that hurts a thin one indeed. My cartoons often grow out of frustration. The situations I deal with are sometimes too painfully close to my own and my readers' existential condition to bring laughter. To laugh when someone approaches an exposed nerve requires courage and a willingness to face life with open eyes. It also requires sufficient skill and taste on the part of the artist to maintain just enough detachment, a quality difficult to achieve.

My "heroes" are little peanut men, images more Sumerian than Greek, inhabiting the bleakest and barest of worlds under the constant observation of a sky filled with dead planets. It is a clear, rational, near-geometric world, except for the men.

My villains are more functional than categorical. Camus has suggested the interchangeability today of judge, accused, and witness. I share his view. Who, today, is not both victim and exploiter, betrayer and betrayed? The enemy is often within.

My own "little world" grew out of the demands of what I felt and needed to say about the world. I suspect that this is true of any artist.

Herblock says the cartoon is an offensive weapon. For the editorial cartoonist perhaps it is. But for me it is more often than not a defensive weapon—and a pretty feeble one at that—for protecting the little scrap of human integrity left in the threatened, frightened, fragmented, heroically unheroic human person of our time.

Cartoons and the Spiritual Crisis

The great majority of cartoons done as folk art deal with ordinary people in ordinary situations or with a fantasy world of stock characters and situations; and most lack the seriousness of great humor. There are cartoonists, however, who have felt the need to penetrate beneath the surface of life and have made the cartoon a means of doing this. Many of these are trained artists who give evidence of knowing the drawings of Picasso, Klee, and Grosz. Many are on speaking terms with the new sociology and depth psychology. In several instances, they have raised the cartoon to a fine art without sacrificing ability to communicate.

[1] Ben Shahn, "The Gallic Laughter of André François," Horizon, May 1959, p. 121.

222

The concerns of these artists are those of many of the other artists mentioned in this book. Their mood is existential. I would like to discuss briefly a few of the cartoonists whom I find most significant and whose work should be called to the attention of anyone concerned with the theology of culture. The list is of my personal favorites, of cartoonists whom I find dedicated to the deepest concerns, who point by implication to the religious dimension of human existence. In each case the artist is involved in caricaturing the spiritual crisis of modern man, the tragic sense of alienation and frustration. Here we see, in a "little world in crisis," the loss of personal identity, the meaninglessness and personal ruthlessness of treating others as "its" instead of "thous," the sense of fragmentation, the crystallization of personality, the decline of sensibility and the loss of the capacity for genuine feeling.

Saul Steinberg is an artist of magnitude and one of the best draftsmen in America. In a magical, fantastically fluid line, Steinberg exposes the tawdriness and fantasy of our materialistic culture. His is a gagless, purely visual humor, often employing visual puns. A sheet of graph paper becomes with a few lines an austere international-style office building. A photograph of an alley with garbage cans and old feed sacks becomes a blighted city. There is no more astute critic of architecture and the culture it expresses than Steinberg. Steinberg's passports are among the most hilarious indictments of pompous officialdom ever done. Steinberg's wit and the style of his drawings have won him a steady following in the New Yorker. His books are more biting and provide a more sustained view of his world.

William Steig is also a fine draftsman, possessing more diversity of style than Steinberg. He expresses his concerns delightfully and pathetically in a number of books. The alienation of modern man and his futile defense of a little segment of his embattled personality is drawn beautifully in The Lonely Ones. In a scrawling, heavy, expressionistic line, Steig brings back all the forgotten pains and terrors of children in a "big peoples'" world in his Agony in the Kindergarten, which should be a basic text for every teacher's college in the country. Steig turns loose a whimsical, sometimes rollicking, sometimes angry, jagged line in Till Death Do Us Part, an existential, clinical peek into the battle of the sexes. The "love" relationships here are light-years closer to reality than the erotic, adolescent cartoon daydreams of the men's magazines. Steig, at his best in these books, is a real humorist and a genuine artist. His view of man is ridiculous, sad, sometimes a little frightening, always compassionate.

Robert Osborn is at his empathetic best as draftsman and commentator in Osborn on Leisure. In this little illustrated essay Osborn has his say

on the great American rat race, the compulsive activism in which most of us are caught. With words and poignant drawings, he pleads for a more qualitative way of life, for art, worship, taking a walk, making love, and for the joy of being.

Osborn is one of the very best draftsmen. He seldom needs or uses a gag-line caption. His latest book, *The Vulgarians*, is delightfully drawn but a bit wordy.

Two of the younger generation of cartoonists who offer much promise, and indeed have already established themselves among the very best, are Jules Feiffer and Interlandi. Feiffer is a tragicomic humorist of the first order. In a nervous, twitchy line, very long dialogue captions (an updating of an old pre–*New Yorker* convention), and multiple drawings from the comic strip, he flays us. We begin laughing at his neurotic, anxious people and end crying for ourselves. It takes courage and a personal perspective to enjoy Feiffer.

Interlandi is not an unusually interesting draftsman, but his line is expressive, and his sense of caricature is keen. He is a genuine satirist whose steel-pointed darts strike often and deeply from his syndicated "Cynics Corner." He deals with the same material as the editorial cartoonists, but with a freshness and absence of cliché.

Feiffer and Interlandi both work in areas of extreme sensitivity and with the profound seriousness of great humorists. Feiffer is indeed "sick, sick, sick" if clear-sightedness is an illness in our age of positive thinking. We can only be thankful that the virus is catching. And Interlandi is certainly a cynic if that is what we choose to call our minor prophets. When these artists confront us, the joke is on us.

Paul Klee, the most tragic and comic of artists says in a little poem:

> Occasionally I'd fool people some,
> I'd put acid in their drinks,
> I'd put poison in their food
> And make it hurt when they mate.
> I founded an order with merrily dancing tears on its banner.[2]

The cartoonist, in accepting his vocation, becomes a brother in this order. There is, I think, a certain faith to be found here.

---

[2] Paul Klee, *The Inward Vision* (New York: Harry N. Abrams, Inc., 1958), p. 37.

XXVIII

Demythologizing "Peanuts"

JAMES T. MILLER

NOT UNTIL RECENTLY HAS THE COMIC STRIP BEEN TAKEN SERIOUSLY, EVEN as an art form, much less as a vehicle of cultural myth. Only with the advent of "Peanuts," with the possible exception of its forerunners, "Li'l Abner" and "Pogo," has any cartoonist tried to picture the driving compulsions and frustrating incoherencies of our time in a continuing situational strip.

Images of Our Modernity

Just as Pogo was winning our affections by introducing us to the realism of power politics, a new strip began in some of our papers. We met Charlie Brown, plain ol' Charlie Brown, just plain ol' Charlie Brown. We then went down the street to Patty, whose first words were "Go away, Charlie Brown. . . . I'm not home!"

Then we met Snoopy, a very human kind of dog, and Shermy, and Violet, the sophisticate, and Schroeder, the sensitive artist and worshiper of Beethoven. But we didn't meet them all at once, and we certainly didn't come to understand them immediately. Only as they became related to one another and came somehow to be defined in reaction to one another did we come to know them.

In coming to know these characters we discovered a new cultural medium

226

in the form of the comic strip. Charles M. Schulz has given us, intentionally or not, a continuing mythic framework for showing forth the basic images of our modernity.

A myth attempts to present images in action, to give a narrative picture of the central motivating forces of the time. Our time seems not to have the cohesion or unity to produce an epic. Perhaps the occasional and somewhat fragmented nature of the comic strip is a more appropriate vehicle for showing forth our world.

With a remarkable ability for allowing characters to grow, Charles M. Schulz has brought us a new microcosm. "Peanuts" fans enjoy this little world not because it is another step in the development of the comic strip as art form. Nor need they be aware that "Peanuts" may be expressing an existential mythology. They like it because it is unpretentious.

Plain ol' Charlie Brown is just plain ol' Charlie Brown. His problems seem fairly simple, but because they are the problems of human relations, of separation and restoration to community, they are also our problems. We always thought the problems not simple at all, but complex almost to the point of being insolvable. Now, we may see our ridiculous rationalizations in the singleness of Charlie Brown's one-block world.

By reducing the drawing to the barest suggestion and depending on a twist of a line for humor, the cartoonist has integrated words, meaning, and action better than any of his predecessors. (Walt Kelly came very close.) By keeping each daily sequence complete in itself and reinforcing the continuity by character themes and theme-situations, Schulz has found a tricky balance which is essential to a continuing strip. A reader can begin anywhere with "Peanuts" and, having seen two or three strips in any order, he will begin to catch on enough to be amused by and interested in these little people.

Schulz has brought a new kind of humor to the comic strip in his situational strips which build up to an urgency, a display of great effort, in the first three panels, only to encounter in the last a simple and unexpected solution, a void or obvious truth, which embarrasses the great effort.

The simple, straightforward answer disenchants our illusions and leaves us standing somewhat ridiculously at the end of having faced ourselves. We laugh at our former presumptions when we see who we really are. As long as we stay to ourselves, what we are does not become clear, but as soon as Charlie Brown asks Patty or Violet to assure him that he is perfect, he discovers that he is just plain ol' Charlie Brown. His worry over being himself amuses us because we know he is exactly what he is supposed to be, and we

227

love him for it. But it is harder to laugh at our own presumptions, not unlike his, when even national policy is determined by "the need to be loved" without loving.

Charlie Brown: The Maze of Original Sin

Who is Charlie Brown? Why do we have such identification with his embarrassments? As the central character, a clear theme grows up around him: a presumption to fame and popularity and the refusal to be one's self lead to rejection from community, a sense of failure and despair when faced by reality, loneliness, and self-pity.

Charlie Brown's introspective suffering amuses us because we know that he is only a little boy and that his problems are not ultimate ones. But when the same things happen to us, we respond just as Charlie Brown does; and, unless we have a much larger world from which to view our failures, we are caught in the same wallow of self-pity and embarrassment that amuses us in him.

Theologically we may say Charlie Brown is caught in the confusing maze of original sin. He tries everything possible to escape his involvement in finitude. Seeking isolation, he takes a running leap into a newfound pile of autumn leaves only to find that he lands in the midst of every one of the relationships from which he thought he was escaping.

With Patty, also a relatively simple character, we find that as Charlie Brown demands her admiration, she simply ignores him, for she is busy trying to secure her own status. She pursues Charlie Brown to assure her that she is beautiful. She arranges parties to make sure that she gets invited.

Very early, the more poised and sophisticated Violet joined with her in a stable social alliance against Charlie Brown and Shermy. Shermy becomes the straight man of the act. While aligned with Charlie Brown against the social ostracism of the girls, Shermy threatens just plain ol' Charlie Brown by being more stable, more capable, by getting the better of him in situation after situation.

Even Snoopy, the sensitive dog with the human desire for recognition, gets the better of Charlie Brown. Sociograms of the "Peanuts" situations would find collaborations of different combinations lining up against each other, but most of them against Charlie Brown. Sometimes Patty and Violet enlist Shermy to play a direct trick. Sometimes among themselves they close the ranks and find their friendship in disliking the same things in Charlie Brown. ("We should wear uniforms," Violet says at one time.) They also hold arguments among themselves to discover which of them likes him more. The lines of separation in their community are never very

229

lasting. The humor lies in these short-lived and easily overcome, in fact, almost unreal barriers.

Schroeder, as a baby, brought out filial instincts in Charlie Brown, though he at first threatened him by knowing more at four than Charlie Brown at six. This part of Charlie Brown's makeup was to be explained more fully upon the birth of Linus and little sister Sally.

From the beginning Schroeder made Charlie Brown look ridiculous. Presented by Charlie Brown with a one-finger demonstration on a toy piano, Schroeder responds by playing Brahms and transforming a toy into a Steinway. Now everyone in the strip has taken for granted rather matter-of-factly that Schroeder can play all of Beethoven and Brahms, most of Bach and Bartók, in addition to the remarkable feat of whistling Sindig's opus 32, no. 3. Schroeder is the twentieth-century artist, sensitive, threatened by commercialization. He adores Beethoven and molds his whole life to his music. He is frustrated because his standards of excellence are not generally accepted. Lucy hounds him to let her inspire him to be a great musician; Charlie Brown annoys him by attempting duets with him on a cigar-box banjo and by misunderstanding as a baseball term his great discovery of perfect pitch. The crowds of his world clamor for him to play simple, popular music ("Three Blind Mice" and "Jingle Bells").

How Schroeder holds out against the popularizers who see in him a threat to their own being is important for us to watch. The artists among us will be pulling for him. Schroeder has brought the judgment of art into this little world. Charlie Brown brought the first hint of it by making a modern snowman along abstract lines. But it took Schroeder to introduce these standards fully. His impatience with a world in which a radio announcer will substitute an accordion solo for Beethoven's *Piano Sonata No. 29* is shared by any honest artist.

Lucy: Scientist and Empirical Philosopher

Just as Schroeder was finding his orientation, another character appeared, even more complex and more exasperating. Lucy is the scientist, empirical philosopher, and fussbudget par excellence. With her latest inventions, she lies always on the threshold of controlling her world, and the prospects are highly terrifying. Lucy, aside from Charlie Brown, is the most involved character symbol, for she combines most of the major sociological factors that have shaped our time.

Science is her major interest: she counts the stars not to keep track or to come to a synthesis, but simply to count them. She begins her life disgraced by expulsion from nursery school and is driven by this early trauma to assert herself loudly and to become a self-educated, self-made fussbudget. Lucille Van Pelt, self-made fussbudget, zooms to frightening pinnacles of success: Miss Fussbudget of 1952, and by 1955, holder of a trophy as "World's Number One Fussbudget." As she says, "You don't win something like that by being sentimental, Charlie Brown!"

Lucy calculates her fussing and her actions; she is the career woman with one driving goal—to achieve fame and to be acclaimed for that achievement. She aims to master her universe so that everyone may give her homage. She shatters Charlie Brown with the twisted logic by which she wins all arguments. Yet, though the *Power of Positive Fussbudgeting* is her text, she is not happy. Hers is a kind of frantic security and a frightened boredom, too stubborn to face any truth outside itself. She is almost a cynical Machiavelli; yet we know her also as a little girl trying to find a home in this world. All of her actions have the same "look-at-me" character, yet she is astonished when we do, making her then look at herself.

If Lucy hasn't yet driven Charlie Brown to a nervous breakdown, she has certainly given her baby brother Linus an insecurity complex. Her domineering has driven him both to introspection and to dependence on his blanket and his thumb stuck in his mouth. Linus, before turning loose of the blanket, had become a philosopher of some dimension. He moved from timidity toward the external world, in which his sister boasts of her security, to a kind of reverence for the mystery of existence. Yet, in spite of Lucy and Snoopy, of persuasion and frontal attack, Linus clung to his blanket, often getting wrapped up in knots in his "security." He continued to keep "one yard of flannel" to place between himself and a nervous breakdown, only recently exchanging blanket for spectacles for his special way of seeing.

Perhaps Linus must be understood as a symbol of the culturally religious man as well as the philosophical questioner. After toying briefly with the idea of becoming a fanatic (wild-eyed or otherwise), he has settled down to a more respectable defense of Santa Claus and a slightly more eccentric admiration for the Great Pumpkin. Yet, for all his dogmatic pronouncements and bizarre projects, Linus is still respected, in Charlie Brown's words, as "the only person I know who can untie a pretzel."

Only one character may be more rejected than Linus, and that is Pigpen. We know little more about him than that we see him through the layers of historical dirt, and we have his profound justification of the *status* quo: "Who am I to disturb the dirt of centuries?"

But we have so far slighted Snoopy, and he resents being slighted. For he is important in commenting on the whole human scene with the prac-

tical realism of his perspective in the animal world. This is not to say that he is free from complexes. He may be even more fraught with them than any of the rest, for whoever heard of a dog with weed claustrophobia or delusions of grandeur that he is a lion or "one of those snakes that squeeze people." Snoopy has both, as well as a growing taste for music.

The common state of each of these characters and of all of us is shared by Snoopy. Each

> Craves what it cannot have,
> Not universal love
> But to be loved alone.[1]

This is why Charlie Brown has so much meaning for us.

Charlie Brown is the plain ol' average man, the all-around fellow who seems to have everything but is ridiculed because his head is like a basketball, an orange, a grape. He loses at checkers and goes bankrupt at the marble game. He feels that he is "not even part of the orchestra." If on Christmas he doesn't receive a single card, we know his feeling of not belonging, and we love him. And we love him also because he is a magnificent failure in manipulating group adjustments.

Remarkably, the others, who are thrown up against him and cause him misery, love him too. For those involved in the situation, it is misery and suffering. From our transcendent perspective, we can find solutions and the whole struggle seems amusing.

Yet we are also filled with pity. Charles M. Schulz seems to have given us a gentle humor of the tragic sense of life, and we laugh at his comic strip.

Maybe if we laugh long enough we may find ourselves laughing at those barriers that are real in our world, at those present myths which separate and make community impossible—especially those that would make us think community automatic and given in conformity to the group. But for that we need a transcendent stance, which brings us back to theology again. Meanwhile, we will read "Peanuts" because it's nice to know someone like just plain ol' Charlie Brown.

---

[1] W. H. Auden, "September 1, 1939," from *The Collected Poetry of W. H. Auden* (New York: Random House, 1945), p. 59. Used by permission of Random House and Faber and Faber Ltd.

BIOGRAPHICAL SKETCHES

MALCOLM BOYD, a former president of the Television Producers Association of Hollywood, is Episcopal chaplain at Wayne State University, Detroit. His books include *Crisis in Communication, Christ and Celebrity Gods, Focus,* and *If I Go Down to Hell.*

CLEANTH BROOKS is Gray Professor of Rhetoric, Yale University. He edited (with Robert Penn Warren) *The Southern Review,* 1935-42. His books include *Modern Poetry and the Tradition, The Well Wrought Urn,* and *Understanding Poetry* (with Robert Penn Warren).

E. MARTIN BROWNE, a British director and producer, has directed all the plays of T. S. Eliot in London and New York. He was visiting professor in religious drama at Union Theological Seminary, New York, 1956-62, editor of *Religious Plays* and *Religious Drama II,* and is president of the Religious Drama Society of Great Britain.

JAMES CRANE, painter, printmaker, and cartoonist, is chairman of the art department, Wisconsin State College, River Falls. He is a long-time contributor of art and cartoons to *motive* magazine, and is author of *What Other Time?*

JOHN W. DIXON, JR., formerly director of the Faculty Christian Fellowship, is associate professor of art, Florida Presbyterian College. He is author of *Form and Reality: Art as Communication.*

TOM FAW DRIVER is associate professor of Christian theology, Union Theological Seminary, New York. He is author of a libretto, *The Invisible Fire,* of *The Sense of History in Greek and Shakespearean Drama,* and drama critic for *The Christian Century.*

FINLEY EVERSOLE is director of the Committee for the Interseminary Movement of the National Student Christian Federation, and a staff member of the National Council of the Churches of Christ in the USA. He has written for several journals including *The Christian Century, The Christian Scholar,* and *motive.*

235

CLARK B. FITZ-GERALD is a free-lance sculptor. He has had numerous one-man exhibitions of his art and has work in several art galleries. He has taught at Washington University, Beloit College, and Phillips Academy.

EDWARD C. HOBBS is professor of theology and hermeneutics of the New Testament at The Church Divinity School of the Pacific and a lecturer in medicine at the University of California School of Medicine.

HANS EGON HOLTHUSEN, noted German author and poet, is program director of the Goethe House, New York. Among his many books, two are in English: *R. M. Rilke: A Study of His Later Poetry* and *The Crossing.*

STANLEY ROMAINE HOPPER is professor of Christian philosophy and letters and dean of the Graduate School, Drew University. He is author of *The Crisis of Faith* and editor of *Spiritual Problems in Contemporary Literature.*

CELIA THAXTER HUBBARD is the founder and director of The Botolph Group, Inc., Boston. One-man exhibitions of her paintings have been held in Lincoln, Massachusetts, Boston, and New York City.

PAMELA ILOTT is director of religious broadcasting for CBS, New York. She is also executive producer of *Church of the Air, Lamp Unto My Feet,* and *Look Up and Live.*

KEITH W. IRWIN, formerly executive director of the Faculty Christian Fellowship, is associate professor of philosophy at Florida Presbyterian College and author (with Roger Ortmayer) of *Worship and the Arts.*

JAMES T. MILLER, formerly program director of the Campus Christian Community, Southwest Texas State College, is a graduate student in the Divinity School, University of Chicago. He was associate editor of *Concern* in 1956, and has contributed articles and poems to *motive* and Methodist church-school publications.

ROGER ORTMAYER is professor of Christianity and the arts, Perkins School of Theology, Southern Methodist University. He is a former editor of *motive* magazine and the author (with Keith Irwin) of *Worship and the Arts.*

GEORGE W. POOL is choir director for North Methodist Church, Indianapolis. He was choral director for a festival of religion and art in Indianapolis in 1961, and has worked with play productions of *Everyman* and *Boy Bishop.*

JULIUS PORTNOY is professor of philosophy at Brooklyn College and author of *A Psychology of Art Creation, The Philosopher and Music,* and *Music in the Life of Man.*

ROBERT E. RAMBUSCH is a stained-glass artist and painter. He has had art exhibits in France, Canada, and the United States and has contributed work to several major Roman Catholic churches in the United States and Canada.

SIR HERBERT READ is a leading British literary and art critic. He has taught at the University of Edinburgh, and lectured at the University of Liverpool, the University of London, and Harvard University. His writings include *The Philosophy of Modern Art* and *The Art of Sculpture*.

DORA CARGILLE (MRS. JAMES A.) SANDERS is a contemporary dance artist and choreographer. She has soloed in a New York television performance with Margaret Fisk Taylor's Religious Dance Group and has taught at the University of Cincinnati and the University of Rochester.

NATHAN A. SCOTT, JR., is associate professor of theology and literature, the Divinity School, University of Chicago. He is author of *Rehearsals of Discomposure, Modern Literature and the Religious Frontier*, and editor of *The Tragic Vision and the Christian Faith*.

ROGER LINCOLN SHINN is William E. Dodge, Jr., Professor of Applied Christianity, Union Theological Seminary, New York. His books include *Christianity and the Problem of History; Life, Death and Destiny;* and *The Existentialist Posture*.

JOSEPH SITTLER is professor of theology, the Divinity School, University of Chicago, and a member of the Faith and Order Commission of the World Council of Churches. He is author of *The Doctrine of the Word, The Structure of Christian Ethics,* and *The Ecology of Faith*.

WALTER SULLIVAN is associate professor of English, Vanderbilt University. He has written two novels: *Sojourn of a Stranger* and *The Long, Long Love*.

ROBERT PENN WARREN, founder of the *Southern Review* and a former professor at Yale University, is one of America's most noted authors and novelists. His novels include *All the King's Men, Brothers to Dragons, The Cave,* and *Wilderness*.

ELWYN A. WIENANDT is chairman of graduate studies in music and professor of musicology, Baylor University. He has published several musical compositions and is author of *Musical Style in the Lute Compositions of Francesco da Milano* and *Choral Music of the Church*, which will be published in 1964.

AMOS NIVEN WILDER is Hollis Professor of Divinity and professor of New Testament interpretation, Harvard Divinity School. His books include *Spiritual Aspects of the New Poetry, Otherworldliness in the New Testament, Modern Poetry and the Christian Tradition,* and *New Testament Faith for Today*.

COLIN WILSON is a young British novelist and literary critic. His books include *The Outsiders, The Stature of Man,* and *Ritual in the Dark*.

SUGGESTIONS
FOR FURTHER READING

I. Art and the Renewal of Human Sensibility in Mass Society

Brooks, Cleanth. "The Crisis in Culture," *Harvard Alumni Bulletin*, July 8, 1950, pp. 768-72.

Fromm, Erich. *The Sane Society*. New York: Holt, Rinehart & Winston, 1955.

Hebert, A. G. *Liturgy and Society*. Naperville, Ill.: Alec R. Allenson, Inc., 1956.

Irwin, Keith, and Ortmayer, Roger. *Worship and the Arts*. Nashville: National Methodist Student Movement, 1953.

Jaspers, Karl. *Man in the Modern Age*. Translated by Eden and Cedar Paul. Garden City, N.Y.: Doubleday Anchor Books, 1957.

Kahler, Erich. *The Tower and the Abyss*. New York: George Braziller, Inc., 1957.

Lynch, William F. *Christ and Apollo*. New York: Sheed & Ward, 1960.

Macdonald, Dwight. "Masscult and Midcult," *Partisan Review*, Spring, 1960, pp. 203-33.

Rosenberg, Bernard, and White, David Manning, editors. *Mass Culture*. Glencoe, Ill.: The Free Press, 1957.

Scott, Nathan A., Jr. *Modern Literature and the Religious Frontier*. New York: Harper & Brothers, 1958.

Tillich, Paul. "The World Situation," in *The Christian Answer*, edited by Henry P. Van Dusen. New York: Charles Scribner's Sons, 1945.

Wilder, Amos N. *Theology and Modern Literature*. Cambridge, Mass.: Harvard University Press, 1958.

II. Literary Tradition and the Contemporary Writer

Eliot, T. S. *Selected Essays*. Rev. ed. New York: Harcourt, Brace & Co., 1950.

Highet, Gilbert. *The Classical Tradition*. New York: Oxford University Press, 1949.

Hospers, John. *Meaning and Truth in the Arts*. Chapel Hill, N.C.: University of North Carolina Press, 1947.

Kettle, Arnold. *An Introduction to the English Novel*. London: Longmans, Green & Co., 1951.

Kuhn, Helmut. *Encounter With Nothingness*. Chicago: Henry Regnery Co., 1949.

Leavis, F. R. *The Great Tradition*. London: Chatto & Windus, 1948.

Nietzsche, Friedrich. *The Birth of Tragedy*. New York: Modern Library, 1927.

Tate, Allen. *Collected Essays.* Denver: Allen Swallow Press, 1959.
Trilling, Lionel. *The Liberal Imagination.* New York: The Viking Press, 1950.

III. Art Tradition and the Contemporary Visual Arts

Coleridge, S. T. *The Friend.* 3 vols. London: 1850. (See especially Vol. II, essays x & xi.)
Arnold, Matthew. *Culture and Anarchy.* 1869.
Buber, Martin. *Between Man and Man.* Boston: Beacon Press, 1955.
Cassirer, Ernst. *An Essay on Man.* New Haven, Conn.: Yale University Press, 1944.
Coomaraswamy, Ananda K. *Christian and Oriental Philosophy of Art.* New York: Dover Publishings, Inc., 1956.
Eliot, T. S. *The Sacred Wood.* London: Methuen, 1920.
————. *The Idea of a Christian Society.* New York: Harcourt, Brace & Co., 1940.
Jones, David. *Epoch and Artist.* Edited by Harman Grisewood. London: Faber & Faber, Ltd., 1959.
Jung, C. G. *The Development of Personality. Collected Works.* Vol. 17. ("Bollingen Series.") New York: Pantheon Books, 1954.
Ruskin, John. *A Joy Forever.* New York: Farrar, Straus & Cudahy.
————. *Two Paths.* New York: E. P. Dutton & Co., Inc.
Tate, Allen. *The Forlorn Demon.* Chicago: Henry Regnery Co., 1953.
Weil, Simone. *The Need for Roots.* New York: G. P. Putnam's Sons, 1952.
Read, Sir Herbert. "In Defense of Abstract Art," *New York Times Magazine,* April 17, 1960.

IV. The Brave New World of the Modern Artist

Fowlie, Wallace. *A Guide to Contemporary French Literature.* New York: Meridian Books, 1960.
Heller, Erich. *The Disinherited Mind.* New York: Farrar, Straus & Cudahy, 1957.
————. *Thomas Mann: The Ironic German.* Cleveland: Meridian Books, 1961.
Hunter, Sam. *Modern American Painting and Sculpture.* New York: Dell Publishing Co., Inc., 1959.
Rahv, Philip. *Image and Idea.* Rev. ed. New York: New Directions, 1957.
Read, Herbert. *The Philosophy of Modern Art.* New York: Meridian Books, 1955.
Scott, Nathan A., Jr. "The Modest Optimism of Albert Camus," *The Christian Scholar,* December, 1959, pp. 251-74.
————. *Rehearsals of Discomposure.* New York: Columbia University Press, 1952.
————, editor. *The Tragic Vision and the Christian Faith.* New York: Association Press, 1957.
Shahn, Ben. "Nonconformity," *The Atlantic Monthly,* September, 1957, pp. 36-41.
Thielicke, Helmut. *Nihilism.* New York: Harper & Brothers, 1961.
Tillich, Paul. *The Courage to Be.* New Haven, Conn.: Yale University Press, 1952.
————. *The Religious Situation.* Translated by H. Richard Niebuhr. New York: Meridian Books, 1956. (Part I, ch. 3.)
Tovish, Harold. "Sculpture: The Sober Art," *The Atlantic Monthly,* September, 1961, pp. 35-39.
Tindall, William York. *Forces in Modern British Literature. 1885-1956.* New York: Vintage Books, 1956.
Wilder, Amos N. *Spiritual Aspects of the New Poetry.* New York: Harper & Brothers, 1940.

V. Is the Creative Process Similar in the Arts?

Aristotle. *Poetics* in *The Basic Works of Aristotle.* Translated by Richard McKeon. New York: Random House, 1941.

Freud, Sigmund. *New Introductory Lectures on Psycho-analysis.* New York: W. W. Norton & Co., 1933.

Jung, Carl G. *Modern Man in Search of a Soul.* Translated by W. S. Dell and C. F. Baynes. New York: Harcourt, Brace & Co., 1933.

Nahm, Milton C. *The Artist as Creator.* Baltimore, Md.: Johns Hopkins Press, 1956.

Plato. "Ion" and "Phaedrus." *The Dialogues of Plato.* Translated by B. Jowett. 2 vols. New York: Random House, 1937.

Portnoy, Julius. *A Psychology of Art Creation.* Kenan Fellow Study, University of North Carolina, 1942.

VI. The Artist and the Problem of Communication

Bell, Clive. *Art.* London: Chatto & Windus, 1914.

Britton, Karl. *Communication.* New York: Harcourt, Brace & Co., 1939.

Cassirer, Ernst. *An Essay on Man.* New Haven, Conn.: Yale University Press, 1944.

————. *The Logic of the Humanities.* Translated by Clarence Smith Howe. New Haven, Conn.: Yale University Press, 1961.

————. *The Philosophy of Symbolic Forms.* Translated by Ralph Manheim. 3 vols. New Haven, Conn.: Yale University Press, 1953, 1955, 1957.

Hospers, John. *Meaning and Truth in the Arts.* Chapel Hill, N.C.: University of North Carolina Press, 1947.

Langer, Susanne K. *Feeling and Form.* New York: Charles Scribner's Sons, 1953.

————. *Philosophy in a New Key.* Cambridge, Mass.: Harvard University Press, 1942.

Maritain, Jacques. *Art and Scholasticism.* Translated by J. F. Scanlan. New York: Charles Scribner's Sons, 1930.

Ortega y Gasset, José. *The Dehumanization of Art and Other Writings on Art and Culture.* Garden City, N. Y.: Doubleday & Co., Inc., 1956.

Rader, Melvin. *A Modern Book of Esthetics.* New York: Henry Holt & Co., 1935.

Santayana, George. *The Sense of Beauty.* New York: Charles Scribner's Sons, 1896.

Tillich, Paul. *Dynamics of Faith.* New York: Harper & Brothers, 1957.

VII. The Artist as Prophet-Priest of Culture

Auden, W. H. "The Christian Tragic Hero," *New York Times Book Review,* December 16, 1945, p. 1.

Auerbach, Erich. *Mimesis.* Garden City, N. Y.: Doubleday Anchor Books, 1957.

Barrett, William. *Irrational Man.* Garden City, N. Y.: Doubleday & Co., Inc. 1958.

Camus, Albert. "The Artist and His Time," in *Resistance, Rebellion, and Death.* New York: Alfred A. Knopf, Inc., 1960.

Clark, Kenneth. "Art and Society," *Harper's Magazine,* August, 1961, pp. 74-82.

Dillistone, F. W. *The Novelist and the Passion Story.* New York: Sheed & Ward, Inc., 1961.

Maritain, Jacques. *The Responsibility of the Artist.* New York: Charles Scribner's Sons, 1960.

Mueller, William R. *The Prophetic Voice in Modern Fiction.* New York: Association Press, 1959.

Sewall, Richard B. *The Vision of Tragedy*. New Haven, Conn.: Yale University Press, 1959.

Shinn, Roger L. *The Existentialist Posture*. New York: Association Press, 1959. (See especially ch. 7.)

Stewart, Douglas. *The Ark of God*. London: Carey Kingsgate Press, 1961.

Stewart, Randall. *American Literature and Christian Doctrine*. Baton Rouge, La.: Louisiana State University Press, 1958.

Tillich, Paul. "Existential Aspects of Modern Art," in *Christianity and the Existentialists*. Edited by Carl Michalson. New York: Charles Scribner's Sons, 1956.

————. "Protestantism and Artistic Style," in *Theology of Culture*. Edited by Robert C. Kimball. New York: Oxford University Press, 1959.

VIII. The Sensibility of the Church and the Sensibility of the Artist

Gilson, Etienne. *Painting and Reality*. New York: Pantheon Books, 1957.

Koenker, Ernest. *Liturgical Renaissance in the Roman Catholic Church*. Chicago: University of Chicago Press, 1954.

Maritain, Jacques. *Creative Intuition in Art and Poetry*. New York: Pantheon Books, 1953.

IX. What Is Christian in a Christian Literature?

Holthusen, H. E. *R. M. Rilke: A Study of His Later Poetry*. New Haven, Conn.: Yale University Press, 1952.

————. "Meaning and Destiny in European Literature," *Chicago Review*, Spring, 1961, pp. 1-19.

Kierkegaard, Soren. *Either/Or*. Translated by David Swenson and Walter Lowrie. 2 vols. Princeton, N. J.: Princeton University Press, 1944.

Rilke, Rainer Maria. *Duino Elegies*. Translated by J. B. Leishman and S. Spender. New York: W. W. Norton & Co., Inc., 1939.

————. *The Notebooks of Malte Laurids Brigge*. Translated by M. D. Herter Norton. New York: Capricorn Books, 1958.

X. Christianity, Myth, and the Symbolism of Poetry

Abrams, M. H., editor. *Literature and Belief*. New York: Columbia University Press, 1958.

Eliot, T. S. Essay on "Dante." *Selected Essays, 1917-1932*. New York: Harcourt, Brace & Co., 1932.

Hopper, Stanley Romaine, editor. *Spiritual Problems in Contemporary Literature*. New York: Harper & Brothers, 1952.

Jordan, Robert M. "The Limits of Illusion: Faulkner, Fielding and Chaucer," *Criticism*, Summer, 1960, pp. 278 ff.

Krieger, Murray. *The New Apologists for Poetry*. Minneapolis: University of Minnesota Press, 1956.

Madden, William A. "The Divided Tradition of English Criticism," *PMLA*, March, 1958, pp. 69 ff.

Shapiro, Karl. *In Defence of Ignorance*. New York: Random House, 1960.

Vivas, Eliseo. *Creation and Discovery*, New York: The Noonday Press, 1955.

Waggoner, Hyatt H. "The Current Revolt Against the New Criticism," *Criticism*, Summer, 1959, pp. 211 ff.

Wimsatt, W. K., Jr., and Brooks, Cleanth. *Literary Criticism: A Short History*. New York: Alfred A. Knopf, Inc., 1957.

Wimsatt, W. K., Jr. *The Verbal Icon*. Lexington, Ky.: The University of Kentucky Press, 1954.

XI. Poetry and Religion

Eliot, T. S. "Religion and Literature," in *Selected Essays*. New York: Harcourt, Brace & Co., 1932.

Jarrett-Kerr, Martin. *Studies in Literature and Belief*. New York: Harper & Brothers, 1955.

Lynch, William F. *Christ and Apollo*. New York: Sheed & Ward, 1960.

Santayana, George. *Interpretations of Poetry and Religion*. New York: Harper & Brothers, 1957.

Scott, Nathan A., Jr. *Modern Literature and the Religious Frontier*. New York: Harper & Brothers, 1958. Especially chs. 1, 2, 5.

Tate, Allen, editor. *The Language of Poetry*. Princeton, N. J.: Princeton University Press, 1942.

Tillich, Paul. "The Religious Symbol," in *Symbolism in Religion and Literature*. Edited by Rollo May. New York: George Braziller, Inc., 1960.

Wilder, Amos N. *Modern Poetry and the Christian Tradition*. New York: Charles Scribner's Sons, 1952. (ch. 1.)

XII. The Existential Temper of the Modern Novel

Eliot, T. S. *After Strange Gods*. New York: Harcourt, Brace & Co., 1934.

Holroyd, Stuart. *Emergence from Chaos*. Boston: Houghton Mifflin Co., 1957.

Hulme, T. E. *Speculations*. New York: Harcourt, Brace & Co., 1961.

————. *Further Speculations*. Minneapolis, Minn.: University of Minnesota Press, 1955.

Husserl, Edmund. *Ideas*. New York: The Macmillan Company, 1931.

Merleau-Ponty, Maurice. *La Structure du Comportement*. Plom: 1942.

Progoff, Ira. *The Death and Rebirth of Psychology*. New York: The Julian Press, 1958.

Sartre, Jean-Paul. *What Is Literature?* London: Rider and Co.

XIII. Camus: The Argument from the Absurd

Barnes, Hazel E. *The Literature of Possibility*. Lincoln, Neb.: University of Nebraska Press, 1959.

Brée, Germaine. *Albert Camus and "The Plague."* "Yale French Studies, No. 8."

Guicharnaud, Jacques, and Beckelman, June. *Modern French Theatre*. New Haven,: Conn.: Yale University Press, 1961.

Hanna, Thomas. *The Thought and Art of Albert Camus*. Chicago: Henry Regnery Co., 1958.

————. "Albert Camus and the Christian Faith," *The Journal of Religion*, October, 1956, pp. 224-33.

Maquet, Albert. *Albert Camus: The Invincible Summer*. New York: George Braziller, Inc., 1958.

Thody, Philip. *Albert Camus: A Study of His Work*. New York: Grove Press, 1959.

XIV. Contemporary Drama in the Catholic Tradition

Auden, W. H. *For the Time Being.* New York: Random House, 1944.

Claudel, Paul. *Two Dramas.* Translated by Wallace Fowlie. Chicago: Henry Regnery Co., 1960.

Eliot, T. S. *The Confidential Clerk.* New York: Harcourt, Brace & Co., 1954.

————. *The Elder Statesman.* New York: Farrar, Straus & Cudahy, 1959.

Fowlie, Wallace. *Claudel.* New York: Hillary House Publishers, 1958.

Gheon, Henri. *Christmas in the Market Place.* London: J. Garnet Miller, 1943.

————. *The Mystery of the Finding of the Cross* (incorporating *The Way of the Cross*). Chester, Pa.: Dufour Editions, 1956.

————. *The Art of the Theatre.* New York: Hill & Wang, 1961.

Greene, Graham. *The Power and the Glory.* New York: The Viking Press, 1946.

————. *The Potting Shed.* New York: The Viking Press, 1961.

Jones, D. E. *The Plays of T. S. Eliot.* Toronto: University of Toronto Press, 1960.

Sayers, Dorothy L. *The Man Born to Be King.* New York: Harper & Brothers, 1949.

————. *The Zeal of Thy House.* New York: Harcourt, Brace & Co., 1937.

Williams, Charles. *Thomas Cranmer of Canterbury.* London: Oxford University Press, 1936.

————. *Seed of Adam and other plays.* London: Oxford University Press, 1948.

XV. Thesis for a Playwright Still in Hiding

Bentley, Eric. *In Search of Theater.* New York: Alfred A. Knopf, Inc., 1953.

Fergusson, Francis. *The Human Image in Dramatic Literature.* New York: Doubleday Anchor Books, 1957.

Halverson, Marvin, editor. *Religious Drama I.* New York, Living Age Books, Meridian Books, Inc., 1957.

————. *Religious Drama III.* New York: Living Age Books, Inc., 1960.

Tillich, Paul. *Theology of Culture.* Edited by Robert C. Kimball. New York: Oxford University Press, 1959.

XVI. The Gospel in So-Called Secular Drama

Bentley, Eric. "What Is Theatre?" in *What Is Theatre?* Boston: Beacon Press, 1955.

Michalson, Carl, editor. *Christianity and the Existentialists.* New York: Charles Scribner's Sons, 1956.

Tillich, Paul. *Theology of Culture.* Edited by Robert C. Kimball. New York: Oxford University Press, 1959.

Wilder, Amos N. *Modern Poetry and the Christian Tradition.* New York: Charles Scribner's Sons, 1952.

————. *Theology and Modern Literature.* Cambridge, Mass.: Harvard University Press, 1958.

XVII. The Image of Man: Criterion for a Religious Movie

Agee, James. *Agee on Film.* 2 vols. New York: McDowell, Obolensky Inc., 1958, 1960.

"Are Foreign Films Better?" *Saturday Review,* December 24, 1960.

Bainbridge, John. *Garbo.* New York: Doubleday & Co., Inc., 1955.

Fitzgerald, F. Scott. *The Last Tycoon.* New York: Charles Scribner's Sons, 1941.

Getlein, Frank, and Gardiner, Harold C., S. J. *Movies, Morals and Art.* New York: Sheed & Ward, 1961.

Powdermaker, Hortense. *Hollywood the Dream Factory.* Boston: Little, Brown & Co., 1950.

Ross, Lillian. *Picture.* New York: Rinehart & Co., 1952.

Seldes, Gilbert. *The Great Audience.* New York: The Viking Press, 1950.

West, Nathaniel. *The Day of the Locust.* New York: Random House, 1939.

XVIII. Television: The Quest for a New Art Form

Bachmam, John W. *The Church in the World of Radio and Television.* New York: Association Press, 1960.

Boyd, Malcolm, *Crisis in Communication.* New York: Doubleday & Co., Inc., 1957.

Fischer, Edward. *The Screen Arts.* New York: Sheed & Ward, 1960.

Gunn, John M., editor. *The Seeking Years.* St. Louis, Mo.: Bethany Press, 1959.

Lynch, William F., S.J. *The Image Industries.* New York: Sheed & Ward, 1959.

Parker, Everett C. *Religious Television.* New York: Harper & Brothers, 1961.

XIX. Mid-Century Man and His Music: A Christian View

Ewen, David. *Complete Book of Twentieth Century Music.* New York: Prentice-Hall, Inc., 1952.

Fassett, Agatha. *The Naked Face of Genius.* Boston: Houghton Mifflin Co., 1958.

Ferguson, Donald N. *A History of Musical Thought.* New York: Appleton-Century-Crofts, Inc., 1948.

Graf, Max. *Modern Music.* New York: Philosophical Library, 1946.

Lang, Paul Henry. *Music in Western Civilization.* New York: W. W. Norton & Co., 1941.

Mellers, Wilfrid. *Man and His Music.* (Vol. IV of *Romanticism and the Twentieth Century.*) Fair Lawn, N. J.: Essential Books, Inc., 1957.

Sachs, Curt. *Our Musical Heritage.* New York: Prentice-Hall, Inc., 1948.

Stuckenschmidt, H. H. *Arnold Schoenberg.* Translated by Edith Temple Roberts and Humphrey Searle. New York: Grove Press, 1960.

Vlad, Roman. *Stravinsky.* Translated by Frederick and Ann Fuller. New York: Oxford University Press, 1960.

XX. Jazz as a Christian Expression

Beaumont, Geoffrey. *20th Country Folk Mass.* (Fiesta FLP-25000.)

Davison, Archibald T. *Church Music: Illusion and Reality.* Cambridge, Mass.: Harvard University Press, 1952.

————. *Protestant Church Music in America.* Boston: E. C. Schirmer Music Co., 1933.

Halter, Carl. *The Practice of Sacred Music.* St. Louis, Mo.: Concordia Publishing House, 1954.

Lovelace, Austin C., and Rice, William C. *Music and Worship in the Church.* Nashville: Abingdon Press, 1960. (Ch. 1, "Worship and Music.")

Ostransky, Leroy. *The Anatomy of Jazz.* Seattle, Wash.: University of Washington Press, 1960.

Routley, Erik. *Church Music and Theology.* (No. 11 of "Studies in Ministry and Worship.") Philadelphia: Muhlenberg Press, 1960.

Smith, Henry Augustine. "The Expression of Religion in Music," in *The Arts and Religion*. Edited by Albert Edward Bailey. New York: Macmillan Company, 1944.

Saunders, Earl. "Jazz and the Holy Spirit," *motive*, October, 1960, pp. 8 ff.

Stearns, Marshall W. "What is Happening to Jazz?" *Music Journal*, January, 1961, pp. 48 ff.

Wienandt, Elwyn A. "Jazz at the Altar?" *The Christian Century*, March 23, 1960, pp. 34 ff.

Summerlin, Edgar. *Liturgical Jazz: A Musical Setting for an Order of Morning Prayer*. (Ecclesia ER-101.)

XXI. Contemporary Dance in Christian Perspective

Amberg, George. *Ballet*. New York: Mentor Books, 1949.

Duncan, Isadore. *My Life*. Garden City, N. Y.: Garden City Publishing Co., 1927.

Fisk (Taylor), Margaret Palmer. *The Art of the Rhythmic Choir*. New York: Harper & Brothers, 1950.

Kirstein, Lincoln. *Book of the Dance*. Garden City, N. Y.: Doubleday & Co., 1942.

Kschessinska, Matilde. *Dancing in Petersburg*. Garden City, N. Y.: Doubleday & Co., Inc., 1961.

Meri, La. *Dance as an Art Form*. New York: A. S. Barnes & Co., 1933.

Lloyd, Margaret. *Borzoi Book of Modern Dance*. New York: Alfred A. Knopf, Inc., 1949.

Martin, John. *The Dance*. New York: Tudor Publishing Co., 1946.

MacDougall, Alan Ross. *Isadora*. New York: Thomas Nelson & Sons, 1960.

Nijinsky, Romola. *Nijinsky*. Garden City, N. Y.: Garden City Publishing Co., 1941.

Sachs, Curt. *World History of the Dance*. New York: W. W. Norton & Co., Inc., 1957.

Terry, Walter. *The Dance in America*. New York: Harper & Brothers, 1956.

XXII. The Catholic Imagination and the Painting of Our Time

Gilson, Étienne. *Painting and Reality*. New York: Pantheon Books, Inc., 1957.

Maritain, Jacques. *Creative Intuition in Art and Poetry*. New York: Meridian Books, Inc., 1955.

————. *The Responsibility of the Artist*. New York: Charles Scribner's Sons, 1960.

Murphy, J. Stanley, editor. *Christianity and Culture*. Baltimore: Helicon Press, 1960.

Ortega y Gasset, José. *The Dehumanization of Art*. Translated by Willard R. Trask. Garden City, N. Y.: Doubleday Anchor Books, 1956.

Sedlmayer, Hans. *Art in Crisis*. Chicago: Henry Regnery Co., 1958.

Selz, Peter. *New Images of Man*. Garden City, N. J.: Doubleday & Co., Inc., 1959.

Sorokin, P. A. *The Crisis of Our Age*. New York: E. P. Dutton & Co., Inc., 1957.

XXIII. Art Beyond Celebration

Brion, Marcel, et al. *Art Since 1945*. New York: Harry N. Abrams, Inc., 1958.

Gombrich, E. H. *Art and Illusion*. New York: Pantheon Books, Inc., 1959.

Haftmann, Werner. *Painting in the Twentieth Century*. 2 vols. New York: Frederick A. Praeger, 1960.

Hauser, Arnold. *The Philosophy of Art History*. New York: Alfred A. Knopf, 1959.

Huyghe, René. *Ideas and Images in World Art*. New York: Harry N. Abrams, Inc., 1959.

246

Malraux, André. *The Voices of Silence: Man and His Art*. Garden City, N. Y.: Doubleday and Company, Inc., 1953.

Ponente, Nello. *Modern Painting: Contemporary Trends*. Cleveland: World Publishing Co. (Skira), 1960.

Shattuck, Roger. *The Banquet Years: The Origins of the Avant-Garde in France*. Garden City, N. Y.: Doubleday and Company, Inc., 1958.

XXIV. A Sculptor Discusses Contemporary Religious Work

Gombrich, E. H. *The Story of Art*. New York: Phaidon Publishers, 1952.

Henze, Anton. *Contemporary Church Art*. New York: Sheed & Ward, 1956.

The Interpreter's Bible. 12 vols. Nashville: Abingdon Press.

Kirchergerät, German periodical on church art.

McClinton, Katherine Morrison. *Christian Church Art Through the Ages*. New York: The Macmillan Company.

Views of the Biblical World. Chicago, New York: Jordan Publications. ('Printed in Israel.)

XXV. Contemporary Christian Architecture and Catholic Faith

The Bishops of Germany. *Directives for the Building of a Church*. Collegeville Minn.: The Liturgical Press, 1949.

Hammond, Peter. *Liturgy and Architecture*. New York: Columbia University Press, 1961.

Henze, Anton. *Contemporary Church Art*. New York: Sheed & Ward, 1956.

Lercaro, James Cardinal. *The Christian Church*. Collegeville, Minn.: The Liturgical Press, 1949.

Reinhold, H. A. *Speaking of Liturgical Architecture*. Boston: Daughters of St. Paul, 1961.

Schwarz, Rudolph. *The Church Incarnate*. Chicago: Henry Regnery Co., 1958.

Weyres, Willy. *Kirchen: Handbuch für den Kirchenbau*. Munich: Verlag Georg D. W. Callwey, 1959.

XXVI. The Matrix of Form in Church Architecture

Cassirer, Ernst. *Philosophy of Symbolic Forms*. 3 vols. New Haven, Conn.: Yale University Press, 1953, 1955, 1957.

Fiddes, Victor. *The Architectural Requirements of Protestant Worship*. Toronto: Ryerson Press, 1961.

Halverson, Marvin P. "Form and Meaning in Architecture," *The Christian Century*, March 27, 1957, pp. 387 ff.

Hammond, Peter. *Liturgy and Architecture*. New York: Columbia University Press, 1961.

Hayward, John F. "Plumb Line on Church Architecture," *The Christian Century*, May 4, 1960, pp. 535 ff.

Hirzel, Stephan. "European Church Building Today," *The Christian Century*, February 19, 1958, pp. 209 ff.

Lynch, William. *Christ and Apollo*. New York: Sheed & Ward, 1960.

Santayana, George. *Reason in Art*. (Vol. 4 of *The Life of Reason*.) New York: Charles Scribner's Sons, 1934.

Sittler, Joseph. "A Hammer, the Incarnation and Architecture," *The Christian Century*, March 27, 1957, pp. 394 ff.

XXVII. Little World in Crisis: A Tragicomic Caricature

Coastes, Robert M. "Contemporary American Humorous Art," *Perspectives USA,* Winter, 1956.

Crane, James. *What Other Time?* Nashville: Source Publishers, 1953.

Dean, Abner. *What Am I Doing Here?* New York: Simon & Schuster, 1947.

Feiffer, Jules. *Sick, Sick, Sick.* New York: McGraw-Hill Book Co., Inc., 1958.

————. *The Explainers.* New York: McGraw-Hill Book Co., Inc., 1960.

Hollander, John. "Paul Klee" and "The Passport" reviewed, *Perspectives USA,* Winter, 1956, pp. 163-66.

Novick, Julius. "Jules Feiffer and the Almost-in-Group," *Harper's,* September, 1961, pp. 58-62.

Osborn, R. C. *On Leisure.* New York: Simon & Schuster, 1957.

————. *The Vulgarians.* New York: New York Graphic Art Society, 1960.

Shahn, Ben. "The Gallic Laughter of André François," *Horizon,* May, 1959.

Steig, William. *The Steig Album.* New York: Duell, Sloan & Pearce, Inc., 1943.

Steinberg, Saul. *The Art of Living.* New York: Harper & Brothers, 1949.

————. *The Passport.* New York: Harper & Brothers, 1954.

————. *The Labyrinth.* New York: Harper & Brothers, 1960.

XXVIII. Demythologizing "Peanuts"

Morrow, H. "Success of an Utter Failure," *Saturday Evening Post,* January 12, 1957.

"A Child's Garden of Reverses," *Time,* March 3, 1958.

"Good Grief, Curly Hair," *Newsweek,* March 6, 1961.

Schulz, Charles M. *Peanuts.* New York: Holt, Rinehart & Winston, Inc., 1952.

————. *But We Love You, Charlie Brown.* New York: Holt, Rinehart & Winston, Inc., 1959.

————. *Go Fly a Kite, Charlie Brown.* New York: Holt, Rinehart & Winston, Inc., 1960.

————. *Good Ol' Charlie Brown.* New York: Holt, Rinehart & Winston, Inc., 1957.

————. *Good Grief, More Peanuts!* New York: Holt, Rinehart & Winston, Inc.

————. *More Peanuts.* New York: Holt, Rinehart & Winston, Inc., 1955.

————. *Peanuts Revisited.* New York: Holt, Rinehart & Winston, Inc., 1959.

————. *Snoopy.* New York: Holt, Rinehart & Winston, Inc., 1958.

————. *You're Out of Your Mind, Charlie Brown!* New York: Holt, Rinehart & Winston, Inc., 1959.

INDEX OF NAMES AND TITLES